100 VOICES
AMERICANS TALK ABOUT CHANGE

2.23.2012

for Elizabeth —

In the constancy
of change and the
comfort of what
endures.

Mary Clare

Written By
Mary M. Clare, Ph.D.

Illustrations By
Morgan Blair

Cover Artwork By
Aaron Foster

LOUDMOUTHPRESS

To the ancestors with gratitude.

To the generations to come with devotion.

And with renewed faith, to us –

the ones creating the changes in between.

For to be free is not merely to cast off one's chains, but to live in a way that respects and enhances the freedom of others.
  ~ Nelson Mandela
    via Anthony Davis, North Dakota

Show a people as one thing – as only one thing – over and over again, and that is what they become. When we reject the single story, when we realize that there was never a single story about any place, we regain paradise.
  ~ Chimamanda Adichie, Nigerian novelist
    via Preston Maxwell, Oregon

Once we are wrongly convinced, then we find no end of doubts, distortions and misconceptions to feed our wrong convictions, night and day, to prove how right we are.
  ~ Sogyal Rinpoche
    via Susanna Kelland, Colorado

Introduction

Change is a word Americans fell in love with in the months leading up to the 2008 U.S. presidential election. By the time we got to the polls, regardless of which candidate we were supporting, all of us wanted what the word change promised. Then, on November 4, the word became a sentence, "Change has come to America."

Change had come. Some of us were elated. Others were lukewarm, disappointed or even furious. But no one could deny the change. Barack Obama had defeated John McCain, the Republican candidate to become the first American man of African heritage to serve as our nation's president.

As I watched and lived through these times, I found my social-psychologist self noticing the enormous importance we had given to the idea of change. Words like change and hope and values are big words. They carry a powerful emotional punch, but they can also be amorphous and imprecise, the meaning varying by the person using them. People say words like that to one another and assume that they both mean the same thing. That's not always the case.

We can associate great feelings with a word like change and we can even think we are all working toward the same thing. But if we never stop to state clearly what we mean and then what we'll recognize as signs of change, meanings can become confused and people can feel betrayed if ideals don't materialize as they expected.

This book began as an idea that formed from such musings in the days surrounding the election. What if I went straight to the source? What if I drove around the country asking Americans about change? To start, I came up with three questions:

- When you say the word change what do you mean?
- Alongside change, what is important to have remain the same?
- What would be signs that positive change is occurring?

Then, the day after the presidential inauguration, I began to ask questions and to listen. My goal was to record one hundred voices in one hundred days. I made it. In the hours of taping and driving I experienced one of the greatest privileges of my lifetime – listening to everyday Americans from all walks of life speak of their hopes, ideas and stories in response to those three simple questions.

In the weeks preceding the January inauguration day, a series of necessary preparations was set into motion. First I decided to announce, via email, to 60 friends and family members that I was committing to drive the continental U.S. for the sole purpose of hearing what Americans thought about a specific word. Then followed the cascade of requirements for making it real. I made travel plans, care-of-the-house plans, who-would-I-interview plans. And I tended to the things I hadn't quite anticipated like equipment for recording and maps.

On the front end of a new project, it is always fortunate when signs appear to tell you that you're in flow. By January 21, 2009 I was completely surprised to have drawn the attention of several people in their 20's and 30's- some from the neighborhood, and some from the graduate school where I teach.

"Very cool," they said. "Thanks," I replied. "You need a brand," they said. "A brand?" Ok. "Not so sure what that is. Can you teach me?"

Over coffee and an evening of soup and bread at my house, we came up with a plan. The trip and the project would be called EX:Change to signify listening and speaking about American change. We planned to create a logo with letters in purple, with punctuation – a colon – made up of a red dot and a blue dot. There would be a website and a blog. "Really?" I said. My next question was predictable. "What's a blog?"

The other sign that the flow was progressing came in response to my email announcement. Within two weeks of going public to friends and family there was not one section of the entire country where I would be without a place to stay. Friends, friends-of-friends, friends-of-friends-of-friends generously volunteered their homes and hospitality. The first theme of EX:Change was emerging. Americans have enthusiasm. They show it through the kindness of sharing.

As if they were written in some universal memo, details of the trip and project continued to fall into place. The interviews materialized and American voices spoke out- in ways both predictable and not. Time passed, circumstances and efforts lined up and the 100 voices are now here for you to read and to ponder.

I present the interviews in seven sections, organized by region. This structure follows the journey – its natural alchemy of time and places and people. The grouping also allows you, the reader, to form your own connections between ideas and themes as they overlap and diverge. Right from the beginning, you will hear strong opinions and perhaps wonder about, or even crave the counterpoints. Over time these emerge with later voices from other parts of the country.

Following the mapped route means following chronology. Over the miles and time three important variables were shifting -- my comfort with the project; public events; and geography.

The first influence was undoubtedly my sense of ease with the project. To start, I spoke with people I knew. When I began approaching strangers, they were still folks in my neighborhood. Once I was on the road, I became increasingly comfortable approaching people I did not know.

All the while time and events in our country continued to shift. The early enthusiasm following the inauguration began to wane by late February, while I was in Georgia. By Pennsylvania, David Snyder (076) said, "Has it really only been 50 days?" Many of the one hundred voices emphasized the fact that real change comes quite slowly. Many used the word patience. The headlines continued to challenge our sensibilities and it became apparent that eventually, fatigue and anxiety can trump patience.

Quieter than the eternal contagion of mediated events like the 24-hour news cycle, the third influence, geography, may tell more about America and Americans. How the land affected the content of these interviews intrigues me because, for one thing, it's romantic and, quite honestly, it serves as an excellent vehicle for structuring this book.

I remember being six years old and overhearing my parents speculating about television with a few friends. They were all bemoaning the inevitable influence that TV would have on homogenizing English as a spoken language. They were concerned that standard-TV-English would eliminate dialects and diminish the richness of America's regional cultures. I must note that this conversation occurred between bridge hands in our living room in Sweetwater, TX (i.e., rural West-by-God-Texas).

Clearly, this is an adult translation of a childhood memory, but the things I heard that evening left a major impression on my young mind. Over the years I've watched to see if their prediction came true. What I found in the voices from the EX:Change trip seemed only to prove the opposite. American regionalisms are alive and well. The chronological and geographic presentation of the interviews affords the possibility of discerning the more subtle regional differences among the voices.

Nonetheless, strong and recurring themes crossed all regions of the country. The 100 voices shared concerns and insights on education, economics, environment, health care, family and the wars. There was frequent commentary supporting a theme of cooperative leadership, great interest in seeing elected and other public leaders overcome insubstantial ideological differences to cooperate in the interest of the people. As common was the related theme of civic engagement – "being the change," organizing to assist with positive changes, having and honoring structures (social contract) for setting and pursuing shared goals. Both of these themes were linked with real expression of democracy.

From the onset, the defining parameter of EX:Change was to represent American voices – as broad a range as I could find. This became another way the project drove itself. The geography of the journey guaranteed variation in regional settings, but I was continually astonished by my fortune in finding people from across such a wide spectrum of ethnicities, ages, sexual orientations, spiritualities, socio-economic circumstances, physical abilities and political leanings. Of course, the representation is somewhat incomplete. I can't claim to have a perfect cross-sampling of our country's citizens, but the range in these 100 voices is impressive.

In that range, I paid particular attention to hearing the opinions of people who hold political views that are different from mine. Admittedly, I was jazzed about the election. I even worked for the Obama campaign, traveling to Austin to volunteer and participating in "get-out-the-vote" initiatives in Portland. For the EX:Change, I wanted to listen to people who did not vote the way I did. I couldn't always tell, especially during impromptu interviews, but McCain supporters came my way nonetheless. I contacted several friends to help find people who supported Sarah Palin in particular. Both Obama's presidential campaign and Palin's entry into vice presidential candidacy engaged first-time voters, many of whom had been eligible to vote for years.

These conversations across political rifts take courage for everyone involved. I am grateful to and for every person who spoke with me. But I have particular appreciation for the people who entered into these interviews knowing we would likely not agree in matters of politics. Their willingness and our conversations demonstrate one of the most fundamental goals of EX:Change – to listen and speak across our differences.

The EX:Change project and the narrative in these pages exist for many reasons, but each has its temporal grounding within our own history. The idea for 100 Voices arose out of President Obama's 2008 election and the publication of this project comes with the dawn of the 2012 campaign season. Beyond anything I could have imagined back in that January, I have been privy to timeless wisdom in these one hundred voices – unsung, unpretentious and, from what I could tell, dauntless. Quite a relief. Quite a resource. Now to draw on that wisdom. Hmmm. That would be democracy, wouldn't it?

Another American moment that coincides with this book's publication will be the tenth anniversary of 9/11. Anniversaries are moments in which we take care of ourselves and one another. They help us recharge our joys and they can also help us tend to our grief. Much will be said about that horrific time – about the way it continues to demand two things – that we change and that we stand clearly together on what we value.

The unimaginable becomes renamed as crisis or tragedy. In the end, no single word works to encompass an entire experience. Still, with the odd combination of terror and providence, times such as these offer profound opportunities to grow as a people. The days just following the events of September 11, 2001 at the World Trade Center in New York were thick with anticipation. In waiting, in listening as Americans, with people across the globe, I do believe we actually matured a little in our humanity. Our government then relapsed into war and culture demonizing and we aren't out of that mess yet.

Nonetheless, we continue on. The sensibilities of American people do not remain the same but a good deal of our wisdom may resound over time. The one hundred voices of EX:Change reveal that we do have profound capacity for maturity in the face of sudden change or unexpected events. This book and these voices are not limited to the historic moments surrounding the inception of an idea or the publication of a book. Instead, among the musings and occasional rants contained within these pages we discover a bounty of ideas, ponderings, and wisdom that offer enduring inspiration for the people of America from Americans themselves.

With infinite thanks to EX:Change volunteers and to the visionary expertise of the people of Loud Mouth Press, the sounds of 100 Voices return to the American people as we stand together for embracing the challenge to keep our democracy vibrant and alive.

Mary M. Clare
September, 2011

100 Voices
Americans Talk About Change

One hundred days, one hundred voices. This is what I learned about change in America:

- We are always free to focus on our differences.
- We are free to fear one another.
- We are free to be at war.
- We are free to oppress and to resist oppression.
- We are also free to ground public action in the strength and endurance
- of our vast similarities.
- We are free to love.
- Being alive demands courage, whatever our choices.
- In life, we may never avoid change and we may never avoid connection. In this we are not free. We are, however, free in our responses given these realities.

On December 31, 2008 I made a decision. Or maybe it made me.

For many weeks the echoes of the recent national elections had struck some ineffable harmony with the strains of my life- the stress in work, the earnest brilliance of my graduate students, my daughter being on the bright threshold of her adult life 6000 miles away and the fact that I had just turned 51. That night those vague notes took on a faintly discernable melody. Then, an idea came to me.

Change is change. Hope is hope. One is impossible to avoid. The other can give us the courage to live with that fact.

In the everyday life of an American adult, it is easy to slip into long stretches of feeling irrelevant. I, for example, am a white woman raised in the South, who has now lived for decades in the Pacific Northwest and is solidly into midlife. The anxious search for meaning and purpose, especially as affecting boomers, seems to be typical of adult life in the United States. What I can say from my own experience is that both the desire to contribute and fear of inconsequence exist. On that New Year's Eve, these feelings were definitely lurking.

I sat on the couch. The living room was dark. Rain fell against the tall window behind me making a muffled sound like kitten paws hitting the floor. The glow of the same laptop I'm using right now was blue on my face. I watched my fingers. I watched the words. I had the sense of being slightly removed from the person who was typing- the confident, wise, adventurous one. I'd always liked that side of me.

The idea forming on the screen was, in retrospect, a natural extension of my career so far. I am a social scientist. I spend a good deal of time watching and thinking about the way we interact as human beings – how that interaction works and doesn't and what might make it more fulfilling – you know, peaceful and happy.

The *EX:Change* project wasn't just some random cool idea. Alchemy remained its defining feature, but even alchemy arises from constants. For *EX:Change* to exist, there had to be the constant of a capacity for listening. Likewise, for my career to exist, it had been imperative that I develop and employ a quality of attention based in listening skills that remains respectfully curious and open to the unexpected. The *EX:Change* project logically followed my experiences with research and teaching, particularly as they continued to be influenced by circumstances in the country, in my family and in my own life.

As the project developed, I could see its basis in social psychology given its focus on the way individual lives and behaviors are affected by living in society with other people. To exist within a society, it helps us to identify what we mean by words like *change*, especially if we want to experience the satisfaction of being heard and understood.

An example of the importance of clarifying meaning can be found in the field of cognitive psychology with regard to the idea of happiness. When we can describe for ourselves the conditions that bring us happiness we are more likely to seek and achieve those conditions and less likely to blame other people when we don't. More recently, research in positive psychology indicates people are happier who place their focus on pursuing positive goals rather than on avoiding what they fear. With the word *change* drawing such attention and enthusiasm around the presidential election, it seemed that similar benefit would come from being clear about what we wanted and would recognize as changes.

Although the project drew on my academic training and scholarship, I feel that it's essential to distinguish the collection of interviews in this book from formal research. In methodology-speak, this project would be categorized as ethnographic, but its presentation here is unique. How? OK. Indulge me for a bit of defining. Ethnography is an approach to research that has its roots in anthropology. Because the one hundred voices were only responding to those three general questions –with nothing but room for interpretation – the transcripts could one day be submitted for formal ethnographic analysis.

Ethnography works with big, seemingly simple questions. The findings can only emerge as the responses come in. Instead of conclusions being hypothesized ahead of time and proved or disproved by the data as they are with more traditional scientific methods, ethnographic findings shift with each new bit of input. In the end, the conclusions may become part of the ongoing human story.

As presented here, these interviews are a collection of voices, they are data for you to consider without the presence of formal scientific interpretation. They are ethnographic, but from a purely scholarly standpoint they are not formal ethnography. Nonetheless, like any good story, these data are priceless when it comes to getting insights into everyday lives.

Also like any good story, and like science or any approach to human observation, nothing that I conclude in these pages comes from anywhere beyond my own viewpoint as it has been formed by my experience. I entered into this project as an academic social scientist. I also entered from the middle of an individual life with its unique combination of history and circumstances. I brought my identity as an American who was heartened by the turn of events surrounding the 2008 election. All of these things influenced my experience of the *EX:Change* and the story I tell here.

That rainy New Year's Eve, the project felt timely, even urgent. We were ready for change. Yet, within that enthusiasm I had the more somber awareness that if we don't learn to listen to each other, our fear could likely do a lot of pretty epic damage, and very soon. Would that be an entirely bad thing or could we really learn from such actions? One way or another we must mature beyond the contentious and destructive ways that define too many of our current behaviors. We always have more peaceful options and I suspect they are not nearly as impossible as we think.

Sitting in the dark, this computer on my lap, I watched myself press *send* on the email describing the seedlings of the *EX:Change*. I pulled out my daughter's DVDs and, for no discernible reason, watched *Fifty First Dates*. The movie made me smile. The sound of fireworks came and went. The year turned to 2009. Had I really just signed on for my very own American road trip?

This many decades into life it can be all too easy to slip into repetitive routines – get up, go to work, go to sleep. Even without suffering amnesia like Drew Barrymore's character in the movie, we often do the same things over and over and over again in our daily lives. Occasionally we feel a glimmer of self-awareness. "When did I start getting four shots of espresso in my nonfat latte?" or "Am I really drinking that much wine at dinner?" The self-medication cycle creeps stealthily around the wall of denial.

There's a character in the cosmologies of many Native American tribes known as the trickster; often an animal, sometimes more human-like, the trickster tends to break the rules of nature. I've been most often been told of Coyote. Coyote is fearless and brilliantly adept at masquerading in ways that pull us away from our integrity and into habits that are both ignorant and harmful. Imagine a scamp, hell-bent on wrecking havoc – on screwing things up. In recent years, however, I've started to be able to understand the trickster as a teacher.

In the first few weeks of 2009, Coyote seemed to be showing up around every corner. Not so much in the form of self-medication but most certainly as divots in the fairway of self-confidence and resolve. The random bumps and digs usually took the form of skeptical questions and doubts. "Can I really afford this? What will I do with the house? How will I keep contact with my daughter? I don't even have a current will. And what about my love life?"

This is the paradox. This is Coyote as teacher. Every time circumstances trick me into choosing bad habits of mind or behavior, I have the chance to see them for what they are. I have the ability to choose which path I take. Either way, I inevitably learn about myself. Coyote shows up and makes me prove myself a little.

This time I stepped beyond the trickery of doubt. I found myself feeling curious and courageous all at the same time. Instead of stirring up worried anticipation of the reality of driving from sea-to-shining-sea and back again, I spent most of my time wondering about the American people themselves. From the beginning I expected to find that we carry hopes and dreams more similar than at-odds. I anticipated that people would naturally want peace and well-being. Then as voice after voice accumulated in the Flip camera, I became surprised with how true that prediction was. We do all want clean air and water. We do want the best for our children and for our communities. We do want the best for the world.

Less consistent in the interviews, but at times quite clear and strong, I saw that people are attached to (*even in love with*) the polarities built into our public life. Part of why the red/blue phenomenon of extremes in our politics remains so intense and divided is that we depend on the "evil other" to define ourselves as righteous. We need the opposition we hate.

But, I'm getting ahead of myself. In front of you are the ideas, hopes and dreams of one hundred people I talked to over one hundred days beginning on January 21, 2009. Each voice spoke to what this change in America might mean. They assigned words to the things that everyday people want our country to be and to become. On Day One, I thought my role in all of this was simply to perform a detached scholarly service. I couldn't yet see how personal and intimate this investigation was. As important as these hundred voices might be to contemporary social discourse, and as significant as they might be as conduits of history, I was also about to find out how much I myself needed the reassurance, guidance and real sense of American community I was soon to experience.

PORTLAND, OR
—
1.21 to 1.31.2009

- When you say the word change what do you mean?
- Alongside change, what is important to have remain the same?
- What would be signs that positive change is occurring?

001 Lena Baucum
Wilsonville, OR

Lena Baucum is a 30-something teacher for English language learners in the Woodburn, OR public schools. She works primarily with immigrant and migrant youth. Lena is also an artist who creates large and intricate paper-cut images like the breathtaking black & white dragon fly filling the wall above her dining room table. This morning, we sat beneath that image to talk. Lena is a woman of mixed race and today thoughts of that reality were top on her mind.

Lena: I'm tentative about how much I'm willing to think we can change, but we're at a point where if things don't change dramatically it's going to mean some really ugly consequences. Still, because of the American spirit, the way we work hard and have essentially good hearts, I'm excited for the possibility that we won't continue to be seen as an awful group of people who prey on every other country in the world. At the same time I wonder if we've put too much faith in one human being. How many times has Obama said, "This isn't going to be done by one person?"

Also, part of me is also waiting for a dismantling– for people to begin to pick him apart bit by bit. Anyone who is mixed is worried about that. You get told on one hand, "If you're a little black, you're all black." But on the other hand, you get things like people handing you Ebony and saying, "Here. Obviously you need some culture." The message: "You're not black enough." It goes back and forth. Obama being a generation older than me, I can't know what all of that has looked like for him. But I know in my generation you get dismantled. I'm afraid I'll start hearing, "Well he never was really black." "Well you know he doesn't do 'this' so therefore he isn't one of us." I've known all kinds of black people and I'd say there's not a whole lot of commonality. People tend to pull the generalization when they want to, when it serves their purpose.

There are a lot of wounds to being black, but there's also a lot of cordiality. It's beautiful. Especially if you look at the way the old Southern women speak and talk to each other–the way they take care of each other. It shows up in the way we as black people interface with young people. It's very different from the white culture. The fact that a black mom will walk up to black child, it doesn't matter if it's their child. If they're misbehaving it's like, "What are you doing? You sit back down in that seat right now." It's loving. It's taking care and taking responsibility for giving children good skills for being in the world.

When people ask, "Do you consider yourself black or white?" I think "both and none." Being mixed has all kinds of pieces to it. In my travels I've been stopped more than once in immigration and told, "Excuse me, ma'am, the immigration line is over there. This is the U.S. citizens' line." They don't touch or talk to anyone else in the line and I can read the sign. I'm thinking, "Is this because as a nation we don't recognize

Lena Baucum *Wilsonville, Oregon*

diversity as part of who we are?" Another example is the magazine called Diversity Incorporated. I always laugh as I flip through it because there's no one who's not black in there. That doesn't mean diversity either.

I think our country is more ready for a black President than for a female. I don't have children but at some point I might and I was imagining my kids in the future asking me who I voted for in this election. I thought, "What do I do, turn to my son and tell him I voted for a person who was white, or turn to my daughter and tell her I voted for a man?" Either way it's bad. Gender is still a major issue in our country. Our culture has left out a piece of how we're supposed to treat one another especially between the sexes. Sometimes my female students allow guys in their classes to say things to them that make me think, "No." I pull them aside and say, "Listen. The largest struggle you're going to have in your life is not being Hispanic. The largest struggle you're going to have in your life is being female. You need to make sure you start drawing boundaries where you want them now and get practiced at it."

More than anything, I'm looking for all kids to be able to see themselves as respected members of our society. For the kids I work with, that means the way immigrant populations are dealt with and perceived needs to change. We do have an illegal immigration problem but our policy and practice are wretched. Years ago, there was a joke that a "friendship ditch" was going to be built along U.S.–Mexico border. It was ludicrous. Truly a joke. And now we have a wall? You build an 8 ft. wall, they build a 10 ft. ladder. The issue is not about a wall or a ditch. It's about the economic relations between the countries. Are we going to change those? Are we going to change the fact that our taxes pay INS officers to walk into a pub, accost the Mexicans and demand to check their paperwork. Do they check everyone's paperwork?

Our public policy supports things that are inconsistent with who we really are. We may have a corrupt government half the time, like every other country in the world does. We may have individuals who do bad things just like everywhere else. But on the whole the Americans are really good people.

In every country I've visited I have seen that. People are genuinely good. What would it take for us to start there and not hurt each other as nations for long and sustained periods of time? If we look at what we're all doing today and how it's going to affect three generations from now, the dialogue will become more cooperative because it's around our children and our children's children. Instead of every generation going into a deeper, darker place we could actually improve things. But that means dialogue. It means the way we treat people we think of as "others," will have to change.

002 Art Garcia
Portland, OR

Art Garcia and I met on the streets of downtown Portland. He was selling *Street Roots*[1]1, Portland, OR's newspaper about life on the streets. That was seven years ago. Now he works for the paper coordinating vendors. Art is also a veteran of the war in Vietnam who, "decided to go into the army because it was the best job option I had." By the time he came back from the Southeast Asia his well-established dependence on substances led him "through a hundred jobs or more" in a life punctuated with prison terms, and finally to being homeless and on the streets. Relationships like the one I have with Art teach me that when differences might create barriers, time and being true to your word are keys to building the trust that supports friendship.

Art: These days, people are talking about change because they're scared. They're scared because they're in a routine about fear. But we're not as bad off as people say. America's not that bad. I was thinking about it this morning. About Obama. Actually he's not changing anything. They used that word change in the campaign but he hasn't changed anything. The people change the direction of this country. Everybody around the change has changed it. The people are the change.

Still, we need to catch up if we're going to make change that's any good. I just got a cost-of-living raise on my disability check and it's still way under what it takes. I'm barely scraping enough to pay rent. Housing is ridiculous. Rent, gas, food. I don't know about containing food prices because of farmers' survival, but there's got to be some way we can afford to live.

I see a lot of teenagers on the streets. I talk to kids who left because their mom can't make it. They say, "I feel like I'm a burden. I'm going to get out and make my own money." It's too bad because they should be in school. Makes me wonder. In this country a 15-year-old kid can't afford to go to school? Part of the problem is they don't have the clothes and everything like that. They don't want to go to school because they don't want to look bad. They want to look like the other kids. They don't even have the money to buy lunch. Change that way is a terrible downward spiral.

The veterans are struggling, too. I'd sure like to see our troops coming home. These wars are costing too much. The country might have made money for awhile, but we're losing it now. It's time to get people back home. Fortunately, there's a little more understanding about what returning veterans need. I have heard there are problems with equipment supply over there. A lady colonel was saying they're having to buy their gas masks and flack jackets. I don't know where all that government money goes. Follow the money trail. Somebody's getting it.

Also about change, we still don't do real well with racism. People on TV and in the news they try to make it sound better, but I don't think it is. Living on the streets, there are still big racial differences. Prison is full of it. Racism.

---

1 *Street Roots tag line reads, "Real news from the streets." Its mission: "Street Roots creates income opportunities for people experiencing homelessness and poverty by publishing a newspaper that is a catalyst for individual and social change."*

I spent a lot of time in prison–mostly state prisons. I was in Folsom about ten, twelve years. The Department of Corrections actually encourages racism by segregating on race. Prisoners have to join one gang or the other or they're on their own. Like in California you have the Northern Mexicans and the Southern Mexicans; you have your black groups–your Crips and Bloods; you have your Asians and your whites. Everybody's split up. That's how the prison officials set it up. If you say, "nobody," they put you in with anybody and then you're in trouble.

There's a lot of killings in there. In the corporate prison the officers were killing people. There was a big thing on 60 Minutes about that. The officers were putting opposing gangs in the little compound yard at the same time–it's called the cage. They'd let them loose and watch from up on the catwalk. After one of those guys killed another one, they'd shoot the one who lived.

They do that to keep the prisoners at each other and not at them. But if the prisoners are constantly fighting and killing on the inside, they're not going to change when they get out. There's thousands and thousands of people in prisons who think that way. Then they have kids and their kids think that way. By the time those kids are teenagers they're out on the streets. I don't see how change can come with that way of teaching racism. Besides, prison is a money making situation–one of the biggest money makers in the United States. Right up at the top of the list.

Last time, I was in prison 30 miles from my hometown of Paso Robles. When my brother came to pick me up, we went by. That was the first time I saw people pushing shopping carts there. I said, "Man; in this town?" We never had that before. People holding up signs. "I need help." Paso Robles. It's really El Paso de Robles, but they call it Paso Robles. It's right there on the coast near San Luis Obispo. Nice, beautiful place. People were happier in the late 50's and 60's. When I was a kid my foster parents never bought anything on credit. We didn't believe in credit.

Change for the homeless is what I work for now. The idea is that being a vendor for *Street Roots* gives people with no economic options the chance to become active on their own behalf–to sell the paper and apply their profits to shelter, food and eventually enough stability to find and keep a better job. It takes commitment and a positive attitude. Those are two of the hardest things to come by when you live on the streets.

003,004 Kate Bodin & Georgiana Nehl
Portland, OR

I found myself wrestling in those first days with my own brand of shyness. As fate would have it, I got a chance to warm up slowly. After Art, I met with two middle-aged, white women artists. I have been friends with Georgiana Nehl for some years now and Kate Bodin is her boss. In addition to each making their own art, Georgiana is a full professor with the Oregon School of Art and Craft and Kate is the school's dean. In age, race, gender, education and economic status these two women are quite similar to me, which was an important reminder of the powerful practice of looking for the familiar in the strange and the strange in the familiar.[2]

Kate: Hmmm. Change. Well really, it feels like I was born to make changes. I have a habit of listening, thinking, seeing the large perspective and then being able to discern viable ways for getting from A to Z. That all influences me as a leader.

I've learned most about change from circumstances in my life. Huge changes began for me when I met my birth mother. It wasn't disabling, but wondering about the woman who brought me here always loomed as a major question. When I had the chance to meet her a few years ago, I had the experience of falling through a lot of the uncertainty. What I fell onto was the solid ground that had always been there in my adoptive family and in my own self. Suddenly all my striving to find better and bigger became more practical. Lots of anxiety dropped away and left willingness. I saw the importance of being willing not only to hold the vision for change, but to live the change all the way through.

So, I've learned that nobody can go into change without being completely committed to healing. The country and the world are hungry for this–for the integrity of action that is consistent with all this language of change.

Georgiana: That kind of leadership requires community. It requires bringing the voices and perspectives–what is around and behind the concerns and brilliance of all people into the intelligence of leadership. And the healing has to occur before change can take hold.

Kate: Yeah. That means good change is not inflicted–it is not imposed. It involves bringing in the vision and interests of everyone involved or affected. But sort of ironically, good solid change also requires conventional top-down authority. Leadership for positive change can't move forward without consensus. That happens in the conversations leading toward decision. Still, decisions must be made and inevitably some stakeholders are disappointed. But when listening to all voices is not just an appeasement, when it is real and respectful dialogue, the disappointment is easier to move past. Soon another change point arises and different stakeholders make the compromises. I'm compromising all the time in the interest of change.

Then there's the question of what signifies change. That's a hard question. It's more global. Right off the top of my head these days I'd say I'm hoping we see Obama really and truly connecting with global leaders. We'll see that in something as basic as productive conversation. The percentage of the U.S. population and the large numbers of people around the world who are excited about Obama symbolize hope for a different way of leading and governing. If we can extend that into issues like Palestine/Israel, Iraq/Iran and those conflicts begin to be rectify toward real peace, that will be a huge indicator of positive change.

Georgiana: For me there are two main signs. One will show up soon in how our new

---

2   *Variations on the phrase are used in disciplines as variant as engineering, anthropology, artistic photography and creative writing. I've always associated it with Barbara Myerhoff in her rich ethnography of elderly Holocaust survivors living in Venice Beach (Number our Days), but with this writing have learned it likely originated with Novalis (1772-1801, aka Friedrich von Hardenberg), a German poet writing late in the 18th century.*

leader interacts with others. If he remains open, heartfelt, non fearful and honest we will all learn to share better. Over the longer term, change will show up more concretely in things like the energy we use, our cooperation across country lines, and our coming together in new formations of leadership.

We need new structures for political discussion and action. We need our leadership to move from us-them thinking to clear understanding that we're all in this together. This will show up in our putting out heads together instead of being so territorial about "I'm right. You're wrong." This is a drastic change and it must happen at the level of leadership–both political and social. Most human community still relies on leaders to validate any way of being–and certainly to validate any change. We need the values behind "we're all in this together" to become deeply established as the paradigm that applies to everything.

005 Se-ah-dom Edmo
Portland, OR

Se-ah-dom Edmo (Shoshone-Bannock/Yakama/Nez Perce) is in her early thirties and already a leader. Between meetings, she stopped for tea and to talk about change. Her work coordinates the Indigenous Ways of Knowing project at Lewis & Clark College. Her mission, professionally and personally, is to support tribal sovereignty. Se-ah-dom's public life gives every indication of her leadership skill and is influenced powerfully by her experiences as a mother, a daughter, and a community member.

Se-ah-dom: When I think about change, I think of how everything is in the process of becoming its opposite. Things that are becoming alive have been dead. Things that have been silenced will constantly struggle to have a voice. Things that have had great voice will become silent. In my mind, that goes toward creating a synergistic balance between opposites; teetering and then becoming balanced.

Lately I've been watching people I know and feeling that their spirits are being fed by really luminous things. We can see these ideas and energies coming from people's bodies. They still look the same but they exude something different. So with change, I think of things becoming the opposite and I think of changes in the spirit and being of people.

What always stays the same is my belief in people's ability to gain moral insight through their sympathy and empathy toward other people. I don't think that's something we could change. Anyone in a moment of sympathy or empathy makes a commitment. That is when morality is formed. We can't take that away from people, and it's something that seems to be happening more now than it has before. There is more listening.

It's kind of a funny time to be on the brink of change. A lot of folks are scared about the economy and I don't think I've ever felt as safe. It seems like there is a different take on what success is now. I'm not as concerned about buying into the economic hierarchy to measure personal worth. I like this new measure of person to person connection, so I'm not really worried about the economy taking a downturn. I think most people have

Se-ah-dom Edmo *Portland, Oregon*

become more concerned with things that are way more real, way more valuable, and more enduring than economic status.

The new presidential administration will have a lot of opportunities to support this kind of change. I hope they don't adopt the tactics and hierarchy of the dominant culture in order to get what they need. I've seen a wave of dominant tactics in the past years when other federal administrations allowed their thoughts and motivations to get overtaken by greed. I hope that never comes this time.

We'll start seeing positive change with the creation of programs and systems that more readily reflect our interpersonal belief systems. If we say diversity is important, we will start seeing evidence of that value in systems and policies supporting how we conduct social programs and public engagement. We will start seeing real service across diversity everywhere and not just in isolated boxes.

People in the dominant culture will be forced to walk their talk until they realize their talk is their value system and their walk is important and good for everyone. I think everybody wants to believe they're good and right and that they make good decisions. But the things that Peggy Macintosh[3] talks about in terms of unearned privilege are real forces. There are many people who unconsciously work against wanting under-represented people to really have opportunity and education toward professional roles. Those people benefit from unearned privilege they don't see. And, of course, they don't want to give up the spots they feel they're entitled to.

Even though I believe everyone has the ability to experience and learn from empathy and sympathy, policies like affirmative action can make it so they don't allow themselves those experiences. They put up guards because they're scared to lose something. They don't realize what they are already losing when they give up their own choice—when they, too, are run by the dominant model by being in a hierarchy that holds some people worth less than others. They give up their personal moral integrity. They give up their ability to make free choices.

I believe that there is a Creator and a God. When those people come to the point when time is over for them on this earth, they are going to have to answer for their behavior and their way of doing things. Even though I sometimes make poor decisions and knowingly or unknowingly have not defended or come to the aid of people who are different than myself, I have done the best I can to always incorporate responsibility for empathy and sympathy into my way of doing things.

Road Note

Listening to Se-ah-dom's words, it was impossible to ignore their historical precedents. Some readers of this book may not be familiar with Native American history, so more information seems important here. You'll see I use these road notes from time to time to keep the *EX:Change* journey present in the way that it had already begun to weave these voices into a pattern uniquely American.

Se-ah-dom is a descendant of Celilo Falls, the cooperative tribal community that was flooded on March 10, 1957 by the construction and subsequent opening of the Dalles Dam on the Columbia River. Her father was 11 years old when he

---

3 *Peggy McIntosh. Lecturer and writer on white privilege, male privilege and equitable curricula. http://www. speakoutnow.org/userdata_display.php?modin=50&uid=93*

stood on high ground with his family to watch the inundation of their home. For thousands of years Celilo had been a major center of economic activity for the tribes of the Pacific Northwest. People from all over the continent made their way to the Falls to trade for salmon. Then the day came, just over fifty years ago, when the domestic well-being of dozens of tribes and a major economic infrastructure were suspended indefinitely in the name of electricity and power.

This story of the Columbia River gorge and Celilo Falls became the story of all people living in the Pacific Northwest and bears the truth of many people I interviewed in the beginning of the project. Their lives have also been affected by historical moments like the arrival of the European explorers and pioneers, the immigration of Chinese people to build the country's railroads, and the internment of Japanese people in refugee camps during World War II.

As I have listened over the years to the stories of the first people of this land, I have seen that contemporary Native Americans are descendants of change. They have been oppressed and subjugated to tyranny and displacement and yet cultural and communal resilience, what one leader calls "Indian Renaissance," help them endure. "And surviving and thriving is not just for Indians," he said. "All of us together change to keep this thing going."

006 "Leila Bowen"
Portland, OR

Leila Bowen (her requested pseudonym), another young leader, is a manager for the coffee shop that sustained me as *EX·Change* emerged and grew. In her mid 20's, Leila has wisdom way beyond her years. And yet she's conflicted about her future and what path to choose. She has already spent years as a campaign organizer and while she struggles with what she calls "economic aristocracy," she is also greatly encouraged by the younger voters who are bringing a new voice to America. Originally from a middle class Mormon community, Leila took a bad turn that ended up taking her way too close to a life on the street. From surviving that experience, she maintains a creative inner drive that is both dauntless and compassionate.

Leila: My first wish is for us to move past race, gender, sexual orientation and appearance as the ways we judge each other. Instead, I would like to see a different set of measurements; like paying attention to energies, demeanor, respectfulness, body language. That would allow strangers to get to know each other without the vague skepticism around appearance. Of course, this is asking a lot. Too many people fundamentally don't care about others and see everyone else as wrong or manipulative.

Hopefully our new leader can inspire people to change their perceptions. In my work I interact with a large range of the public and I've already seen some movement. I certainly don't expect Mr. Obama to wave a magic wand, but from the first time I heard him speak I knew he was willing to talk about our problems without pointing fingers. He understands where we are and the opportunities we face. If people watch that enough, they'll begin to learn how to do it themselves.

A lot of it has to do with the experiences people have as young citizens in the schools. My personal experience with the public school systems was disastrous. I am the type of student that gets straight A's, leads group projects; the one teachers love because of my curiosity and fairly open mind. But I didn't graduate high school. I lost interest. I was not challenged and I felt stifled. I was especially enraged when the GED test did not incorporate anything taught after my sophomore year. If that is the case, then keeping students for two extra years is nothing more than a monumental waste.

So, we need to change our educational system. We pay more taxes and approve more bonds but the quality of education continues to decline. It is time to bring in experts who are not tainted by bureaucracy to reformulate our whole approach to learning in this nation. It will be a painful restructuring, but it is critical to avoid being left in the dust with all hopes of sustaining our economy gone.

007, 008(+) Alegria Cupit and her preschoolers Portland, OR

I spent the next few days getting ready for the road: I took my Mini Cooper to the shop for one last check up; lists of plant-watering and fish-feeding tasks were distributed to people watching my house, tentative itineraries were emailed to family and my bills were all paid. On January 29, the opportunity came to me to hear from some of our youngest citizens, students at Schoolita Alegria, a bilingual preschool focused on Spanish and English. This morning, the children spoke from perspectives that adults usually overlook. The voices numbered here as 007 and 008 include Alegria herself and the eight three-to-five year olds who sat in a circle, vivid and entirely present in the way children remind us that we all can be.

MC: The first thing I want say is, "Good morning."

Children: Good morning.

MC: It is so good to see you. I have a question. There's a word we use in English that you've probably heard. The word is, "*change.*" Have you heard that word?

Child 1: Yeah. Cambia.

MC: "Cambia" in Spanish. Exactamente! Bueno. OK. So, somebody put your hand on your heart and tell me what you mean when you say "*change.*"

C2: It means change your toy.
C3: If it's legos.
C4: Change the toy to some other toy.
C1: Change markers.
C3: Put one marker back and use another marker.
C5: Like change your clothes.

C6: Change your clothes into your pajamas.

MC: Do you know that the grownups in this country have been talking a lot about change?

C7: They have?
C5: Because the economy is changing.
C8: It's Obama. I watched Obama.
C6: I watched Barack Obama get elected.

I have another word. The first word was "change." The second word is "same." What does same mean?

C6: The same means like you're the same as another person.
C3: Like me and Fiona, we have both light skin.
C4: Like the same toy.
C5: The same paper.
C3: Like we all have one of these (*points to the letter 'i'*). Look you have one (*points to another child's card*)
C2: But not me. (*continue comparing letters*)
C6: The same is Alegria wrote our names with the same pen.
C8: Look. You can fold it! (*folds his name card*)

MC: OK. Here's one more word. Tell me about "hope." What does "hope" mean to you?

C2: It means that you mean something.
C3: You hope for to happen.
C2: Like a baby.
C6: It's like that you hope that Barack Obama gets elected. Because John McCain and George Bush aren't good Presidents.
C3: George Bush is a funny name. George Bush is a bush with eyes.
(*all start saying funny things about bushes*)
(**C8**: *one little boy sits quietly*)
C6: So somebody says, I hope that George Bush does not, is not is the President.
C5: Because he started two wars.
C4: He started three wars.

MC: What are other things that people hope for?

C3: You hope for a toy you want.
C5: You hope for a teddy bear.
C3: Or you hope for an art project thing or you could get your own princess set, a princess castle like me. I have a princess castle.
C2: I have a Dora.

Alegria: I just explained to the children this morning. Where's Mary going? Who can remember?
Children: All over Portland.
Alegria: And all over to the U
Children: United States!
Alegria: And what is she going to do? I don't think I told you that. She's going to talk to a lot of people about...what did she talk to you guys about? Was it cheetos, was it chores?
Children: Change.
Alegria: Change. You guys said it. Say it again.
Children: Change!
Alegria: Wish her a happy trip. Buen viaje.
Children: Buen viaje.

MC: Gracias. (*lots of hugs*)

C3: You smell very good.

MC: I'm so glad. And thank you for the good wishes.

Road Note

My daughter is in her early twenties, so it's been awhile since I walked out of a preschool. Leaving the children that morning, I had the pleasant experience of being flooded with memories of my life as a preschooler's mom. Their wisdom resides in their freshness, in their complete freedom from pretension. I remembered my five-year-old handing me a note, one of her first attempts at writing. It read, "BasBaLL has aLot uverules anD so Duse sowingBy sara." (*Translation: Baseball has a lot of rules and so does sewing. By Sara.*)

I walked from the Scoolita Alegria to a neighborhood coffee shop. As I set up my computer to send some last emails before I left, I wondered if I was ready to initiate a conversation with someone I didn't know. Social interaction has a lot of unwritten rules. One is, don't pursue an unwelcome conversation. A man was sitting and enjoying his coffee with the paper. He seemed not to be in a rush, so I decided to gather my courage and give it a try.

009 Nick Minnis
Portland, OR

Nick Minnis and I exchanged eye contact. I leaned forward, said my name and offered my hand. He smiled and said his name in return. After some small talk, I told Mr. Minnis the story of *EX:Change*. He was intrigued. I said, "Would you be willing to let me interview you? I've got this super tiny camera and a permission form. What do you think?" Nick Minnis, a laborer on an uncommon day off, was into it.

Nick Minnis: Change overall? It's going to be different for everybody. Any change has got to be better than what we've had the past eight years but from today's market we're going down, down, down. Anyone who can step up and show interest in doing something better; well, that's the change people are looking for.

I might be hanging myself here. You can look at it as blacks are now top dog, but blacks don't think it's really going to be different. The government is still run by the people already there. Still, to have a woman running for President, that was a change. To have a black person running for President, that was a change. And he won. So, the change has already started. Now, it depends on what we intend to do with it.

Anything that's done well will be received by everybody. Everybody will benefit, not monetarily, but by changing their life. They'll get a job. They'll get a pay raise. They won't have to sweat about losing their job. Stuff like that is change. I'm not a politician. My world is small. I work, I provide, and I sleep...very little. (*laughs*) Just waking up every day is the only thing I can be sure will remain the same, but stability comes from alleviating the fear of what's going to happen next. How bad is it really going to get?

If we're talking about President Obama, then he's already made changes they're publicizing. He's listening to people – to foreign people. You can't just consider what's right for America. What's right for everybody? Why not find out how to avoid stepping on toes and be allied so that we all gain? It goes from there.

Common sense should tell the American people that even with a new president, you can't just have the soldiers home from war in six months. I don't think they can take them out of Afghanistan. And with the Iraqi people – we go in there, we disrupt their way of life and then just leave them? That's not right. You don't do that.

We think we did them a favor, but I think it was a big mistake. I view things differently than a lot of people. Saddam Hussein had his way of flexing muscle. They were pushing him around, but he was in control. The random and widespread killing we see now wasn't happening when he was in power. We cut the head off and now everybody wants to be in charge. So here we go. Civil war. Who's going to end up on top when we finally leave? It could be worse. I could be better. Whoever is in charge is going to be better off for himself and not so much for Iraq. Whenever we do leave, whoever's got the most money, the most power and can hurt the most people is going to be in charge.

There's no difference from the way it was when we first came to America. Americans so called "discovered" this country and you know what we did to the Indians. All of that grew into slavery. Back in the cowboy days, they say the country was uncivilized without laws. That's what they have to do in Iraq, make laws. But the majority of the people have to want it. There's still too much fear for the people to step up.

The Iraqis are fighting for what they think is right. They don't want an outsider telling them how to live. The early Americans had their first war was with England for the same reason. They also fought the Indians that already lived here. They fought for territory and because of the clash in the lifestyles. It's all the same. The Indians were doing it before we got here with warring between the different Indian Tribes. The guy with the most braves and the most determination ruled the most territory.

The same thing in Iraq. Superior power is going to win – whatever sect, you know Shiite or whatever. We came here with guns. The Indians had bows and arrows. Someday there will be other forms of power besides military, but that has to happen here first before you can expect the world to accept it.

Can we be without military force? It's going to be a struggle the same way it was for us to elect a black president. Change to peaceful ways of negotiating and working things out will evolve over time, but not as long as people keep flexing their muscles with weapons. The main thing everybody wants is a better life for their kids.

The Republicans say, "Why should we take care of these people the Democrats have programs for? Everybody should provide for themselves." But everybody can't be at the top. I guess there's always going to be a left and a right.

It's not always destructive, though, depending on the individuals. Even in church not everybody is on the same level of Christianity. There's always that 10% that are going to be different. You can pick out ten people you think are good people. When the discussion starts, one somebody is going to stand out and disagree. Somehow you have to come up with that happy medium. What that is, only God knows. (*smiles and laughs*)

It's going to take a while, a lot of talking. Speaking from the black – I don't want to speak for blacks, but from my perspective being a black man. Because of the history behind us and what I have observed in my lifetime, I will feel I'm going to be shortchanged. I will feel that until I see some definite improvement. If they tell you that you can be equal, but you never make any gains, you're going to say, "Nothing has changed." So why should people apply themselves? It's really a catch 22. It's going to be a long process breaking down racial barriers.

What I would like to see is this. Obama wants everybody to assist him with these changes, but there's nothing out there saying what we need to do. If his team of people knows, put it out to the public. What changes? Not the grand scale, but what can we do down in the communities to actually start building change as opposed to just throwing the word out there. I'm ready, but I don't have any guidelines. A list of some sort would help a lot.

010 Bao Pham
Portland, OR

I thanked Mr. Minnis and went back to my table. A few minutes later, a man who had been selling Street Roots on the corner of East Burnside came in to get warm. Bao Pham got some water and sat down at the table next to me. Bao has an enormous personality. He smiles and jives with people walking down the sidewalk, and ends up selling a lot of papers that way. I offered to buy him some coffee. "No thanks. I already had my quota," he joked. For a second time, I initiated an interview a stranger. Boa Pham agreed.

Bao: Change. We need big change. Like having jobs come back home. There's no jobs and that's why we're getting new vendors every day. What's going to happen next month when the economy gets worse? I'm not going to work if there's many more vendors. I hit different spots, different locations and people are saying, "We've already got the paper." That tells you how many people are selling it.

I'll make a grand a month on the paper but that's not enough to live on. A hotel room costs $80. You gotta eat. That's another $20 a day. It's expensive out there. The cheapest motel is $58. If you get a cockroach motel that's $28, but that's where you get your bug bites – like all this stuff, (*points to bites on his face*). I'm going to look for another job. I'm just doing to this part time on the side. I'm the top vendor, and I tell you it's just enough to eat on. I don't know how the other guys are making it. They're buying rolly cigarettes instead of regular cigarettes, and they're eating at Sisters of the Road4[4]. It's been tough out here.

And it's going to get worse. Six more months, you'll see. People will be jumping out of windows. The true survivors are guys like me who know the streets. You never lived on the street. What would happen if you end up homeless? How are you going to handle it, you know what I'm saying? The shelters are packed. You ain't going to be able to sleep out in the snow. You don't know how to do that. You don't know how to get cardboard and go underneath for shelter and put up a tarp. You don't know that kind of lifestyle.

I went to Salvation Army last night, they turned us away, 48 guys. I slept outside, got up, went and got me breakfast, went to the office, got my papers, and it's been slow this whole morning. This has been a bad day, 9 papers. It's hard sleeping outside. As you get older, it's worse for your body. I'm 40 almost, 37 years old. I still have a full set of hair, though. (*smiles*)

I've lived on the streets five or six years off and on. I held jobs and had an apartment and stuff. But when you get into crisis situations like getting laid off, you eventually have no choice. I don't have a heroine problem. I don't have major serious problems. I drink a little bit, but not every day. It could happen to anybody, man. What's going to happen if you end up not being able to pay for your mortgage?

I came from Iowa and ended up getting laid off from a printing company in California. I started pan handling first. I did real good – 60-80 bucks a day. But you've got to know how to work it. Life's not been really fair, so you have to know the streets and how to fly signs like, "Hey, I'm out of insulin." You fly sign, and people give you money. You do what you've got to do, but I don't like doing that. I really don't like manipulating people. But hey, I'm sleeping in the snow. Going out to look for work during the day without a good night's sleep, that's pretty hard on a body. You haven't showered for three of four days. It's rough.

Could you imagine if you had no money? I went without anything for 2 Ð months before I started pan handling. Then flying sign. I had to throw that gig in, but I don't like it. It takes my pride away. This takes my pride away, too, selling papers. But it's also a good cause. I feel a little better doing it to get the news out.

If we talk about change – well, you drive around the city, don't you? You see how many people are homeless. Every corner people are holding signs. We need to bring jobs back home. This laying off people is not going to work. There's going to be more suicides coming. We need to create jobs, now. Right away. Hybrids, whatever – Natural gas running cars. And you have to end the war, period. Not one war – you have to end both wars. It's draining us. End both wars and bring jobs back home.

I'll tell you that right now. I would rather have a home, a job, a place to stay – not sleeping out in 3 feet of snow. Last night was cold, man. It was 29 degrees where I slept.

4 *Sisters of the Road Café. Food for people of the street; community-driven, nonviolent solutions to the calamities of homelessness and poverty. http://sistersoftheroad.org/*
6a *George Grigorief died in a cemetery in Portland on January 9, 2009. He was Iranian/Russian/American, a military veteran, and homeless. Dying Out There Amanda Waldrope Street Roots.*

And the fog came in. I went down to Salvation Army and they were out of blankets. I had my two sleeping bags and they gave me this little thin blanket. I was like, "What am I going to do with that?" So, I used it to cover my feet. I'm sleeping out tonight, too. There's just too many people – 4600 homeless people and only 4 shelters.

I'm not worried about selling papers as much as I am concerned about getting this information out to the people. That's my life project right now. I want people to know it's hard for us out here. George didn't need to die. And there's 1000 Georges that are dying out there. George didn't need to die that night and neither did the guy who died last night. You didn't know that? Yeah, a fire fighter announced him dead down on 6th Street last night. Froze to death. Shelter turned him away at 10 p.m.; found his body at 4 o'clock this morning.

There was no room. He had no blankets. He was about eight guys in front of me at the shelter. Thin as paper. Froze to death last night. You didn't know about that? The fire department went down there and checked his pulse and he was dead.

There's 1000 Georges. George was just one. There's 1000 Georges out there that die and we even don't know. And a lot of them have family. George came from a good family. He served in the military. He served for this country – went to Viet Nam. Came back all messed up. That's what happens. That's why I sell the paper.

KLAMATH FALLS, OR to SAN DIEGO, CA

—

2.2 to 2.10.2009

- When you say the word change what do you mean?
- Alongside change, what is important to have remain the same?
- What would be signs that positive change is occurring?

KLAMATH FALLS, OR to SAN DIEGO, CA
2.2 to 2.10.2009

The sun was shining and the temperature was warmer than usual on this particular Groundhog's day, 2009. Had I been in Punxsutawney, PA this would not have been good news, especially for the winter-weary. In western Oregon, there was no possibility of the missing shadow, that mythic promise of an early spring. That was just fine by me.

In the days since January 21 I had collected ten voices for the *EX:Change-* seventeen if you counted each brilliant preschooler. As our interview wrapped up, Nick Minnis (009) had asked me, "So what do you think about change?" I hedged. This project wasn't supposed to be about my ideas, just about everyone else's. Right? Mr. Minnis continued, "But you're calling it *EX:Change*. Exchange is like this. It's Ex + Change. That equals exchanging points of view. It's communicating. It can't be just a one-way thing."

I realized later that Nick Minnis had 'busted' me. What made me think that I could position myself as the only one asking and answering questions? I'd read enough linguistic theory to know, or at least remember, that the role of questioner is a power position because it controls the conversation. Mr. Minnis may or may not have known it, but he was calling me out and into the dialogue I had said I wanted – one with all of us listening across our differences.

Today I would set off on the highway south. As I moved through final preparations, I thought about how change always implies the existence of a constant. One can't exist without the other. I remembered the two questions that arose when I spoke with Kate (003) and Georgiana (004).

- What is familiar in the strange?
- What is strange in the familiar?

For example, I considered the privilege of having the ability to take this trip in the first place. It's easy for privilege to be so familiar it can't be seen. With Kate (003) and Georgiana (004), I had also recognized a bit of the strange in the way all three of us use so many words. I watched how the number of words and complexity of our sentence structures increase with our bounty of passion for life and its concerns. To spend a career this way, researching the human condition, is not only unusual, it could be considered somewhat of a luxury.

There's no avoiding the facts of this privilege. It's not a condemnation; it's circumstance. It's opportunity. I am fed and housed and educated. I have a job. I can talk philosophy over coffee. I can go for long walks and think things over. I can drive around the country out of curiosity with a Flip camera. These privileges in my life are uncommon but action that is enabled by privilege has the potential to improve the quality of many lives. The caveat is in making the familiar strange; that is, in being willing to see when my good fortune exists at a cost to someone else. The follow up to that kind of awareness is using my privileges of access and time to do all I can to help dismantle the systems of oppression and repair the harm.

Early in this project I would have the opportunity to interview two very wealthy men and with an affluent older couple. These four people remain the richest I know to date. The men followed up on their interviews with the decision to withdraw their words from the project. Both of them cited the importance of reputation and anonymity as reasons. Financial success often involves holding your cards very close. The result in the case of this book is that their insights on change and social circumstances are unfortunately not included here. Nonetheless, based on our interactions, I sensed that both of these men understand the social responsibility and influence inhering in their privilege.

Each of us holds some measure of privilege with the option of using it for positive social change. However, sometimes even the most well meaning intentions can cause harm of staggering proportions. For example, in the late 1800's the Friends of Indians, a group of white religious leaders, social reformers and government officials began the 'Indian boarding school movement.' The idea was to educate Native Americans with European-American standards in order to "kill the Indian, save the man." Entire generations were separated from their families, punished for using their languages, beaten and finally shamed away from their cultural identities.

Another danger of acting from a position of privilege concerns denial. As we continue public debates on discrimination and harassment, people from systems of privilege can respond in several ways. One set of responses comes out of awareness; using privileges of access to address harmful circumstances. In contrast are two reactions that both avoid taking responsibility and side-step creative action. The first is to becoming angry or dismissive; to deny any participation in or benefit from harmful actions. The second is to become paralyzed in response to the enormity of the damage caused by unfair privilege and to do nothing for fear of causing more harm.

"Yeah, yeah, yeah." So many thoughts on the dawn of the road trip. I carried another load down to the car and imagined my daughter warning me against over-thinking things. "Give everybody a chance to show up and live kind lives, Mom. We can do it."

Ok. I actually do believe clear down to my toes in the essential kindness of people. But here's the deal. Kindness doesn't always get expressed. As it turns out, it takes major courage on top of basic manners for any of us to see our potential to be kind to fruition. From what I can tell so far, the courage to comprehend and then take action to repair oppression in any form depends on listening well. It depends on being fully present in this world. That's why I was packing my car. I wanted to know about change and I wanted to know if it was possible for us to listen to each other.

Everything was ready. I had maps. I had the tiny Flip camera with its tiny tripod. I had batteries and my sleeping bag. Since a Mini Cooper requires that stuff be spare, I had packed only a small bag with a road trip wardrobe – minimal, versatile and washable.

The house was secured; the weather was sweet. I hit the road.

Just after dusk I stopped in Roseburg, Oregon for a decaf latte. The only coffee place I could find was the drive-through Dutch Brothers, where a guy was working alone and I was the only customer. When we got into conversation about the *EX:Change* trip, he wanted to know if it was partisan. I said, "It's American." He mused, "I think we're all star struck. We can't put change all on one person." He wished we could rise above our differences to identify a few major points of agreement – things of substance that matter to Americans – "things we can work on together. It's a privilege to live in this country," he said, echoing my recent thoughts, "We need to take care of it."

011 Calvin Hecocta
Klamath Falls, OR

The next morning I was near the Oregon-California border, in the foothills of Mt. Shasta. Over the phone, Calvin Hecocta (Paiute/Modoc) warned me to drive slowly over that pass, especially by Klamath Lake. He was right. The high desert roads were icy in the morning shadows. An activist, counselor and teacher, Mr. Hecocta is widely recognized as an inspiring leader. His sixty years of advocacy for the environment and indigenous rights demonstrate wisdom as the ground for his action.

Calvin Hecocta: As a change, I would like to see an international tribunal for indigenous peoples from across the globe. So far convening this kind of event has been blocked.

Here is an example. The tribal people of Belize have been attempting to make the indigenous voice heard relative to the oil drilling policy and practices of that government. The people wish to have their testimony heard. They have the assistance of an attorney. It is too likely, though, that the U.S. will flood the Belize government with money to support drilling and overwhelm the indigenous voice. If that fails, typical U.S. practice is to create a military coup that results in massacres of native peoples.

This has been the U.S. government's pattern across South America and every other region of the world – Iraq and Pakistan, for example. The U.S. has to understand its impact on the world. It has to understand indigenous rights. That is the change that is needed.

The change I expect? Very little. There will continue to be changes to benefit the global industrial complex but none for the people. Unless we survive about 10 years, then we might see change.

In myself, the indicator of change would be for me to believe in this country. There are things that could move me in that direction. For example, the current president will have to allow charges to be brought against Bush, Cheney and all others involved in the colonial war against Iraq. If he does not support that expression of justice we will continue the status quo as inherited. To say, "Forget all that stuff and let's just move forward," is to proceed the same as always. We'll see if Obama does anything about it or if he's just the same as the rest of them.

I would say the Democratic and Republican political parties are one and the same in the crime family of the current U.S. federal government. The mafia is small time compared with the federal system. The American people must come forward to reject the Republican/Democrat philosophies and adopt policies that support the States becoming independent nations working in their own boundaries to help the people they know are there.

In all of this, mine is not a fringy militant voice. I am speaking as a citizen. My hope with every speaking engagement or other teaching I do involves the waking of people. When they wake up to see they are being lied to by their government and representatives, they will speak out and take action against the deception.

The problem begins in a school system that creates the dumbing of America. Our youth need to be re-educated to reveal what is expected of them. They are currently being trained in total silence – in passive acceptance. There's also a powerful disconnect with the environment. The connection I speak of is with the soil, the waters and the plants – with the forest and water beings – with all the people there – the flyers, beautiful birds.

Together with waking up to our intricate interdependence with all beings, change requires psychosocial shifts. The psychological things we must deal with are evident in symptoms of mental and spiritual disconnection. If your mind and heart are not right because of confusion in your belief system then you are unable to have an understanding of the natural environment.

You look at the child within. I deal with that child within me, and with the teenager and the adult and the old man. I deal with all those pieces every day. If my mind and spirit are not in balance with the four ages inside me, then the tendency in imbalance is to shut everything out. Isolation then creates spiritual death. This is the sickness of our Nation and its citizens. That's where we're at.

Empires do collapse once the peasant workers come alive and get their spirits back. I'm trying to remember that song. Years ago in school we all stood and sang that song, maybe the state of Oregon song. In it there was something about, "the land of empire builders." If you get a bunch of youth singing that – a whole state of young kids – they'll come to believe in the illusion.

The other day I was at the library and there was this movie: Beckett. You know that movie? It was a good one. I checked it out and lost it four times. I compare that movie with what's happening in this country: The "kingdom" and its fight with God and God's People. I ask myself, "Am I just a part of the babbling brook or am I a part of the movement of the stones?"

When life has been given to you, you must take it very seriously. I was raised in Beaty, Oregon by a Paiute dad and a Modoc mom. I was born on December 7, 1942. I remember standing on a mountainside looking down on the valley with the Old Man. The Old man told me I would be a spokesman for my people. For a short time I thought he was meaning the people in my tribe – my clan. My grandfather eventually explained the Old Man was meaning the people that have no voice: The trees and the people that live there – the swimmers and the flyers that have not voice – the children. I was told that by the Holy Man. Every day I live with respect for that responsibility.

How many young men have received such instruction around the world? Too few. This has led to our psychosocial unrest and illness. In this country and others individuals, families and communities have become profoundly deprived of spiritual connection because of the absence of rites of passage for youth. An important change would be to look at these rites of passage again as a blessing – as a mainstay of strong community and good government.

When the US government outlawed the ceremonies of the people, that denial led to the total separation of people from their connection to and belief in the Natural

World. The ceremonies were replaced by the Pledge of Allegiance, by the waving of the flag and the singing of the National Anthem. Vital and ennobling rites of passage were replaced with the trivial shout of "God Bless America."

God did bless America a long time ago. The question we must ask, the question of today's change is, "What have we done to that blessing – the blessing that is the Natural World? What have we done with that blessing in the name of being American?"

Road Note

. I left Calvin and Klamath Falls to drive south. Around my neck was a necklace he had made of shell and hematite beads with a polished bone carved in a flat spiral hanging in the center. "To keep you safe on your journey," he explained.

Highway 97 drops out of Klamath Falls onto the long northern shoulders of Mt. Shasta. In local lore, the mountain is said to have a power and presence deserving of profound respect. On the horizon for miles, with the blue sky seamless behind it, the mountain held me captive. In its February robes it was enduringly indifferent and benevolent all at once. I pulled out the Flip camera to get one more shot. The power clicked on. I turned to the mountain and spoke. "One more view of Shasta." Then there was the sound of gravel beneath the tires. There was a pole bent and crashing across the top of the car. No doubt, a few choice words flew from my mouth, but just as readily an extreme calm and presence of mind synchronized every nerve and muscle that was needed to steer the car back onto the road.

"Wake up call," I thought, and then repeated the words out loud. I am driving alone on the highways of America. That is both a responsibility and an opportunity to pay attention and stay focused -- to endure the excitement of magnificence while resisting the temptation to multitask. How lucky to get this early warning and escape with such relatively minor consequences!

012,013 Tara Loyd & Brett Wiskur
Walnut Creek, CA

The next day, at Mike's Auto-Body in Walnut Creek, I met Tara Loyd, the receptionist. The single mom of a 4 year old, Tara was on for an interview and asked if her friend could join us. Brett Wiskur is an auto-body technician who specializes in fixing body damage like dimples from hail. Married and in his early 30's, his joy is being on whitewater. As Tara and Brett spoke about change in the stark body shop break room, they unwittingly provided a model for how a friendship can be big enough to sustain ideological differences.

Brett: To me change is a shift in consciousness from what we've been preaching–closed mindedness and politics of fear–to reaching a new level as people. Not staying on the same path just because we've followed it so long, but making change across the board.

Tara: I think we're going to try something new. I hope Obama really means what he says about change. I hope he's not just a good talker. So far, instead of going with what they think inside the government, he's going outside to listen to regular people. He's trying something different and that's what change means.

Brett: Change nowadays is a political statement about what we the people don't want. We don't want the government in gay marriage, in steroids, in baseball, in religion and all these things. The situation has spun out of control and that's what needs to change.

Tara: Yeah. I do hope people stop caring so much about other people's personal lives. Like, really there are so many bigger things.

This is my first election, the first time I've been interested. For young people, it was clear Obama cared about reaching out to the people. What I keep hoping is that we will get more focused on what we as Americans need instead of helping everybody else.

Brett: But there's a catch 22. If we just focus on Americans and don't focus on the globe, we miss that we're all in this together. Trade touches every part of the world. Every single person is a part. We're all going to end up the same color–a global tribe. Look at the internet. Even before technology, we were always connected anyway. Diseases stretch across the planet in a day. It's just nuts. If we don't act as a human race, we're going to fail as a species. The guns blazing, stay the course mentality–the lack of respect to other cultures and countries doesn't work. That's the change in consciousness we need. It's not all about us. We have to sacrifice for the better of people all around.

Tara: Well, whatever.

Brett: Are you saying we're spending money on the world when we should be spending money on our schools and our education?

Tara: Yeah.

Brett: You've got a small child.

Tara: I just watched the news yesterday and saw they're going to add to the death row unit in San Quentin. They are going to spend huge amounts of money because inmates are crammed in death row. If they're in there, I don't really give two shits... sorry...if they're crammed. When I was having a child at 19 years old, I made a little bit over $1500 a month. Living in the Bay Area, that is nothing–nothing. But I couldn't get any public assistance. So, I hope they change by not just helping people that don't want to help themselves. The people who really want to work (*points to herself*) are struggling.

Brett: I have barely a high school education. She didn't graduate high school.

Tara: I'm a drop out.

Brett: Exactly, so for the two of us to be able to feel this type of involvement, to look into national issues and have this much interest; that's where it needs to be. The level of

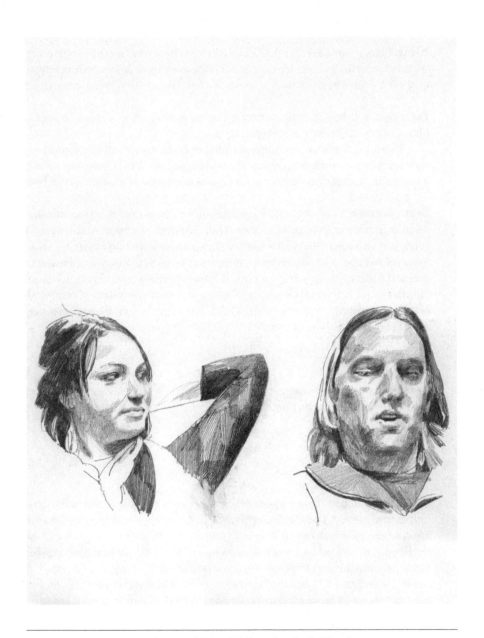

Tara and Brett *Walnut Creek, California*

ignorance blanketing the United States before this campaign is the reason we haven't changed.

Tara: I agree.

Brett: (*whispers to Tara*)

Tara: I was thinking about that, swear to god. He whispered family values. I hope that gets better in this country. The last 20 years, my whole life I've heard divorce, divorce, divorce. Family feuding. My parents are divorced, but thank god I grew up in my dad's Italian family. We're all very close and still have traditions. You know what I seriously hope stays the same? Christmas. I'm tired of saying Happy Holidays because we have to fit everybody's need. Why are we ashamed to celebrate Christmas?

I know this sounds small to some people. Still, I hope God doesn't get taken out of the schools. God gives people hope and that's tradition. It didn't screw up my aunts' and uncles' lives because they heard, God. If you have your own personal belief, that's alright. I think they're trying to change too much of everything to fit everybody's needs. (to Brett) I know you don't like that. But some things don't need to be changed.

Sometimes I feel like I do sound a little racist. That's why I don't say things because I don't know who's going to get offended. I just think we should stay how America–not stay the same because that's contradicting what I said about change. I think we should ... (*long pause*). I don't know.

Brett: (*leans toward Tara and smiles*) We generally agree to disagree.

Tara: Yeah. We agree to disagree.

Brett: (*to Tara*) You see everybody being politically correct and so you try to be that way too, so you don't hurt anybody.

Tara: To be honest, I think that because I'm in my twenties I'm really confused about everything. I want people to have all these rights and freedom. At the same time I want to make sure not to lose some things. For instance, my grandparents came here from another country–from Sicily. When they arrived, they changed. They adapted to what America was in the 1910s. They learned to speak English. They learned the values of Americans because they wanted to live in America. I just don't like when so many people come here and try to not do that.

Brett: Mexican immigration?

Tara: I don't want to press 1 for English. Some people think, "Oh, she's racist." But I think we're trying too much to help other people when we need to help ourselves first. We need to fix our own problems and smooth our own rough patches.

Brett: It can start in the family and with traditions. No matter what, we're still all connected. When the change in consciousness happens, we'll have a more open minded community. The wars that pertain to religion won't need to happen. Our outlook on foreign policy will be more open-minded. We think we're open-minded, but as a country we actually have a pretty decent sized stick up our ass. Still, with the election we've changed this much over how long?

Tara: A couple of months. A year.

Brett: We've got a black president. I can remember my grandma talking about black bathrooms. She was living in Tennessee. There were black water fountains. I can't fathom that. In the same way, I know that some day we'll be saying, "Can you believe that gays couldn't get married?" It will be the same as the Civil Rights Movement. It's like major periods of change require a conflict or maybe a Depression. Something negative has to happen before a positive happens. It's like an intervention on addiction; you have to almost hit rock bottom before it will start to get better.

That's where I think Obama maybe set himself up for failure. The idea of change is such a powerful thing–everything is already in change and will always be changing. But what are you supposed to look for, "And, February 5th it changed"?

Tara: People are waiting for him to do all the changing, but we need to be the change. We can't expect everybody to plunge in totally since we're still living our same daily lives, but we should all do whatever we can. You can't just hope this one person is going to change America.

Brett: Still, everybody is waiting. He put people in place to work for that change. That's what he claimed he could do, so let's see if he can do it. That's why we elected him.

Tara: Yeah, you're right, but we all need to be the change—Gandhi—we wish to see in the world. I think most Americans are ready to do it. We may want Barack to inspire us or show us some things that need to be done, but we've got to stop relying on government to fix everything.

014 Laura Geduldig
Oakland, CA

The car was okay, so the trip was still on. I was staying with Terry and Barbara Gutkin, friends who have known me over half of my life. Terry was the department chair at the University of Nebraska where I did my doctoral work. Now, they are family to me. A few years ago they moved to the San Francisco Bay Area to be near their children. The unexpected extra days in Walnut Creek gave me the chance to interview them and their daughter, Laura Geduldig. To begin, Laura, a mother and a life coach sat with me on the floor of her parents' guest room.

Laura: I can't even think of the word change without Barack Obama coming to mind.

I felt the Bush Administration was just so awful and so rooted in a narrow worldview. Barack Obama came and said, "Things can be different." Then you flip on the radio or the news and there's this horrible economic crisis. It is actually terrifying. Even still, I feel there's a great possibility we can shift in a new direction. The ship is sinking but the tide is turning. That's how it feels to me.

I'm an ultra-positive person. I've been lucky enough to make some major shifts in my life, to steer the ship in a new direction. I'm not saying it's easy. I'm not saying it doesn't take work and healing and perseverance and falling off the horse and all of that. It's all learning. You try something and you learn from it. Then you go back, try something else and learn from that. What we need is the belief that change is possible and that we have what we need to create the lives we want. That includes knowing love is present and available. Love is what allows people to feel happy and whole and it shows up in connection to others – in community.

Again, that Barack Obama thing. He could not have won without the resurgence of belief in community among all the grassroots people who believed change was possible. Americans are finding these connections again by finding connection to the highest power in this country – the president. For Obama to be successful, that has to continue.

At the same time and just as important are love and change in the family. So much is perspective, the way you hold a situation in your heart. My youngest son is having movement, gross motor skill issues. At six months we realized a problem with putting weight on his legs. He didn't crawl. We had to do MRIs. We had to see pediatric neurologists and keep countless physical therapy appointments. He's nineteen months now and he's still not walking. But he's close.

During this period I have worked to love him for who he is. I'm not going to say I haven't gone to fear, but I have tried hard to stay out of it. Fear can envelop and take you places where you can't think straight. I come from a lineage of worry and fear. I love my mom, I love my grandma, but they are definitely worriers. One of my biggest change decisions in parenting is to break the cycle of worry. I do that when I stay really present for my son, for who he is, for his journey and his process.

I have to be aware – really mindful and aware. With Gabriel, I've tried a mixture of being relaxed and at the same time being hyper tuned in. I'll watch him get in a position we've been working on in physical therapy. No one else would notice, but because I'm really tracking, I see it. I could be focusing on the things he's not doing, but instead I notice him move his legs for the first time in some little way. That fills me a little bit. I recognize "OK. Maybe that was a micro step." I take that inkling and use it to guide him or me a little further in that positive direction.

A phrase I use a lot is, "point your toes in a direction." Even if you don't know how to get there, figure out the direction you want to go and point your toes. Inevitably you'll head that way. Oh, and don't expect change to go quickly. That's important. It's a whole journey. Even if it's something I want really bad – and of course I want to fast-forward – I usually can't. But, when I'm facing the right direction each step is powerful. I point my toes and take the next step. Sometimes I have to sit down and rest. Sometimes I take three steps back. But as long as I've got the right trajectory I can be a part of really great changes

015,016 Terry & Barbara Gutkin
Walnut Creek, CA

Later, at a nearby East Indian restaurant, Terry and Barbara voiced their own fervent hopes for the future of our country. They hold the broader view of boomers with grandkids; citizens in their sixties with acute awareness of how intensely our actions affect the generations to come.

Barbara: I would like to see major change in the way America interacts with other countries. That's what change means to me. I would like to see more cooperation, less exploitation, much less violence and aggression; much more supporting other economies and working together for everyone's benefit.

Terry: I would like to see change at every level; systemic change, cultural change. I'd like to see change in our government, change in our economics, change in the way we treat people, change in the way people think about one another in this country. We have a world view of rugged individualism. I see the value of it to an extent, but it's also very destructive. It results in everybody looking out and caring only for themselves. I would love to see that change.

Take the current public response to the GM workers. Americans talking about other Americans they resent because they work in car companies and are making more than the people working in non-unionized Japanese car companies. There was another mindset when I was growing up in Brooklyn and my dad was a union organizer. The union mindset says, "We ought to raise the standard of living for people who are not doing as well." The public attitude now is, "No. We have to take our own citizens and lower them economically because someone else doing better takes from my plate."

That's why as a nation we're so intoxicated, so obsessed with the idea of cutting taxes. Nobody wants to spend anything that doesn't come back to them personally and immediately. We just want to invest in ourselves. We don't want to invest in the commons. We don't want to invest in the nation. If you have a problem, you help yourself. If you don't help yourself, screw you. Whatever happens to you happens to you. You're on your own. The rest of Western society doesn't think that way. There's more of a net, a community, a network through which people help each other. They're going to surpass us as a country, and rightfully so.

Barbara: Well, I think the American people actually are very decent. We donate a lot of money. For instance, with the tsunami, Americans opened their pocket books to the Red Cross and so on. The instincts of the American people are good. That's part of our history, part of our stable political system, and part of our educational system.

The government often doesn't truly represent the people. Instead they represent moneyed interests. When decisions are guided or made by Americans as a whole, when it's not just slogans, when they really understand a circumstance; with school bonds, for example, I see Americans open their hearts and support their communities.

Things with the economy are very personal. There's a good chance we will have to simplify our lives. But it might actually end up creating more happiness rather than less. My hope is people will realize consuming more is not going to make them happy. In fact, debt is a huge burden. When I was growing up there weren't large shopping malls. There weren't credit cards. People just bought what they needed. We weren't miserable because of that. Sometimes I'd only have one pair of shoes, but that was ok. It could be that we'll go back in that direction–families helping each other. We may need to take people into these large homes like we have. Can we really just let people have no place to live?

I think this election has been personal to Americans. In my lifetime, and I'm 62, I would never have imagined an African American would be elected president. I was lucky to grow up in New York City in integrated public housing. That was a real privilege in a lot of ways, but around us there was so much racism. It speaks to very good things in the American people that the racism could be put aside and people would actually vote for who they believed would be the best president. That's really hopeful and positive.

Terry: : I partially agree with Barbara. The American people are good when they see a problem, but they're also very good at not seeing problems. I always hesitate to say things like this because I'm not in any way implying that Americans are Nazis. And, I think in Nazi Germany, anybody who wanted to could have seen what was going on. They got very good at not seeing because they didn't want to see. I'm sure the German people are good people, too, although I don't know that many German people. But when you choose not to see, you don't act and everything seems ok. Later, when you do see it, it's like, (*gasp*) "If I had only known."

There's a lot of that here. American people choose, and it's not entirely their fault, to have the wool pulled over their eyes so they don't know what the U.S. does around the world. They don't realize the misery and brutality, the countless number of police states we've established and the oppression that comes from that. All they know is the good things we do because that's all they're told. They're also very busy. One way to perpetuate ignorance is to make sure people don't get enough to live on. This is a primary reason for "trickle down." It keeps people very busy. As long as they're busy scampering for food and keeping a job and trying to be sure their kids are raised without being on drugs and blah, blah, blah; they don't have time to pay attention.

The main thing that is right about this country is the positive side of the entrepreneurial spirit. The double edged sword is a good metaphor for the up and down sides of the pioneering drive of Americans as they moved across the country from ocean to ocean. That movement came from the energy of entrepreneurialism. It also resulted in genocide of the people already here. That contrast is vintage American. The unbridled energy and creativity is miraculous. Very often, though, success has very destructive effects. We fulfilled our collective destiny by managing to cross the whole country, but we killed almost everybody in our path. If we could do one thing with out the other; maintain the energy and creativity and cause no harm.

We have such a bad track record. Right now, we do all these great things but we're destroying the earth as we do it. We're destroying the environment, we're destroying each other. So, I would like to keep the drive and energy and lose the other part. One is vintage American and is really spectacular and worth keeping. The other part is also vintage American, equally spectacular and catastrophic. It has to be done with.

Maybe just one other thing. We should keep the ideals this country was founded on. The Declaration of Independence, the Constitution and the Bill of Rights are beautiful documents as I know them. The ideals and what they stand for are an important step beyond the Magna Charta. Those documents are a glorious and incredible expression of freedom and humanity.

Barbara: The particulars of change – I will be reassured if I see more restraint, less sending over arms as a first solution, more diplomacy as a first response and support for groups economically, for instance the Palestinians. Of course I want to see change in Guantanamo with people actually being charged with crimes instead of being held indefinitely.

I would also like to see less sexualization of women. Even though women have risen in a lot of professions that did not include women, oppression continues. When 9/11 was happening what really counted for the people stuck in those buildings was saying goodbye to their families. I would like to see families work things out more. I've spent most of my professional life working with children. I know that it would be good if families could stay together.

Terry: Obama's election is an enormous sign of good change. More evidence will come when this country gets over its fear of gay people, when it gets over its xenophobia around immigrants. Those will be signs.

I also have a postscript that you can edit out. The sign of change I want to see is this: I want to see the Yankees finish in last place. At least for 50 years straight. If they finish in last place for 50 years straight, I might forgive them for existing. I might. (*laughter*) I forgot to say that before. When that happens, we'll know for certain the Universe is coming to peaceful terms with itself.

017 Bob Bliss
Walnut Creek, CA

On the morning of February 7, only one day delayed, I loaded up the profoundly dented, but no less road-worthy, Mini Cooper. The view through the new windshield was crystal clear. I turned the key, the motor purred and the coffee habit I'd naively tried to curb reared its head. I mean, could this really qualify as an American road trip without coffee? In line at the corner coffee shop, I met Bob Bliss, a delightful man who reminded me of my uncles. His easy manner and quick wit were comforting and typical of American descendants of Scots Irish.

Bob Bliss: Well we sure need national medical insurance. Every country around us has it. Some aren't so good, but they've got it. Because of insurance costs, our companies are paying 18% to 20% more to manufacture things. That's why we can't compete. Our schools are burdened because of medical expenses. The military's costs would go down; everybody's expenses would go down with national medical insurance. The best medical system in the world costs its citizens 9%. We spend almost 20% because of our messed up situation. Can you imagine? You simplify the whole economic and social system with national medical insurance.

Almost 60% of all bankruptcies are caused by medical issues. It all could have been stopped in the 1940's except that the Republicans nailed Harry Truman in 1946 when he pushed for national medical insurance. "He's against the American doctor. We all love our American doctor." Stuff like that. A year later, England passed national medical insurance. It was Harry Truman's medical plan. You find it in France, in Spain, in countries all over the world. We don't get diddle. You sure you want to take this down?

In my opinion America has been handicapped by the Republicans. My family members were old time Republicans. At the turn of the century, the Republicans were liberals, not conservative. The parties have changed shape. It started after Taft got in and screwed everything up. Then along came Ronald Reagan. With Reagan, the rich paid for the Republican Party, so he gave the rich big tax cuts. My son and his wife received $23,000 back on George Bush's tax plan in August. I asked him, "So are you going to vote Republican, now?" He said, "Dad, I'm an American. I've got an MBA. How can I vote for Republicans?"

This country runs on money. Where does it come from? It comes from your taxes. If you cut off the money coming in from the tax payers, you have to borrow. Where do you borrow from? You borrow from China. Now, China won't take our money anymore. They can't get rid of our money. They can't hand it out.

This country has a lot of good things, though. I'm a farmer, rancher. I know this world lives off the sun. The rain is from the sun, the wind is from the sun. The oceans are caused by the sun. In one way or another all our main energy reserves including oil go back to the sun. We waste all this solar ability. When Ronald Reagan came into the White House the roof was covered with solar cells. First thing he did was to take the solar cells off. That's the kind of moron he was.

I want to see this country back to using its head. Just common sense. I've known some Congressmen and other people in Washington. They all kind of shrug their shoulders. I have a Congressman friend I asked, "How many Senators and Congressmen do you admire for their intelligence?" This man is very, very sharp. He said, "About 20%." He said there are more idiots sitting in the Senate and in Congress than he can believe. Educated, but still idiots. What are you going to do? You have to stop electing them.

I guess I started thinking more politically the day I turned 21. I was in combat in Korea and had to stand guard duty from midnight to 4 a.m. on my birthday. I didn't tell anybody it was my birthday because the guys would say, "Let's go get drunk and get laid." I'm on the front line that's the way they'd give a tease. At end of the night, wouldn't you know, I get guard duty again, 8 p.m. to midnight. So, I spend 8 hours on my birthday standing guard. I'm standing out there about 11p.m. feeling sorry for myself. I think, "What am I going to get out of this?" Then I think, "You know what I'm going to do? I'm going to prove this war was caused by a political problem." The Korean War was; all these wars are. So I decided to keep myself informed and to be active supporting good leadership.

We need great leaders like Kennedy and McCarthy – Eugene McCarthy the Congressman from Boston. I supported both of them. Here's a story. Years ago my wife was a teacher. We'd taken students back with us to D.C. We saw a crowd moving down the hallway of a Senate office building – a host of people following somebody. One of the guys with us says, "I'm going to see what's going on." He came back in about twenty minutes and said, "I just saw McCarthy carrying two chicken buckets full of money."

Every year the bursar goes around and gives Congress members plastic envelopes with money in them. Back then you got $100 or $250 for incidentals in the office. McCarthy had brought it all back. The bursar said, "I've been here 26 years and you're the first man to bring back so much as $1. Besides that, I haven't given you money in nine years." Amazing story. Too bad that kind of integrity is a freak thing.

I just want the world to go right, you know. I've got these great grand kids. I love them. I can't get enough of the little monsters. I have a sign on my door that says, "I've childproofed my house, but they still get in." That's the way I feel about them. They're fun. You know, they run up and kiss me. They climb into my lap and I'm just a bowl of jelly. It's fantastic. God's been very kind to me. Knock on wood. (*Knocks on his head and laughs*).

Road Note

After I turned off the camera, Bob told me about his job with the Kennedy administration. Apparently John F. Kennedy had a very bad back and Bob's job was to carry him down sets of stairs. I have to say I felt a little bummed to be behind schedule. I had to make Santa Barbara for an interview that afternoon and was already pushing the boundary of my timeline. Can you imagine the stories this man could tell? I pulled onto the highway and found myself wondering about the chances of ever finding Mr. Bliss again.

Meanwhile, the road felt great. Dented as it was, the car hummed. The highway to Santa Barbara was easy. I pulled into town and called another of my influential professors, Jane Conoley, the current Dean of the Gevirtz Graduate School of Education for the University of California.

018,019 Marshall & Carol Ackerman
Santa Barbara, CA

Jane had arranged for me to visit with Marshall Ackerman who had served as the inaugural and long-term publisher of Prevention Magazine since 1950. Prevention was the first American publication to define and promote the genre of health-focused magazines. Now in his late eighties, Marshall and his wife Carol, a retired school psychologist, live in the hills above Santa Barbara. Jane and I accepted their invitation to afternoon tea.

Marshall: (*laughs*) Nobody wants to go on the record. This is too much generalization. Many people do not want to go on the record with their thoughts because they are afraid they are going to be different from the majority–that people will respect them less when they find out what they think. So, they are reclusive–Is that such a word, "reclusive?" (*all agree*) I do some surveys for Gallup. I tell them that one of the problems they have is asking people who don't want to say what they think. The big fallacy of the whole democratic system is that the good people won't run, because the good...

Carol: That's right. So run. You never would.

Marshall: No, the good people won't run.

Carol: That's you.

Marshall: OK. I'm a good person.

Carol: I always told you, "Go run. Put your body and your mind where your voice is." Go run. If you can do better, go try.

Marshall: No.

Carol: Well, there we go. That's the end of that. (*laughter*)

Marshall: I used to be too young. Now, I'm too old.

Carol: Some years ago I decided to get involved in politics. It seemed entry level would be as a committee woman. You have to sign up for it so I did. I was very proud of myself—my first step. That evening, I got two telephone calls. One was, "Why are you running against my wife?" I said, "I'm not running against your wife. If she wins, I'll support her and if I win, she'll support me." He hung up. The next one was a man who said, "It doesn't bother me that you're Jewish, but I know that other people would be bothered by this." I hung up on that one and decided I can't take the heat of the kitchen, or whatever you call it. I got turned off by politics in Pennsylvania.

Marshall: OK. But you could get turned off without announcing that you were going to run, because the politics is the same anyway. So, why are you voting for all these people who don't want you to run because you're Jewish?

Carol: Marshall, at one point applied to a country club that had no Jews. People told him, "Go ahead, we're all behind you." So, Marshall applied and the person who recommended him got a letter saying–what did the letter say, "We don't take Jews"?

Marshall: No, they didn't put it in writing.

Carol: What did the letter say?

Marshall: It said, "We're sorry to tell you that we have rejected your application." The only reason I applied was that all the executives in my company were members and we had all our meetings there. So I said, "OK. Put my name in." I wasn't aware I was sticking my neck out pretty far. But we solved the whole thing. Every time thereafter when we were invited to the country club–you know for dances and fundraisers–we'd send them a copy of the letter rejecting me with a note saying, "I'd like to come, but they won't let me in." That was in Allentown, 1980. I got over it a lot quicker than Carol did.

Carol: It's still happening here in Santa Barbara. But that has nothing to do with change.

Marshall: It has everything to do with change.

Carol: It's not going to change, though.

Marshall: I've always felt the basis of civilization is the family. I took a course at Harvard with Carle Zimmerman2. It was on the family. His main point–it took a whole semester to make one point–was how valuable and important the family is. I think I took the course because I have always felt that way. I watched when I was growing up. Carol didn't like my mother, but nevertheless, there was a family structure for all of us throughout the Depression and the Wars. That's gone for children now. Long gone. The percentages now of the, what do they call it, the mother, father, children–nuclear family–what's the percentage now, like 20?

Jane: 23-24%

Marshall: So you can call that the deterioration of our society. There is really no more family. Even among affluent, educated, intelligent people the parents don't pay any attention to the children. I'm generalizing, but I see this and hear of it very frequently. People are going their own way as individuals, not as family members. That bothers me. I don't think I can do anything about it except to cry on your shoulder.

I guess I'm a real cynic about this. If change means things get better, obviously I hope we'll change. But, where's the motivation going to come from? The motivation for most of our society is money. If people don't have money they'll try to change something so they can get money. I don't visualize people trying to change something so their children will stay home at night. The things that need to change aren't going to change. Write that down.

Carol is now listening to CNN all the time. I find it not offensive, but not entertaining either. It's just a bunch of people talking and then they go back and say the same thing over and over again but they don't tell me anything.

Carol: It's opinions.

Marshall: Well, what do I care about Anderson Cooper's opinion? Does he care about my opinion?

Carol: I don't know.

Marshall: I know. I know. He doesn't care about my opinion.

Carol: He has a job to do and he's doing it.

Marshall: He's an entertainer.

Carol: People watch television because they want to communicate with people similar to them. They want confirmation that they're not unique or isolated. They want to know that other people are doing the same things and having he same problems. They want to have companionship. They want sympathy. That is why there are questions and answers and, partially, why Mary is doing this. She's going to write a book about people and what they think. Someone's going to buy it and say, "Gee, that's what I think."

You and I maybe don't care what other people think of us. This is because we have a job and we're comfortable. We don't have the worries other people do. But most people want to see other people with the same worries. They want to read about it, too, to know they're not alone.

Marshall: What benefit is that?

Carol: It makes them feel better–makes them not want to kill themselves.

Marshall: But that doesn't really do anything for society to give people some comfort.

Carol: Yeah, but society is made up of individuals. If there are enough people who feel better about something, they'll become a group and maybe there's action. People want to be one of something.

Marshall: It just came to me. When people aren't happy together, they get a divorce. What if you don't like your child, can you get it reneged?

Carol: No. I can't conceive of not liking a child. Neither could you.

Marshall: Carol, when I married you, you didn't want to have any children.

Carol: That's right. You wanted seven.

Marshall: I think you're exaggerating.

Carol: Or maybe it was six. (*big laughter*)

Marshall: Hey, we're getting away from the subject here.

You have to think at so many levels about the family. If you think about the people in poverty, they have a different reason for letting the family come apart. They have no incentive to keep the family together. I think of the poor people. Without enough resources to feed a whole family, they split up. It's not their fault probably. It's nobody's fault. That's where the change has to start. We have to say we don't want to have ghettos where families can't survive and never get to do the things that you and I could consider luxuries like going to a concert. Such things never enter their minds because they have no resources. We're lucky. We think about things like that and sometimes we even go somewhere. Not as much as we used to.

Now we're old. We're taking physical therapy just to try and hold our own. It's a change. Sometimes it's a change you don't want to happen, but you can't stop it. It's inevitable. The steamroller is going to go over us sooner or later. There's not much you can do about it. You can postpone it a few years. Sometimes you even die.

Carol: Couldn't be.

Marshall: Well. One of the things that bothers me so much is when my contemporaries die. It's frightening. They're too young to die. (*laughs*).

Anyhow, everybody wants their health to be better. It doesn't matter how good it is, they want it to be better. Some people have the motivation to do something about it and some of us don't. It's very hard. I did some exercises this morning. I try. Then I stop and say, "I can't do this anymore because it hurts." It's so easy to say, "As much as I'd like change, I don't want it to make me uncomfortable." How do you change and be comfortable? (*laughter*)

Carol: You don't want to do what you have to do to have the change.

Marshall: Oh, I would do it if it didn't inconvenience me. (*laughter*)

020,021 Jane & Collie Conoley
Santa Barbara, CA

The next morning I got to catch up with Jane Conoley and her husband Collie, an academic couple that has been together for over thirty years. During my doctoral studies, I lived in a spare room in their home in Nebraska. Jane was my mentor in a doctoral program in Texas and her move to UN-L was the reason I applied to transfer there. In exchange for my room and board, I took care of the Conoley's young son, Collin and cleaned the house from time to time. Jane, the daughter of an Irish family from the Bronx in NY and Collie, from Texas, met in graduate school. They have had plenty of time together to think about families and psychological health.

Jane: The best time to talk about change is before nine o'clock in the morning, don't you think? The best energy.

Collie: Hmm. I guess I usually think about change in personal terms. My life stance is not acceptance; it's change. When people experience a terrible issue as not being malleable–when they feel it just can't change–that part of life becomes their focus. In my work, that's what I'd like to change.

Jane: To help people change their focus? Is that what you mean?

Collie: Yeah. The wonderful thing about being a psychologist is that you know you're onto a good theory when your own life is good. If the theory I'm using is helping me be the person I want to be then it's good. If it's not, then I shouldn't be proselytizing.

Jane: It seems over the last couple of years you've gotten clearer focus on positive psychology.

Collie: Yeah, the new research about how positive feelings are different than negative feelings has really energized me. I've always had the inkling of the positive approach. Now with theoretical and empirical foundation for it, I can speak more freely and confidently, especially in academic settings. An interesting dynamic for me is explaining positive psychology to practicum students. They think it means being in denial. The fact is, if we are actively running away from or not acknowledging a problem that's when it hurts. Once you admit and understand it you can spend some time fixing it. Emphasis on some. If you dedicate your whole life to avoiding or fixing a problem, your life becomes the problem. You become the problem.

Those us who are reflective can get stuck on what we wish we hadn't done. Say I said the dumb thing, or did the dumb thing. Over and over I back up and rethink that dumb thing. Change is to go all the way through it to the point of saying, "So I did a dumb thing, what would I do next time?" Change is to be finished with self punishing and move on as who you want to be.

Some of the research we're excited about looks at problem avoidant vs. goal directed behavior. If a behavior leads you to avoid a problem, at the very most you feel relief. If you don't avoid it, you feel angry. Anger dissolves relationships. However, if you are goal directed you get a sense of accomplishment when you reach your goal. That gives you energy to move on to other goals. Success creates positive feelings. It's self enhancing. If you fail, you may feel frustrated or sad, but sadness at missing a goal is better than anger at not avoiding a problem. So, change doesn't happen by focusing on avoiding problems. It does happen in moving toward a goal.

Jane: I think of change mainly as persistence. Having a vision, a goal, and pulling different people, resources, opportunities and strategies together. Change of that kind is purposeful. I guess there is a paradox for me. There are changes that happen without my being involved. Thank goodness for that. But my focus in terms of work, family life or personal change, is all about persistence. It's about having a notion of where I want to go and trying to put things together to make that happen.

Nothing doesn't change. Yet even in the face of unavoidable disappointment, hopefulness is important. To me hope is a constant that reflects what you've mentioned, Collie, about the rediscovery of old virtues like patience, tolerance.

Collie: Faithfulness.

Jane: Faithfulness, right. And gratitude. You can avoid heavy discouragement when you know your intention and focus are grounded in commitment to support others. It can be hard to hold on to those virtues. It takes more work than people realize to retain hopefulness, thankfulness, or gratitude. They seem to slip away quickly.

I feel lucky that way. Collie and I live in conditions that are supportive in terms of great relationships, wonderful family, and enough resources. All of that contributes to our ability to retain happiness. There's also evidence that forty or fifty percent of happiness comes from focusing on the blessings that has–noticing good times, savoring moments.

Our experiences lately with older relatives have made some things clearer to us about the quality of people's lives. Aunt Mary spent her life focusing on the positive. At times I thought she was living in a world of denial. But as I get older I realize that wasn't the case. Other older family members are stuck in thoughts like, "I didn't get the relationship I wanted. I didn't have the house I wanted. I didn't have the health I wanted." They ignore the positive things in their lives and that can show up in a passive relationship with life instead of one with goal-directed intention.

Intention and goal directed thinking have public applications, too. We learned from Paul Watzlawik–you may remember his book *Change*[55]–that when you create the greatest good, you create the greatest evil. In a recent talk, he was using the example of democracy vs. communism. If you believe that democracy as we construe it is the greatest good then you're allowed to use the CIA to topple governments or assassinate people because in your fundamental judgment you've got the greatest good and they don't. By contrast if people were to become less threatened by difference that would be a major sign of positive change for the country and the world.

To me a very concrete change would be for gay marriage to become a non issue and for the whole crazy cultural focus on sexual orientation to go away. That would be a significant part of the country learning acceptance. It would be a sign of moving into focusing on goals rather than on what's different about you and me. When people are focused on difference, it represents thinking in terms of a problem, a cultural problem. And of course that relates to the global rise in the last 20 years of religious fundamentalism which is one of the most dangerous things in the world.

022 Bob Potter
Santa Barbara, CA

Jane had mentioned to me that her job puts her in touch with some of the more affluent people of Santa Barbara – individuals who might be inclined to fund university initiatives. Santa Barbara is one of the wealthiest communities in the country. In 2009, the median cost for a home there exceeded $1 million. I drove out of the Conoley's neighborhood and turned south to drive along the ocean front. The stretch of brown sand, silver-gray ocean and general Southern California opulence was suddenly interrupted by the appearance of thousands of small white crosses. "Arlington West," Mr. Potter would later tell me. I parked, grabbed my camera and release forms and walked toward the water. Bob Potter, a veteran of Vietnam stood in the stiff sea breeze with another volunteer

Bob Potter: My name's Bob Potter and this is Steve. We're with the Veterans for Peace here in Santa Barbara. We've been hosting this memorial called Arlington West every

---

5   Watzlavik, P., Weakland, J., & Fisch, R. (1974). *Change.* New York: W. W. Norton

week since November of 2003. Steve got it started, but I've been working on it most of that time. For the past five years we've been asking for change.

We try to demonstrate the necessity for change through speaking about the cost of the current war in terms of human lives – American soldiers, but also Iraqis. So I'd say, in the most pressing instances, change comes when a situation is so impossible it can't continue – it has to be changed.

I would differentiate that kind of urgent change from things it would be nice to change. For example, you might think about changing your car, getting a newer one. But, when your car breaks down, when it's a total wreck, you have to change. I believe we are in a more urgent time right now. But, this is a favorable thing about difficult times; things are so bad they just have to be changed.

A good sign of change would be to see the application of science rather than superstition in public decision making. Many of the decisions made in the Bush administration were based on unsubstantiated prejudices and old wives tales. For instance, the way they reacted to the notion of stem cells by trying to ban them. This is like trying to get the waves not to crash. It's necessary that we move ahead with that kind of technology to save people's lives or to repair what otherwise is irreparable physical damage.

Just in that one area, there was prejudice operating. A number of the Bush administration's reactions to social problems demonstrated prejudice and appealed to people's worst fears about other groups rather than summoning them to do better.

With intelligence, change can come about ahead of time. I'd like to see more of that. I'd like to see us think ahead to a problem and change our policy before it becomes totally disastrous. Global warming might be an example. Things are threatening now, but will become realities later. We shouldn't wait until necessity makes us change. We should change now because we can see what is coming. If you're a good driver, you anticipate possible accidents before they happen. It's no good to wait until an accident is happening and react at the last minute. Both responses involve a change in the direction of the car. One is the more intelligent kind of change.

I look for that to be the hallmark of the new era. I think it is an era where we will use our brains. Barack Obama is above all else, a brilliant man who looks beyond the present situation into the future. That is a great quality in a leader. I believe that we'll measure the success he has by his ability to think ahead – to get the public to start thinking ahead – to anticipate and behave with the intelligence we have to prevent problems.

I'm optimistic. I've got five grandchildren. It's their world I've been worried about, not so much mine. They will have a long time to deal with the consequences that follow our actions.

023,024 Two students from Kathy Goodman's Advisory, High Tech High L.A.
Las Angeles, CA

Beneath the bruised but trusty Mini, the miles rolled on. I found my way to Los Angeles and to the hillside home of Kathy Goodman. Film producer, co-owner of the Los Angeles Sparks, high school English teacher and the childhood best buddy of a friend of mine back in Portland, Kathy opened both her home and her classroom to me. The next morning, Kathy left for school when the day had barely broken. I met her later in her advisory, where the students were mostly Latino and Chicano. Many, if not all, had plans to go on to college and would be the first in their families to pursue a higher education.

Student 1: We use the word change in America a lot. Especially the president, Barack Obama. They say the USA is one of the leading countries in the world for decades. Everything is changing now and we need to change with it.

Student 2: I think what should change is the government–new ideas, new people, new perspectives. But some of our values need to stay the same, especially our care for the planet because it seems to be a very big problem. We shouldn't change is our morals and things like the laws. And even though government really needs to change, the basic ideas of our government are good–that people are allowed to change the government if they're unhappy with it. I think that idea should apply in these times because it seems everywhere you look someone's complaining about our leaders and the economy. Everything needs to be completely redone now following that basic principle.

Student 1: I believe the thing in America that should stay the same is the Constitution because it hasn't changed in a long time. The most important thing that should stay the same is what Thomas Jefferson pointed out, "All men are created equal." Since Americans believe that way, one day everybody will be equal. If someone is rich you don't necessarily let him go first to do something. Americans want a place where everybody is treated equal. I know that's what we want for the future.

Student 2: One clear sign that change has come is that people will stop complaining. It's in our nature to complain, but it will be less. They'll stop complaining about the things they're complaining about now. They will complain about other things.

Road Note

On the road from Santa Barbara to Los Angeles, I thought again about how essential it is to seek out people whose lives are different from mine for this project. In the mixture of visits with people like both Bobs (017, 022), like Tara (012) and Brett (013), Bao (010) and Art (002), Nick (009), Lena (001) the Ackermans (018, 019), and now Kathy's students, I felt the power and necessity of such diversity.

The evidence was stacking up. In the *EX:Change* the Americans that I talked to thus far seemed to accept the breadth and depth of perspective that comes from our differences. We need them so that we can recognize the priorities we actually share in common. It's a blend of the Oregon coffee barista's wish for Americans to combine their efforts and Dean Jane's suggestion that we "focus on goals rather than on what's different about you and me." With our eyes on a shared prize, our differences might turn out to be beneficial in the long term.

Back at 'Arlington West,' Bob Potter's (022), colleague Steve Sherril brought up the physics of the relationship between solid matter and life's more agonizing challenges. "You know, if you want to have a table, an ocean, a flag or anything, negative and positive atomic forces have to be joined," Steve said. "They have to bind together." Given our talk about various armed conflicts, the analogy wasn't particularly comforting It did not make negatives like death and war any more palatable. Still, the three of us agreed that Steve was onto something with the idea of a paradox that anchors human experience. Death, diversity and change are unavoidable, but listening to and learning from them and one another may help us see the opportunities in what we tend to usually avoid.

Santa Barbara's gentle beauty together with its incomprehensible wealth had opened onto the sprawl of glitter and garbage atop graceful lifts and dips of land. Often I could glimpse the pink, red or purple of the lovely bougainvillea blossoms resting helplessly and in the open spaces. The closer I came into the center of Los Angeles the more I felt its buzz and that reminded me of the Arlington West conversation about paradoxes.

I witnessed elegantly curving hills scattered with roadways. The drivers seemed in manic competition for time and space even as the contours of land dipped and rose like Strauss' Blue Danube. The dewy scent of eucalyptus the next morning was as exotic to me as the expensive clothes on bodies standing patiently in line at the Starbucks off Beverly Drive at Mulholland. An hour later, I had found myself surrounded with uniformed high school students. On her way out of the room one of the students said, "Sometimes it's only when things get really bad that we can see the good stuff we've taken for granted." Another paradox.

025,026 Rudy & Colleen Suwara
San Diego, CA

From Oregon on down, the Pacific Ocean was the constant. By San Diego the warm February air was warm and smelled like the sea. Rudy and Colleen Suwara, career professional volleyball athletes, live in San Diego with their dog Blanca. An acquaintance had mentioned *EX:Change* to the Suwaras and they had readily opened their home to me. When I arrived, the threesome took me to a room with a wall of windows and with shelves holding mementos of Rudy's triumphant debut with the US Olympic team in Mexico City in 1968. There was also a photo of Rudy with Fidel Castro from one of the US Team's visits to Cuba. The city, the near-full moon and the ocean sparkled through the windows as I slept. The next morning Rudy and Colleen shared oranges and avocados from the trees out their back door and we talked about change.

Rudy: For me there are a few things that are priorities. One, stopping the war; two, national healthcare; and three, better education for everyone. Of course the economy seems to be on everybody's mind right now and I'm also hopeful that will change and improve. Stopping the war is number one for me, though. I don't want us to be this big bully in the world. I'd like to see us working with other countries for positive change.

Also, I really think we're missing it if we don't educate people. In California, we have more prisons than schools. It's ridiculous. If we educated people better, we'd need fewer prisons. Education is and always has been the real key to our future.

Colleen: Along with the specific things Rudy mentioned, a big change would be to have more optimism than pessimism. In general I would like to see all of humanity, all of the world being more optimistic; having more joy than fear and more hope than gloom and doom. We need more of the positive, especially as it shows up in being ready to help instead of fearing someone else.

In the last decade there's been a lot of fear mongering. I would like that to change as soon as possible. When you're fearful, you can't change. When you're fearful, you can't move. You can't breathe.

There have always been the people who are helpful and positive and as a country we've always had this creed of wanting to help the world. Unfortunately in the last decade we have begun acting like we control the world; like we can set the rules for everyone. We used to be loved by other countries. We're not so much loved these last few years.

Rudy: The Constitution and our freedoms are something I've learned to appreciate. In the travels I've had all over the world, I've found there aren't a lot of countries that enjoy our freedoms and prosperity. We're fortunate to have been born or to have come here.

I do not want the government asserting powers like the ones based on the terrorist attack where they restricted freedoms of expression and differences of view. Under the Bush administration you were considered an enemy if you were in any way asking, "Should we go to Iraq? Should we be on the other side of the globe trying to tell other people how to live?" You were labeled a terrorist if you didn't agree with the war. They say we have to fight the terrorists. For me that is a bunch of bunk. Our best opportunity is through communication.

For an example I'll jump to Cuba where I spent many visits. It's a wonderful country with wonderful people. I've always thought we should have solid communication with Cuba. For us to be at odds with them by continuing sanctions that make things harder on their people is not the way. If we opened relations, that would change communism faster than anything. There is no reason not to communicate with other peoples.

Colleen: Obviously and already President Obama has been able to make a change at the grass roots. For the people to elect him was a great change. Now he's got to deal with something even more difficult. The people who are voting on public policy in Congress will be harder to work with. When he's able to succeed there, that will be significant.

As soon as those first brave people reach across the aisle, it's going to be more possible for others who are flexible to follow suit. "If they did it, I can be brave, too." That will make for more and more good change. There will always be extreme thinkers on each side, but I think collaboration is already happening. It's the tough cookie right now. Obama got there. Now the question is can he convince the leadership to work together instead of just being partisan? It's exciting.

Rudy: One more change I'd like to see has to do with the people running companies in our capitalist society. Capitalism works in a lot of ways. But now there's the fact that some people have become so greedy they think they have to have thousands of times as much income as line workers. If a worker makes let's say $100 a week, they've got to make $100 million. It reminds me of right before the French Revolution. The rich people became obscenely wealthy while the general population of workers starved. It's not that way in our country yet, but there needs to be a better sharing of the prosperity.

The first step would be providing assistance in some tax relief to people on the lower rungs of the economic ladder. The principle of taking care of our children is vital. If someone comes in and is a guest worker and the system wants to discriminate and say, "We can't take care of your child," that is appalling to me. I can't accept that we wouldn't want to take care of our own children. As a country, they are our children. They are our future. When we take care of them, we're making our lives better.

027 Todd Franklin
San Diego, CA

Later that day I sat in yet another coffee shop, this time on the campus of San Diego State University. Todd Franklin sat in the retro vinyl chair next to me. He was surrounded by notebooks and intently focused on the huge Finance text open on his lap. His cell phone rang and he spoke in tones that carried comfort and reassurance. He finished his call just as both of us saw a single red tail hawk circling outside the window. I was hesitant to ask for an interview given my respectful awareness of his studying, but changed my mind when Todd flashed his easy and winning smile. He welcomed the break.

Todd: I'm a student. I'm thinking of change within myself–how maybe I want to better myself. Whenever I can remember, I remind myself daily that I want to change. It's funny the word change has become so popular in the past two years, because people change all the time. It's just we finally put it on a piece of paper. We finally verbally expressed what it can mean.

Change to me is a scary experience. I was just on the phone with my brother. He's 18 years old and just lost his job. He's getting kicked out of his house. He's trying to change himself, you know. He's adopted. He wanted to get away from that whole lifestyle and try to be somebody, whatever that may be. But it's not working for him. Things like that beat people down. His voice was like, "What do I do?" He was desperate calling me.

It's like that, you know, day to day change. Once you can focus on yourself and know that you're changing, then you're able to help others. You can teach others how to change as well. It starts with how you want to change yourself–to better yourself or maybe change for the worse, I don't know.

I'll give this personal testimony. I've changed a lot in my life. I study finance but at this point I don't know if I want to do it. I'm facing that change and it's scary because I want to go out there and accomplish the American Dream. I want to get the flexibility and gain the independence that we all so desperately, supposedly, need.

I've changed by being in the Coast Guard, in the reserves. I've traveled Europe, South America. That's changed me. I was born here in San Diego and I've lived here almost my whole life. So living up in Northern California for a little bit, experiencing different environments, meeting different types of people with different perspectives; all of that creates a change within that you don't necessarily explicitly state.

Tod Franklin *San Diego, California*

Your environment changes you. If you don't want change in your life, you're not going to grow. Change is necessary for heading toward any goal a person or a group or the world wants to accomplish. But, we have to start by focusing on a smaller level, a micro-level.

My micro-level would be my life and my family. I never really was a family type of person. I guess I changed that way. I realized no matter where I go in the world, no matter where I travel, no matter what experiences I go through, they're my family. I never really had that feeling growing up, because I was adopted. I grew up in an environment of foster kids. Foster kids are people who are changing daily, and not because they want to change; they are forced to change. Most people don't really understand that unless they've been in it. It's a situation that makes you start to block off a lot of the outside influences and connections that maybe could help you change in the right direction. You're too used to being forced to change.

Everyone has their stories and everyone comes from different circumstances. Mine are what made me change into the person I am. For me, it seems like the only way you can recognize change is if you're searching for it. Like I was saying before, we change daily. We just don't notice. You choose what school you're going to or you get a haircut or you talk to a certain person. Before you didn't know that person, but now you do. It alters your life somewhat.

You have to notice change. Once you start noticing you aren't threatened by it. You learn to see people. You look beyond the common associations you have with the background a person comes from. That's probably the change I've noticed most in myself. I'm just an ant on a big ant hill, but I know from my own life that somewhere deep down all humans have inside of them a conscience. When we're fighting, we can't hear or touch it. That core of conscience is buried under and bombarded with all the different expectations of society and the world. But it's still there. The core: Treat someone else as you want to be treated.

We've become so self-centered in America. That disables change. People aren't communicating with each other when they get stuck in being right. No one's really listening. People need to listen to create change personally and on the bigger global level. Like we're doing right now. You're listening to me.

TUSCON, AZ to SHERMAN, TX
—
2.11 to 2.21.2009

- When you say the word change what do you mean?
- Alongside change, what is important to have remain the same?
- What would be signs that positive change is occurring?

TUCSON, AZ to SHERMAN, TX
2.11 to 2.21.2009

After Todd and I talked in the SDSU coffee shop, I got back in the car to take a giant left turn. *EX:Change* was shifting regions. Time for the trip and the story to head east.

It was late in the day and soon the sun was setting, a classic orange fireball in the rearview mirror. Within minutes, a full moon rose above the eastern edge of the California desert. It was one of those moons that seems to fill much more of the horizon than makes sense. As night came on, the moon assumed its more typical size to serve as a flashlight upon the desert floor. In grey tones, the sand and the scrub of cacti repeat themselves, oblivious to any human notion of state lines and to the thundering 18-wheelers that, besides the moon, were my only companions on the road.

Todd's story stayed with me as I drove toward Tucson. I thought of his honesty and courage. Off camera, Todd had spoken a bit more about being a mixed-race child-first living in foster care, and then adopted. He spoke of having two biological parents with severe mental illness, of worrying about his DNA and trying again and again not to succumb to that rumination. "I keep making choices to be strong and happy," he told me, "My brothers and sisters struggle with poverty and drugs and life on the streets. All I can do is live my life as well as I can and hope they see from that that it's possible." None of Todd's siblings are related by blood and he is surprised, but no less confident with his newly claimed sense of family bond. He attributes that in part to feeling more comfortable with himself and to how deeply affected he was from the time spent traveling the world and living in Northern California. "I am change," he said.

In the world of academic social science, there is a debate about what connotes 'real data.' How can we classify Todd's voice as data? How can we understand the content of his interview and the twenty-six before him in terms of data analysis and interpretation? I'm a bit of an oddball, even in the less mainstream qualitative research circles. Nonetheless, to me, research findings that describe human experiences are always most powerful when they are based in the stories of real lives.

Each and every one of us survives because we're paying attention in life and constantly learning. We do stupid things to push the boundaries. But extreme behaviors can be legitimately lively. They can even be life enhancing. In the world of research, thinking outside the box is vital to the innovations needed for meeting most of our urgent shared and individual problems. At the same time, anyone who does any kind of research is funneling the process through her or his individual ways of knowing and being.

For example, anytime we apply systems of quantitative analysis, those strategies have been conceived and developed within the limits of their authors' ways of knowing. We do our best, but we can't be more than humanly aware. And, it makes a difference who is telling the story – even with science. That's why I prefer listening to the experts, the people who are actually living their lives. Both social science and government institutions miss their purpose if they get overly prescriptive, not listening directly to the people concerned. As the voices up to now have repeatedly indicated, both arrogance and failure to listen are harmful to American community.

I pulled into Tucson past midnight. Dear friends of mine who moved from Portland a few years ago welcomed me and settled me gently into the bed they had made for me on their floor. I awoke in the morning to see the place I had entered the night before – this land of beige and brown, of dusty coral, pink and red. The giant fingers of saguaro cacti were abundant yet each one grew at a polite and considerable distance from the next. Like my time on the road, like the pauses in the narratives of the Americans I was listening to, the saguaro were reminders to notice the spaces in between.

028 Cheri Lynn Carter
Tucson, AZ

I found a coffee shop on Swan Road. One of two purple comfy chairs was free. The other one held a woman I figured to be retired and in her 60's. She was dressed in a business suit, scarf, earrings and wore her hair in a longish bob. As we chatted about Tucson and her work, I discovered that she was newly retired from a career in law enforcement and was working today on business plan for an LLC to become a private investigator. Meanwhile she was making a little money grooming dogs. Cheri Carter has lived in Tucson from the age of ten. She had taken it upon herself to ensure that her two children, a boy and a girl now fully grown, became fluent in Spanish. She did this in part by becoming bilingual herself even though there is no Mexican or Latino ancestry in her family. "To my mind," Cheri said, "It's just irresponsible to have any kind of job in Tucson without both languages."

Cheri: Change? Our government has to change! It has to change to suit the people. Our elected leaders work for the people and not for the government, not for Wall Street, not for the car manufacturers. They have to work for the common good of the common people. That's what change means to me.

What I want to have remain the same is our freedom. Our freedom to go from one country to another without the United States government or other powers that be having any authority to say you can't.

I'm half-Iranian. I'm not allowed to go to my father's country. That is where my father is. I don't even know him. By the rights of the Iranian government, if a person is born to an Iranian father, no matter where he is, that person is an Iranian citizen. I want my citizenship here and in Iran. And I want to be able to go there without having to go through different countries to get the right papers and finally to come back here only to be, you know, tongue-lashed by our government or whoever – homeland security – for going to Iran or to any other "questionable" country.

It's the freedom. The freedom to take a breath wherever the heck you want to take a breath.

I want to see President Obama have verbal exchanges with these countries that the United States hasn't wanted to work with. I want to see him talk to the Iranian government. I want to see him talk to the Chinese government. I want to see him talk to the Afghan government. I want to see him talk to all the leaders of all the countries that we have shunned. Our leaders haven't even been willing to sit down and break bread with them. I mean, that's what you do when you've got a problem with somebody. You sit down with them and you say "hey, let's try and solve this problem between the two of us." If we can't solve it, we can agree to disagree, but we also have to agree to not hate each other.

Right now, I'm hopeful. I'm hopeful! (*laughs*) So there you are. There's my hope and my prayer. And I know that we've got to help.

I haven't flown the American flag since the Vietnam War. I've pretty much stuffed it in the back of the closet. Now I am proud to display it because we have come kind-of full circle as human beings. Instead of enslaving somebody of a different color, we've elected him to the highest office of our nation. That's change.

There's one other thing, too. I've got to say I really am angry at the country's arrogance about Islam. I am Muslim, and I do cover. I wore hijab every day until 9/11. It got ugly after that, though. Real ugly. I got scared and put my hijab away except for going to the mosque

Then a few years ago, I was so mad about having to hide who I am that I did this. [*Cheri, turned around and lifted her bobbed hair from her neck to show tattoo with Arabic lettering in lovely script*]. Every time I show this to someone, they say, "That's beautiful. What does it mean?" and I get to say, "It says Islam. I submit myself to God and live in service to the wellbeing of all people."

Road Note

Cheri Carter's story had completely surprised me. There she was in a coffee shop in Tucson looking like a retired middle class white woman. Man-oh-man, you just can't ever count on first impressions to be true. This fact was turning out to be one of the most essential findings of the *EX:Change* project.

I drove to Albuquerque from Tucson at dawn the next day. I parked on Silver Road across the street from a quintessential New Mexico adobe home – white with a vibrant swag of red peppers on the door. I took a photo. The roads parallel to Silver Road were named for other minerals- gold, coal and lead. This house was at the corner of Silver and Pine, which had parallel streets named for Oak, Maple, and other trees until. A bit farther north the theme shifts and the ores begin crossing with names of esteemed institutions of higher education – Yale, Bryn Mawr, Tulane, Stanford. I walked awhile in this geographic poem – blocks of city streets organized around the intersection of minerals with trees and the institutions that support study for variously understanding, sustaining and exploiting them.

Throughout this and the next day, Valentine's Day, I would speak with three people whose emphasis was on relationships. Like the mapped intersections of Albuquerque, our relations with one another and the world were about to fortify and extend the themes of *EX:Change* thus far. My Tucson friends had connected me with Margaret Randall, a long time friend of theirs from lesbian, literary and activist communities. Luis Vargas, another thinker of immense proportion, is part of the clinical faculty with the Child Clinical Psychology program in the Psychiatry

Department of the University of Mexico's School of Medicine. While completely gentle, he works incessantly as an activist for the wellbeing of people who typically get the short end of the social justice stick. And finally, I interviewed Bruce McQuakay, who I've known since he was in elementary school. At 28 he's already given over half of his life to supporting the wellbeing and preservation of indigenous traditions. All three are activists, devoted to human relations.

029 Margaret Randall
Albuquerque, NM

Margaret Randall was both guarded and generous with her story. She is a living example of 'thinking outside the box' and making extreme choices. The intersections of those conscious efforts have yielded vast benefits- some quiet, some astonishing and all hard won. Such is the life of a scholar and leader like Margaret Randall.

Margaret: I'm a writer and photographer. I'm 72. I was born in New York City and, from the age of 10, grew up here in Albuquerque. I think of Albuquerque as my home, my heart place. The landscape here is incredibly important to me.

I spent about a quarter of a century in Latin America. I lived in Mexico for 8 years, Cuba for 11 years and Nicaragua for 4 before returning to the States in 1984. When I came back I had published many books. I don't know how many. I'm up to maybe a hundred by now. By 1984, a number of those books expressed opinions contrary to U.S. policy in different parts of the world, in particular Southeast Asia and Central America.

About a year after I got home, I was ordered deported. That opened a chapter in my life that was pretty frenetic. From about 1985 to 1989, I was involved in an immigration case related to the government trying to deport me. I had incredible support. I was represented by the Center for Constitutional Rights[6] and supported by artists and writers and other people from all over the country.

I was being deported under the McCaren-Walter Immigration and Naturalization Law[7]–a law that very few people know exists. It's a 1952 law that passed over President Truman's veto. It has 34 clauses under which you can kick people out of the country. Everything from being gay to being a communist, a socialist, an anarchist; but interestingly enough, not for being a fascist. In any case, we eventually won my case in the fall of 1989 and I was free to stay. I continued to live here and was able to come out as a lesbian. I hadn't been able to do that during the years of the case because that would have been another reason to deport me.

During that time, I wrote more books. I just never stopped working. I was on Studs Terkel's show twice and got to know him a little bit. He was also a hero of mine. My work is mainly oral history, essay, memoir, and poetry. I think of myself as a poet more than anything else. I have a book that just came out last week. It is a memoir of my years in Cuba.[8]

---

6 *Center for Constitutional Rights*

7 *McCaren-Walter Immigration and Naturalization Law*

8 *Margaret Randall, To Change the World: My Years in Cuba(Piscataway, NJ: Rutgers University Press, 2009)*

I spent so much of my life living the idea that I was one of hundreds of thousands, millions of people not in a leadership capacity, but just one more foot soldier among so many who truly wanted to change the world. I was on the front lines working in revolutionary movements in Mexico, in Cuba, in Nicaragua. I saw my comrades fall by the way side. They made tremendous sacrifices that are so unspeakable. It is hard for me to think of them at this point especially because, in most cases, what they fought and died for didn't come to be.

Change. One thinks of change a lot at the age of 72. At the moment, and perhaps because of my age, I'm involved with working out the texture and fabric of my own change. There is always the temptation as one ages to feel that all change is negative. You get older, your body responds less immediately, less well.

As a positive change I feel that I'm more able to see things in over arching ways. I can make connections more fully and powerfully so that in my writing and photography I am at the peak of my possibilities. I see connections between all kinds of things; like a plate of food and the Israeli invasion of Palestine. Elements that may seem disparate to most people connect and click in my head. Connections have always been important, but now I do it better or more deeply.

I've been interested in this utterly long campaign because Barack Obama embodies the idea of change in such an interesting, rich way. He's the first black president. But is he black? I think of him as black and white and more like this country. I personally believe that if he had been absolutely black, he wouldn't have been elected. He has, "like most of us-ness." And he's such a smart person. That is a change all by itself. I love the speeches he makes that are so eloquent and his spontaneous responses to stupid and not so stupid questions.

I remember during the campaign the other side ridiculing him for his eloquence. I asked myself why. I think it has to do with Christian fundamentalism. Eloquence is sort of the anti-Christ. It's the devil that seduces you with his forked tongue, his eloquent tongue. This was probably an idea used to court a constituency which is, in my mind, extremely dangerous and growing in this country and in the world. And not just Christian fundamentalism but Islamic fundamentalism and Jewish fundamentalism. We must know all the fundamentalisms and still set out for real change against those obstacles.

As for signs of change, I would be reassured if we cared about education. I would like us to stop saying we have the best educated population in the world. That is absolutely false. Almost every industrialized nation has a better educational system than we do. If we were really to put money into education, if we were to put money into people's health, if our elected and appointed officials suddenly got honest, all of those would be good signs. If the more flagrant abuses of human rights ceased. If states decided same sex marriages were OK as is the case in Buenos Aires, in Mexico City, in Spain. If any one of these things were to happen, if some of the hypocrisy were suddenly to disintegrate, those would be positive signs for me. I don't expect those things.

Still, I really believe in change. I believe the opposite of change is stagnation. I am extremely fortunate to be in a relationship that's almost 23 years old now, an extraordinary relationship. There is the temptation to say you don't want love to change, but it gets richer. To me, change is the currency of love, and fear of change is a very dangerous thing. There are so many connections we can make; new ways of loving, new ways of supporting, new ways of creating. And for me, creativity is change and change is creativity.

In all of this, I find change is reduced to a very personal level. It's what I make, it's the relationships I have. In this way I understand ever more deeply that they cannot prevent us from winning. By "they" I mean the status quo, the corporate world, the military. In the end, they really can't take from us who we are. We hold that. That's what we have and it's worth honoring. I suppose that has to do with getting older too. Perhaps in age you come to see who you are and the relationships you have as most important.

030 Luis A Vargas
Albuquerque, NM

The next morning Luis Vargas met me for breakfast at the Flying Star Café on Central Avenue. Dr. Vargas was raised in El Paso by parents who were activists for freedom of religion in their homeland, Mexico, in the 1920's. "The values that raise us matter," Luis wisely notes, "They tell us who we are and how to live."

Luis Vargas: Did you ever read the book *Change* by Watzlawick, Weakland & Fisch6? At the beginning they quoted the French proverb, "The more things change, the more they stay the same." For me that's always been an indication of what change is not. Change must involve going outside conventional ways of perceiving problems and framing solutions.

To give an example, we can say these economic crises occurred because we used a particular kind of system to understand and respond to them. The previous administration relied heavily on the notions and frameworks of free market enterprise and capitalism. Let's say that government next acts to have more control with the intent of ensuring the system works well, but never questions the system itself. What does that mean? Nothing changes.

You know Maynard Keynes? He said a lot of outrageous things. Among them was the suggestion that capitalism is the extraordinary belief that the nastiest of men with the nastiest of motives will work for the benefit of all. When you consider that possibility you ask, "How can more government control curb that?" We've seen how folks in oversight positions speak the very same language—free enterprise, capitalism and so on—and therefore only perpetuate the problem.

That brings to mind another person—Ambrose Bierce who defined a corporation as a clever entity created to absolve individuals of personal responsibility. The person is not the corporation. The corporation can ignore and distance itself from the everyday people it supposedly serves. When you put the insularity of the economic system together with absolution from responsibility to people you have a force that is very resistant to democratic influence.

In 1968 the president of Nabisco was quoted in Forbes saying something to the effect of, "I envision the day when Arabs and Chinese and Latinos and Kenyans will be drinking Coke and brushing their teeth with Colgate and eating Ritz Crackers." To me that tells us we are not just dealing with economic systems, but with social change systems.

Current economic practices are systems through which we impose our values. We're basically teaching that our way, the American or Western European way–is the right way. We're saying, "Give up your local cultures." Do we really want that? Do we want to wipe out cultures by never questioning the business processes we're embarking on at the mega-level of global corporate activity? Do we want to sit idly saying nothing? We live with and complain about them but fail to see their role in teaching us what we as a country or as communities, families and individuals value. Our economic practices teach us values constantly. Either we don't see it or we feel powerless to deal with such huge forces.

That gets into the whole issue of who decides what our values are. At its most respectful and democratic, defining our shared values involves true dialogue among people of different backgrounds and perspectives to identify what is best for each immediate group and society in general. We must look consciously at what we're doing and espousing now so we can have the dialogue about what we all want to be teaching.

True dialogue among folks who can make a difference could help. Powerful people have huge influence. They could put their efforts into questions like how we use markets responsibly. They could consider the questions I've been suggesting. What values are we teaching? What messages can we give youth that lead to healthy social change?

Most recently this kind of initiative has come from the Bilderberg group. The Bilderberg group is composed of elite and powerful people. They meet secretly every two years to talk about world issues. There are no agendas. Nobody else can attend. Not surprisingly, this group is the subject of conspiracy theories that are probably exaggerated, but also instructive in some ways. For example, there has been concern about the Bilderberg group's composition–elite people with similar values. The group's response was, "We have members from third world countries."

At the time, the richest man in the world was a Mexican fellow. The group pointed to his presence as indication they were bringing in different perspectives. That claim raised questions regarding what happens when someone from a small or oppressed group enters a more powerful group. More often than not, that person gets co-opted. It's human nature. You naturally start to give up the values of your third world country to fit with the culture of the elite. In that process, you wipe out any effect of a different perspective.

The more we eliminate diversity in commerce or composition of think tanks, the more we compromise our ability to change. A local writer here in Albuquerque used to speak with our graduate seminar. He would wait as people drifted in late and then start his lecture by looking at his watch. He'd say, "You know, time is an interesting thing. It runs in English, it marches in French, it works in German and it walks in Spanish." That tells you a little bit about how culture and language influence knowledge.

Moves to eradicate language are powerful examples of threats to change and the flourishing of human community. Eradicating language is not simply eliminating words; it is losing ways of thinking and seeing. Language is an aspect of culture that adds to capability in the way humans know and interact with the world. There's research to show that kids who are bilingual have a cognitive advantage over kids who are monolingual.

Many citizens of the United States want to have only one legal language. That raises questions like the ones related to our economic system. What is implied in that position? It's actually much more than a political statement. Such a policy would impair social change by legislating one way of thinking about things. If we all learn only English, our time will always run. It will never walk, it will never march.

I once heard George Luis Borges speak about the language he most liked for writing. "If I want to get my point across in a specific way or if I want to give instructions, I'll do it in English," he said. "But if I want to affect your emotions, if I want to make a point that gets you to cry or become angry, I use a Romance language." That goes again to what's in a language. It is not a threat. It's a perspective. If it is wiped out we lose strengths and options that can be very beneficial to knowing. We very much need the range of diverse perspectives to discern the best solutions for the society of our future.

031 Bruce McQuakay
Albuquerque, NM

Language, economy and a relationship with the land define Bruce McQuakay's daily life. Bruce (Tlingit/Apache) is a water and sacred-sites activist with a non-profit Native American organization. His advocacy brings him into interaction and occasionally into conflict with the mining companies in the Albuquerque area. Bruce met me that afternoon at a filling station across from his apartment complex. We sat in the Mini. Arizona sunlight angled through the sunroof and onto Bruce's smiling face, his long black braid and red fleece jacket. That image was by far the best Valentine of the day.

Bruce: It's been pretty tough looking for work. A lot of that has to do with what Bush has done in office. I think the change that's promised will bring work back to the United States, but that needs to happen through green jobs as opposed to oil, gas, uranium, and nuclear. And, we need jobs that last more than two or four years. Sustainability.

Through it all, the main thing I count on is our community staying together—the diverse community I have become part of. Here in Albuquerque there are other organizations–Hispanic, Latino, Chicano groups that we work with. Being a Native American organization we've recognized that we need to maintain those connections.

A lot of things that affect us all don't see cultural or color lines. Poverty doesn't see any race. There can be poor white people, poor Asian people, poor Hispanic people, poor Native. Maintaining unity in that sense, that's something that I'd like to have stay with us. It's something we can bring into the next generation–the bigger picture of things that affect us all. It will always be important to have a community of people who support each other to work together for the struggle, I guess. Yes, for the struggle for all people.

Within the last eighteen months there has already been a lot of change. The first African American president, more progressive ideas being more acceptable and social changes starting to take place. An important sign of change would be peace–withdrawing our troops from Iraq and even Afghanistan. Making peace with people in the Middle East where we are currently in conflict. Then, I'm looking for how we move on energy. Oil is not going to be around forever. Natural gas probably won't be around forever. Nuclear energy is not safe in any form. How we progress with that will show us how Barack's gonna handle things. But I have faith in him. I think he won't let us down.

I don't expect an overnight thing, but I am hoping it will get better for people who

Bruce McQuakay *Albuquerque, New Mexico*

are living below the poverty line and people who are having cultural, I guess, despair. We will know things are changing when more opportunities come to economically challenged people. It is time to stop the oppression of people who aren't advantaged and to protect what they believe is important to their homes, or family or communities.

On the cultural despair situation, here in Albuquerque a road was just built through the petroglyphs. That's culturally insensitive. I hope there will come a point where we can cooperate on issues that affect sacred sites and places of prayer. There are vital threats right now here in the Southwest to Mount Taylor. Industry wants to get to the uranium underneath it. Mount Taylor is considered sacred by most of the tribes here in New Mexico and Arizona. And there are the San Francisco Peaks and the aggressive proposals to put a ski resort there. That area is considered a sacred place to Navajos. I'm not sure which other people regard it in that way but I know definitely the Navajos greatly revere the San Francisco Peaks as a special place.

Across America, there are many traditional places of prayer that are under threat. We need to start paying more attention to sacred sites like that. That's one thing our organization is working on; getting a bill passed to make the laws already in place more enforceable for protecting sacred places. I look forward to seeing how that's gonna happen. As much as I can, I'm gonna to be a part of it.

Road Note

My route from Albuquerque, NM to Kerrville, TX took me past hundreds of sacred sites known only to the indigenous people of that land. If it weren't for my time with Bruce, I wouldn't have noted the special significance of this land. Driving on the interstate these kinds of details are easily overlooked and all too often, the experience is dominated instead by being ... well ... long.

On either side of the road the land expands into a vast and seemingly empty terrain. An exception being the brief chorus of rush hour and billboards in Las Cruces and El Paso. In the fifties, the Eisenhower administration began laying out this solid band of asphalt where now it stretches out like a well-worn cattle trail. All day and all night herds of semis trundle across these deserts and onwards through the bayous and farmlands of the Southeast. Their job is to convey commerce between the communities rooted in the land between our shining seas. Dodging in and out of the procession of giants are little cars like mine.

In New Mexico those of us of the smaller wheel-base can get away with 80 mph. In Texas I could nudge it up to 85, but I was back down to 74 or so after sunset when the black signs with white lettering read "NIGHT 65." The unwritten rule: 9 miles over the posted limit usually passes, but don't even think of cresting 10. The word 'usually' and the periodic signs depicting a lone leaping deer are worth taking seriously. One's driving record can be significantly impaired by being lax with either, especially with six hours of paying supreme attention while driving in the dark.

Ragged and saddle sore, I logged another post-midnight arrival, this time at the home of Fred, B.K. and Preston Gamble. Their reception was as effusive as ever. In the Gamble's guest room, Fred had left a giant Mylar balloon and a copy of book of Barbara Jordan's speeches – an iconic leader and inspiration to both of us over the years. The balloon read, "We Love You!" These kinds of homecomings are truly the best.

Fred Gamble had arranged for me to talk first thing the next morning with several of his colleagues at the Schreiner University. Schreiner was a small two-year college when Fred and I were growing up in Kerrville. He went to school there before going on. Now decades later, he serves as the CFO for the small but thriving university. Later in the day I would also have the chance to speak with Mrs. Gamble, Fred's 86-year-old mother.

032 Tomas Duarte
Kerrville, TX

Consistent with a lifelong attribute of affability, Fred has a multitude of friends and acquaintances. He introduced me to the campus painter, Tomas Duarte, who was working in the administration building where Fred has his office. I tucked myself into a corner with the camera. Tomas smiled and said, "That will work real good since I think best when I'm painting."

Tomas: Change. I hadn't really thought about it but I hear it a lot. Everything's gotta change, ya know. Everything changes. Slowly, but it does change. Everything should change. That's what I think. And things should get better. Right now there's a lot of unemployment and hopefully that changes for the better instead of going backwards which it might be for a little bit. It's going to take a year or two, maybe longer for total change.

President Obama, he mentions a lot of change. He can't do any worse than what's been in office prior to him. That change prior to him was going bad. Very bad. It can't get no worse than what it has been. Can't go down anymore, so it's got to go up.

Everybody in my family has their jobs. My sisters, they work in the hospital. I work here–on my fifth year. My brother's a glazer. So we've all got jobs. I hear everybody saying, "You've got a job, you better keep it." I still believe that if I was to quit here and go somewhere else, I'd be able to get employment.

But if you speak only Spanish it's hard. Very hard. Not so much here in the south as it is further north. There's a lot more Spanish speaking people in this area–everybody coming up out of Mexico, South America–headed north. There's not much opportunity down in those South American countries so they're looking for a better life. Some of them stay if they have family here. Others just keep moving north. Sometimes there's conflict as they take the jobs nobody else wants at a lower paying wage than what most other people will take. Most people want $12, $15 an hour, but you're not going to get that unless you show somebody what you can do. You're going to get about minimum wage and then you go from there.

For most working people the main sign of good change will be a wage increase. I'm used to making $100 an hour instead of $10 an hour. It's best when you contract a job. You contract it for so much and then you get it done in a short period of time. That's making money. In less than ten months, my partner and I up there in Michigan made $50,000. It's a big difference from here. The painters up there are in a lot bigger demand than they are around here. I'm just trying to be in demand (*laughs*).

033 Barbara Von Brandt-Siemers
Kerrville, TX

By mid-February of 2009, unsettling economic news flooded the newspaper headlines. Barbara VonBrandt-Siemers, the Controller for Schreiner University has immediate familiarity with the fluctuations and expressions of our economy. When Fred introduced us, Barbara shook my hand and then folded up the budget sheets on her desk sliding them into a wide drawer. As she pushed the drawer closed she said, "They won't miss me for a few minutes."

Barbara: Are you familiar with the book Who Moved my Cheese?[9] I cannot remember the author, but it's a business book. It's about two mice. They live a happy life in a maze with lots of cheese. All of a sudden, the cheese has been moved. One mouse takes out its walking shoes and finds a way to adjust to the situation. It is happy again. The other mouse just complains. The cheese is gone, things are tough and it's just awful. It's a metaphor for the business world. You lose your job and things are just not the same.

The book made a pretty big splash in the business community. Business coaches all quote it. It's in our human resources library, so I checked it out. It was great. If circumstances change in ways we did not see coming and are not happy with, what can we do? We can sit and complain and lament the good times, or we can go out and find new cheese, different cheese–something to restore our contentment. That's what I think of cheese. Oops...I mean "change." (*laughter*)

Of course, I rely on things like security, food and shelter–means of survival. Also peace of mind, that's very important to me. There are things that I worry about–like the budget. "Have I made a mistake? Have I taken everything into consideration?" As Controller for the university, one little mistake can have dire consequences.

For me it's all about peace of mind. Some people say it is all about happiness. To me a big part of happiness is peace of mind, contentment. I want to be comfortable in my surroundings, to have the absence of wishes. Like, "Yep, I have a nice living room, I have enough to eat, I have a nice car." I just have enough of everything.

Sometimes peace of mind comes with huge change, like coming here from Germany. Looking back I think, "My God, that was a bold move." I've never regretted it, not one day. I was a little anxious the day before I left. My mother didn't take it well. She yelled at me and said, "One day you're going to come back and I'm going to be dead. You're abandoning me." I still did it because I knew it was the right thing for me. That was 11 years ago. I'm 46 now, so I was 35. I wasn't a teenager so I already had experiences. I had lived in Kenya. I had a job there. That was another change. It came out of the same motivation to experience another culture, broaden my horizon, do something different.

It might sound like I'm just out there for the fun, but really I take calculated risks. I was in Kenya for four and a half years. Then my boss died. His widow sold all the businesses, so all of our positions became unnecessary in the process. Otherwise I might still be there. After I came back from Kenya, I had a hard time fitting back in the German lifestyle. You know, once you see something else it really opens your mind. Then when

9 *Who Moved My Cheese: An Amazing Way to Deal with Change in Your Work and in Your Life. Spencer Johnson. Putnam Publishing, 1998.*

you go back to all the trivial stuff that people can bring into living, well I was just not happy there. I lived in Germany for two years but I couldn't wait to get back out in the world. So I came to America.

I met an American in Kenya and he already had a place here in Center Point, TX. That's a bit outside of Kerrville. He lived with me for a while in Germany, but didn't speak German and really didn't want to live there. I said, "OK. I'll move with you to Texas, but what am I going to do?" He said, "Well, I know this small liberal arts college in Kerrville. Why don't you get a degree there?" I had not been to university in Germany, so that's how I ended up here.

When I studied here I befriended a lady. She was in her early 20's. I remember she said, "I was born in Fredericksburg, TX and that's where I'm going to die." I thought to myself, "That might be good for you, but it would not be good for me." I would need a lot of rich experience in between. I was born in Alsburg, Germany and I may die there, but between here and there I want to have plenty of change. I want some action, some fun. The good life. (*laughs*)

The good life is not always easy, but in the end it always pays off. All my decisions have panned out. All the changes I've initiated have turned out well. There were some changes that were not what I wanted. The man that I met in Kenya, the one who brought me here, he died in 2000. Of course I thought, "What am I going to do now?" I decided to finish my education here. Then I met my new husband. So, twice. And I'm still here.

Looking back on my life, I'm glad that I got to do many exciting things. I like change. It's not all fun, but there's always another day. I guess it's all in how you respond to the question, "Who moved the cheese?" (*laughs*)

Road Note

I spent the rest of the day with three generations of a family I've known since I was eleven. Until now, I had never spent any quality time with Mrs. Gamble, Fred's mom. In the Texas hillcountry of the late sixties and early seventies, it just seemed normal. The white people all lived around where we lived and then, down Harper and across Town Creek was where all the brown and black families lived. That's where Charlie Delgadillo's dad had his grocery store and where Mr. Wilson, our history teacher and school bus driver lived. Fred came to our house. So did Barbara Villarreal and Diane Wheatfall. But we never went to theirs. At the time I never stopped to consider that.

Meanwhile, Fred and I lived the drama of our teen years amidst Texas high school sports, the Civil Rights movement and the reliable cycle of seasons across the land. Our vantage points varied by where we lived, how we looked and by the way public sensibility had formed and shifted in rural Texas. Mounting civic calls, public incidents and fledgling victories for the end to racial oppressions surrounded us in those years, along with demonstrations of profound rejection for military involvement in Vietnam.

What Fred and I knew more than anything, however, was our friendship - a connection that became particularly strong during the time we both worked out of town on ranch land along the Guadalupe River that had been converted into a Presbyterian conference grounds. The bluebonnets of spring would come and go. The river would welcome us in the summer when we took our breaks sitting on its bank and diving in. Less visible to us at the time were such constants as Mrs. Gamble's personal policy on education, its link to economic health and most powerfully, her quiet reminders to "trust in the Lord."

034 Mrs. Laura Gamble
Kerrville, TX

Today, for the first time, I visited the house where Fred grew up. Mrs. Gamble is now in her mid eighties. Fred and his nine siblings are all grown and have kids of their own. Four of her grandchildren, boys between the ages of nine and fifteen, live with Mrs. Gamble. "Now, I'm raising these four, too," she said, eyes shining above her beautiful smile.

Mrs. Gamble: I've heard about change on TV and in the media. I haven't heard people themselves saying much about change. Whenever people get in a panic they think they need a change. They don't realize you can't fix it in two or three weeks. It may take years. President Obama may be out of office and there will be somebody else in there still working on getting the same things done.

I was raised in Texas. Me and my husband were in the service. We came from Virginia to San Antonio and from San Antonio here. I wanted to settle down, so I said we weren't going to move anymore. Changing schools was too much for the children. I've been in this house for forty-five years. When I moved here it wasn't even paved. The house wasn't like this either. There was no closet space or anything else. I bought it, remodeled it and added to it to make it the way it is now.

I worked for the State Hospital, raised 10 children and then took on the four grandkids in 2003. It's a whole lot different from raising Fred (*her son*) and them. (*laughs*) It's kind of rough, especially when they aren't toilet trained or anything. You just have to start.

They're all in school now. There's a new program so there ain't no kids left behind, but I still think they need to let them learn to do schoolwork for themselves. That one in there, he has a shunt. He has a disability where he's, what do you call it, Special Ed. They pamper him. You see how well he talks and how much manners he's got? At school he's different. He hollers with this and that teacher. They read and do other things for him. We don't. We want him to read for himself. He can do it. He can read. He can ask questions. He can spell. You've got to let him do it. He will say he can't. Let him do it. I told them that.

The main thing is to make sure the children have manners and respect their elders. I wanted my children to have respect. I'm getting these four grandsons to do the same thing. To respect. It takes a lot of teaching. They're not taught that anywhere else. I also want them to have a nice dress code, not clothes down here all saggy. Oh, they look horrible. Hair not combed. If they have character, respect, stuff like that, they can go further than they can just looking sloppy. I'm from the old world maybe. (*laughs*) I would like to see prayer back in schools. That helps the children be more respectful. That kind of change, it has to start at home.

Whatever's their job or whatever they're doing, I want them to be the best they can be in it. Be respectable. I don't want them to think they've got to run over somebody else to get a way in. With education, and manners you'll get what you want. You don't have to take it away from anybody else. It will come to you. I always tell them to pray about it and to be the best they can be whatever they do. I've been saying that all my years.

My children are all educated. They're all teachers or doing something else. I had them studying. They would help each other. These grandkids won't. When their parents were kids, they used to all sit around that table and get their lessons together. They would help each other. They had teachers back then that would come like a truant officer and see what they were doing. Professor Wilson did that. He's dead now. He used to come and check on them at night and see what they were doing.

Jobs right now are hard to come by. I've got a son in Houston. He was working in the Men's Warehouse. They took that whole store and moved it away, so he's got to get another job. They had to sell the store off because the economy is so bad. I feel sorry for everybody, not just some. It is bad. I know the government – it's not going to get better in a week or a month, maybe not even a year.

I guess they have to downsize so they can at least keep making a living with the employees they have. The people that own the business have to do something so they can keep afloat. Farmers and everybody else. Like I said, you hate that it is happening. AT&T and all of them, just downsizing. Everybody's having problems.

I haven't seen this in a long time. Maybe way back in World War II. Of course I was a kid, but you had to get stamps for shoes and different stuff like that. Like I say, we're not making the change. We just have to see how it works out. I'm just hoping and praying it will work out for everybody. My race and every race.

I'm not an outrageous Christian, but I believe. You just have to pray and wait on the Lord. If you happen to be a person who gets a good job, be ready for it. Prepare yourself. Because if you bring your best, then you can stay in it. If they have to downsize and lay you off, keep yourself educated and prepare to be knowledgeable enough to get another one. It may not happen today or tomorrow, but sooner or later, if you've prepared, then you can find something that you can do.

So things are going to change. It's going to be. But these aren't the changes everybody is talking about now. For the big changes in the country we just have to wait and see how it's going to come out. I don't care who's in office it always takes its time.

Oh, I've got to get these kids ready to go to Bible study.

035 Andrae
Kerrville, TX

Typical of Laura Gamble's household, life progressed again into the next thing that required attention. As we talked, grandsons had wandered in and out of the living room. Mrs. Gamble would give a quick look and shoo them away, calling their uncle Fred to get them into the kitchen. When she mentioned Bible study, the 'next thing,' we noticed one of her grandsons, Andrae, standing quietly in the doorway.

MC: Hi Andrae. Was that you she was just talking about, saying you're on honor roll?

Andrae: Yes ma'am. And I know a good person you can ask about change.

MC: Who?

Andrae: Miss Loraine.

MC: Is that your teacher?

Andrae: No ma'am. It's an after school program that I go to. She's always talking about changing lives. That's what the program's mainly about.

MC: Is that what she would say? That change is about changing lives?

Andrae: Yes ma'am. But, she would give a lot of extra.

MC: What would you say? What do you think change is?

Andrae: Change is like when you're running on one thing and you can't get off of it. Almost like a habit. You know you can fix it, but sometimes it's not that easy. You just have to believe in yourself. That right there is a change.

MC: Do you think there's anything that ought to stay the same so that things can change?

Andrae: You mean in this house?

MC: I mean anywhere.

Andrae: The way most people are polite. The way I've been since I moved from Oregon to Texas.

MC: You've seen changes in your own life?

Andrae: Yes ma'am.

MC: And in yourself?

Andrae: Yes ma'am.

MC: How old are you now?

Andrae: I'm 10.

MC: And how long have you been here?

Andrae: Six years. When I came here I started going to a better school and studying harder. Now I'm in G/T (gifted and talented) classes.

MC: Do you like them?

Andrae: Yes. I'm challenged. G/T is a lot more than just studying. Like, for Christmas we bring clothes and toothbrushes and toothpaste for the K'Star[10]1 children. We just did that.

MC: How does that make you feel?

Andrae: Happy because when I think about the K'Star people I know they probably feel like nobody thinks about them because they don't live with their family. When they get gifts from people they don't even know, that tells them that they're important to somebody.

036 Fred Gamble
Kerrville, TX

Forty years later. By now, Fred Gamble and I are family for sure. Our lifelong friendship remains as dependable as the seasons. That evening we sat in his living room as the February day dimmed outside an expanse of windows facing west. Fred laughed and said again, "Mary, it's just so good to see you. And, I'll still swear your mama just spit you out." Fred always did have a crush on my mom.

Fred: When I listen to my president talk about what's going on I want to believe him. And I don't want anyone to doubt my patriotism when I disagree with him. I don't want to continue having somebody piss on my boot and tell me it's raining. The last six or seven years I haven't felt free to discuss my feelings about my government and my government's actions without having my patriotism questioned. So, when I think of change, I think of those things being different.

I want people to assume I am of good will unless I give them reason to believe otherwise by my behavior. I want you to assume that I'm intelligent enough for us to have a discussion. I don't want you feeding me your position loud enough, often enough that you think I'm going to believe like you do. For example, there is a vast difference for most Americans between the war in Iraq and the war in Afghanistan. You lump them together and call them fighting terrorism often and loudly. If I question your thinking, you question my patriotism. I do understand why we went to Afghanistan and I don't understand why we went to Iraq. Assume that I am well read and exposed. You assume that I'm not.

Implicit in that is my retaining access to information when you're pissing on my

---

10 K'Star http://www.kstar.org/

Fred Gamble *Kerrville, Texas*

boot and telling me it's raining. If I hadn't had access to real, good, and various sources of information I wouldn't know the difference in the two wars. It is also important to me, obviously, that I stay healthy and free enough to take advantage of access to information.

What I'm looking for is to see people in dialogue. People talking and listening who before thought dialogue was me shouting at you and you shouting at me. I'm not going to wake up on a particular day and see, "Oh my god, they're really talking." But I think I will look back over time and say, "They're talking. We're talking." Then, you will trust me enough to let me know what you feel about an issue. You will know that I'm not going to hate you for it or jeopardize your job or jeopardize your friendships or whatever. It's something that happens slowly and in small pockets like a yeast bread. With right conditions for long enough, even minor set backs won't stop it.

A lot of people want real dialogue and collaboration to happen and I hope their spirits aren't dampened when a year from now–after Obama's 100 days, or the first year or the first 18 months IT hasn't happened. IT will happen, but we won't know exactly when it does.

In many ways, significant change is already here. If you go back to the late 60's and the Martin Luther King era, it wasn't universal but the vast majority of blacks were very proud of Dr King, his approach and what he was trying to accomplish. But that was coupled with fear. You didn't want to say anything about your pride. You didn't revel in it. You didn't get excited about it. You were hopeful, but that's a totally different feeling than excited. Now there is excitement. Maybe it's because the end of major oppression seems near or maybe the consequences of expression aren't as dire, but I've never seen anything like what I think I see now. Nothing close.

Dialogue in the country has not completely changed yet, but what I see is a pep in the step, a glide in the stride that wasn't there before. People of at least equal if not immensely greater faith back in the late 60's weren't able to have the pep in the step, glide in the stride. There were different social requirements. But I do see that now. It's something that's communicated without conversation.

Like Colin Powell's recent speech. He said something about the way blacks are responsible for blacks. He was talking about Barack Obama. He told a story of growing up in Brooklyn when that community had their first black bus driver. The man was not working on the bus, not fixing the bus. He was driving the bus. Powell talked about how exciting this was for black people in Brooklyn. There was a black bus driver in charge of a bus that was going to leave Brooklyn. This wasn't a local bus. It was a Greyhound kind of thing. In the midst of all the excitement there was one thing they all said. "This is great. This is wonderful. We're all so proud of you. And don't you dare wreck this bus!" Then Powell said to Obama, "Barack, don't you dare wreck this bus!"

That's something all black people understand–that in all this excitement there is also enormous pressure. What Powell was saying was, "If this guy wrecks this bus, there will not be another black bus driver in Brooklyn for a generation." If that happens then all the things they've said about why blacks can't do whatever it might be come back as, "Told you!"

What was funny was that here was this erudite, macho, intelligent guy who you don't think would have the same feelings you've had. Feelings like, "Oh my god. I was so glad the guy who shot Reagan wasn't black." Hearing Colin Powell's speech was like,

"Damn, Colin. I didn't know you dealt with the same stuff I've been dealing with." The guy was Secretary of State, Ambassador to the UN but even he was has these feelings. He said it in a joking way, but you understood it. Like so many black people, he was saying, "This is so exciting. We're all behind you. But do not wreck this bus." He looked right into the camera and said, "Barack, don't wreck this bus."

Of course, people laugh. I don't think they understand Obama's burden. It's very different to have someone like Powell be able to say out loud that he has that trepidation. The overwhelming majority of us want our president to succeed, and for people of color, whether they're black or Hispanic or other people of color, this is a little different. A very big part of what you want for your kids and your grandkids and your great grandkids rests with this guy. And I know that's why I see people moving around differently, stepping differently and taking more chances. Our dreams are within reach.

037,038 Tommy Carpenter & David Martin
Kerrville, TX

On my way out of town the next morning I stopped only slightly astonished to find a Starbucks on Junction Highway built with windows and a terrace looking out on my beloved Guadalupe River. Things do change. Just as I finished a blog entry, two men- one in his forties, the other in his twenties- came in and sat near me. They were planning ways to support the three hundred youth attending their Baptist Church. The younger man, David Martin, was the youth minister. He, Tommy Carpenter and I started up one of those coffee shop conversations, but this one had a familiar home-folks twist.

Tommy: My friend says love has a twenty part definition. He's got it on a wrist band. He says if you don't know what the twenty parts of the definition are, you don't know what it is and how are you going to know what to do with it? It's the same thing. If you don't know what change is how can you know what you're doing?

I'm a very dominant personality. For me, change is finding out what needs to be changed, taking the first steps and then enlisting those around me who feel the way I do. I build teams so I like to get people involved making things move.

Dave's ministry is about three or four hundred kids cycling through our church every Wednesday. My goal in getting involved in the change there is getting a team built so we can get youth involved beyond the level of just showing up to church and then going back to school and whatever they did before. Really it's the next step in activating change in their lives. If they're going to say, "I'm a Christ follower," what does that look like? What does that do? How does that act?

David: When I was driving in this morning, I was listening to the news. They were talking about how there's a 6% bump in inflation today. I thought of that poster with Barack Obama that, of course, said Change. I thought whether he's attacked for this or not I still wonder what change means. These reports were coming out from January, so he'd only been in office a couple of hours at best and can't be blamed for today's inflation. Still, what is change you can believe in?

I think change is ambiguous. It's different for every single person in this coffee shop. Anybody you put on that camera will have a different idea of what change is. Change has to start in the heart before it ever makes any type of visual effect in our lives. That would be my version of change.

Tommy: The big constant, and I'm going to go back to the Bible–God is a God of love. To keep our lives centered on God and the work he did on the cross with his son Jesus Christ dying for our sins. That doesn't change. There are certain values with that. Family values are one set of values that never changes. We've kind of blown that apart trying to redefine the family and redefine society around that. But society always evolves and always will. The constant that never changes is love. I show love towards you through my behavior. That's constant, that can't change.

It's easy to dehumanize people and then to mistreat them. That can turn into killing each other off because we don't consider the others human in the first place. For example, we don't get along very well in America right now. You're a Democrat, I'm a Republican. Either of us can get into this, "You're an idiot" philosophy instead of "We're humans. We live in the same place. We should get along." We do all come from the same place. (laughs) The source of life is one in the same. We can't lose that perspective.

David: I can't top that. (*laughter*)

Tommy: If a person doesn't want to believe in the Bible, believe in God, you still have to believe in something bigger than you. If you don't live for a cause that will outlast you, then your life will change at every whim. That's why democratic societies have a hard time. We chase the latest and greatest instead of living something bigger than us. As a country, we don't live for our kids' and grandkids' generations. That's something bigger than us. Instead, we live for right now. If it's uncomfortable right now, we've got to make a change. What's wrong with self sacrifice?

David: He's right on. And I would say the first sign of a good change is motivation. That requires me to have a resolve that regardless of what seems to be hindering me, I will push through. The greatest and the best minds our country ever produced had that perspective. Regardless of circumstances, inadequacies or lack of talent, the passion was there. They knew what it was going to take and they gave that.

Tommy: Two specific occurrences in our country right now make me think change is possible and coming. One is working with the youth. They have a lot of dissatisfaction and mistrust. "There's got to be something better," is their thought process. When youth see something better, they typically run toward it instead of away from it. They're fed up with the machine of a society we have now. If enough of that generation gets frustrated, they will bring change. We've seen that before in the cultural history of our country.

Then there is the downturn in spending and people wanting to save more money. We're frustrated with, "Spend, spend, spend–me, me, me." People are starting to say, "Let's pay off debt. Let's save some." That's a sign of good change. It's hard on the economy, but it's good for the family. And there's my thumbnail analysis.

David: Man, we've held court. I think we've solved all the world's problems. (*laughter*)

Tommy: There's one more thing that seems important to say. Seems to me we've been majoring in the minors instead of the majors. We can get back to that little stuff, you know. It's time now to focus on the big issues and work together as American people toward those solutions.

Road Note

The Guadalupe river of my childhood rolled as gracefully as ever beyond the steps that led down to the parking lot. Every interview left me with a feeling of gratitude. Every one left me with more I wanted to learn about and each of them refined the shape of EX:Change. Talking with Tommy and David reminded me again of the issue of political differences. You know, the red/blue thing. True or not, and particularly since the first election of the second President Bush, the American people have seen red and blue as mutually exclusive, often antagonistic and ultimately, as categories that we have no choice but to fit into.

I've often wondered how truly polarized we are. Although it does seem easier to identify differences than to notice our shared sensibilities, at some point it becomes like trying not to see the space between the saguaro cacti in Tucson. The opportunity to listen to Tommy and David gave credence to what I had been suspecting. When I sincerely listen to people who differ from me in their religious orientations, political positions, and socio-economic circumstances, I gain unique perspectives on priorities and values that we share in common.

Tommy and David's interests overlapped with what I'd heard from Se-ah-dom Edmo (005) and Leila Bowen (006) in Portland, from Colleen Suwara (026) and then Todd Franklin (027) in San Diego, from Cheri Carter (028) in Tucson and Bruce McQuakay (031) in Albuquerque. The hopes and wishes of each of these Americans ultimately center on the well being of family and community and on positive leadership from our elected officials. The EX:Change voices so far agree that the well being of each of us depends on the well being of all of us. Like Calvin Hecocta (011) says, it is time for "waking up to our intricate interdependence with all beings."

039 Shelly Knox
Aledo, TX

My next stop was Aledo, Texas, an exclusive bedroom community of Fort Worth. The houses are enormous, easily 4000-5000 square feet, sitting on large lots with fenceless backyards bordering a private golf course. That warm February afternoon, Shelly Knox left her teenage daughter in charge of two younger brothers so we could take a fifteen minute walk on the golf cart path, Flip camera in tow.

Shelly: Most of us in America are just normal real people. That's who we want leading us, normal real people. The change I think is necessary right now is for the people we've entrusted with running our country to get the politics out of their decision making. Instead of doing things for greed or political gain, I want them to do things that help the average American. I think that's been missing. We need honesty and straight forwardness. Right now we need to put differences aside. We're in a crisis. We need real people helping us figure out how to solve this mess.

The stock market drop really hit home. That's what affects my life the most. In our family, we've put things like the war and all that on the back burner. I'm sure there are people who would like changes in those areas, but with my husband being in the financial arena we need change in the stock market.

That starts with everybody buckling down to quit living above our means. So many people, especially in a suburb like where we live, are keeping up with the Joneses. We're guilty of it, too. So, one of the main changes we need is for people to hunker down for a little bit. That's hard because we also need people to spend money to keep the businesses going. (laughs) What do you do? It's a catch 22.

Right now in this moment I hope for change to get people working so we can secure our children's future. I have three kids. I told my third grade son this morning at breakfast, "It's a really good thing that you're not graduating from college this year looking for a job because it's hard right now. You wouldn't have near the opportunity we did when we were graduating from college."

My husband has a lot of friends and family who are clients. He takes that on as a heavy load. He feels so responsible for the loss of all these people's retirement. He worries more about them than he does about us.

My kids are so funny. They know the stock market's been a roller coaster for six months. Just crazy. We all watch the stock market to see what kind of mood daddy's going to be in when he gets home. (*laughs*) Even my four-year-old will ask me, "Mom, is it up or down today? Is it up or down?"

I live in an area where, I don't know what the exact percentage would be but it's very high Republican. I didn't vote for Obama. Now that he's elected, I have the highest hopes for him. I'm not angry or bitter. Where the Republican party was going was not good. I would not vote for George Bush if he were running against Obama.

I struggle because I hate it that when you say you're a Republican and you're associated with George Bush. When I look at the moral things that each party stands for, I am straight Republican. But now that we have Barak Obama, I'm rooting for him. We need him. I mean, I think that he's that kind of normal real person I was describing. I see that. Now that he's in office, I'm impressed with him. I hope he does the right thing and I hope he's got the right people around him to influence him positively. I also hope he stays true to his realness. I hope he doesn't get in there and get influenced by the politician types. In four years I would love to say, "He got us back on track." That's what we need.

I haven't been real involved in politics. We've been fortunate to have a real happy life so far. We both have good college degrees and good jobs. We can raise our kids. We've been blessed. We've never needed something we couldn't get. We live in a great community. So, I haven't felt the great need for change until this financial mess. My mother laughs at me because I will go days without watching the news. It's depressing and I'm such an optimist that I'd rather not hear it. I'm sure as my kids get older that will change and I'll pay more attention to things that go on.

We probably all want the same thing. You can get nit picky. You can say, "Well I believe in this and so and so believes in that." But you're never going to get everybody in America to agree and there's no reason to try. I have two parents who both have political views completely opposite to mine and it's fine. We just agree to disagree. Nobody gets hostile.

You probably aren't going to learn anything from talking to me. We're just a family that's always at the baseball field or the football field. We live this life of raising these kids and aren't very politically active. Still as a parent, your main priority is for things to be good for your kids. Sometimes you don't realize they are good until everything tanks.

Maybe we needed all this turmoil. You don't appreciate things until something like this happens. Life is full of change and I guess change is good. But it tests you, it stretches you. It's been real hard for me to accept change sometimes. I'm hoping the changes we make in the near future work so we can look back and say, "That was rough, but we made it through." I do have hopes. I have high hopes. We'll see.

040,041,042 Olivia Bailey, Holly Perkins, Margo Ryan Dallas, TX

I drove on to Dallas that evening to stay the night with Juliana Perkins, a friend from college. Juliana was characteristically enthusiastic about the EX:Change project and ready to offer her voice. "Before that, though, what about talking with a few brilliant young Texas women?" She was referring to her daughter, Holly, and Holly's friends, Olivia and Margo. That idea led the next day to a lunch date at a super loud nouveau-Mexican-fusion-sit-down-fast-food place in the Highland Park neighborhood. The three young women joined us in their school uniforms, seniors at the prestigious Hockaday School, and shifted a little reluctantly into talking about change.

Olivia: Change. That's a hard one.

Margo: Bad to worse. Bad to worse.

Holly: Change. I have no idea.

Margo: Everybody's always changing.

Olivia: Yeah.

Holly: Yeah.

Olivia: All of us are going from high school to college.

Margo: To living in a dorm instead of at home.

Olivia: Living without parents. (*smiles*)

Margo: It changes rules and curfew and–just change.

Holly: You might make an actual decision that might actually affect your future.

Olivia: Yeah. But I don't want my connection to these people to change (*touches Holly and Margo on their shoulders*). My friends, my family. My relationships.

Margo: But will you change? You're probably going to change in college. Like going to a different city, you know?

Olivia: Well, I'll gain experiences. I don't know if I'll really change.

Holly: To change you have to have something you want. You have to have a goal. You can change lots of things randomly, but it's not going to do any good. You have to have an idea of where you want to end up. We all want to go to college, to get jobs.

Olivia: My highest priority for change is the economy.

Margo: The economy and how the world sees us. It's been really bad.

Holly: Education and the environment. Education first because if we raise a bunch of idiots, then we'll never have a future.

Olivia: The environment, education and health.

Margo: The environment is really important.

Holly: But it won't be as important as everyone having their own education, their own job, their own means. Education affects everyone who doesn't have jobs, who can't get their own healthcare.

Olivia: Yeah, and education would create more awareness of the environment overall. I don't think many people are aware of how bad it is.

Margo: I guess I'm hopeful, but there's a lot that needs to be done. I think it's going to take a long time. We need to be patient with everything that needs to be done not just here but everywhere.

Olivia: We all tend to be cautious about change because there's obviously the risk that something could go wrong and get worse

Holly: I'm hopeful, but I don't think I'm really optimistic. So much needs to change so quickly. It doesn't seem realistic for things to get better enough to make a difference even in the next couple of generations. People I know personally will be fine, but in a broader sense, we're probably not going to do very well. It's because people are getting less educated in a world that needs us to be well-informed and thoughtful. There's more knowledge, but people are becoming less educated. At least in America. So much can come from people just being educated. So many problems can be fixed with that.

Olivia: And so many people are motivated only for themselves these days. If being more eco-friendly, for example, doesn't benefit them up front, they don't want to do it. There are so many things that might not benefit them immediately but would benefit coming generations. They just look short term at their lifetimes. Maybe they think of their children, but not their grandchildren and what would benefit them.

Margo: A lot of people are just very naïve. They don't know what's going on and what they need to do and they don't really want to know. They take what's easy and take what's cheaper. I think that in the future we really need to focus not necessarily on doing what's easiest, but doing what's best for everyone and for future generations. Like Holly said, we need to support education–to increase awareness in people so they know and learn about things that influence life now and into the future.

043 Juliana Perkins
Dallas, TX

Juliana Perkins is one of the happiest and most integrated people I know. Like anyone, her life is far from perfect; nonetheless, she consistently radiates confidence, optimism and nonjudgmental acceptance. Her acceptance extends to anyone she encounters, as long as they aren't cruel – she will draw the line. Juliana is a rather amazing study in demographic contrast. A nurse, wife, mother, and social activist with progressive leanings, she was raised in Dallas by a Sicilian father and a Texan mother and lives now in the most exclusive of Dallas neighborhoods, just three blocks from the new home of George and Laura Bush.

Juliana: Let me think. I'll start with the current political climate. I didn't like how things were going the last–certainly the last eight years and probably prior to that to a certain extent. All the verbiage about being kinder and gentler I'd like to see that actually be real and not just talk. For example, it's not kinder or gentler to subsidize people who are not trying to help themselves. You're not doing them any favors. A lot of people need a break, and what they need is to be given the means to help themselves.

I should also say I am happy when people are passionate about their beliefs and ideas, but I would like them to be more respectful of other peoples' beliefs, passions, and ideas when they differ. That's one way our country has changed that's not for the good. It's been encouraged by the fear mongering that's been so prevalent of late. Not that there aren't fearful things out there. But it's been used as an excuse to amp up ideologues to a point that is not even remotely helpful.

Some of our ideologues are on paths that are not that far away from the Islamist extremists. The seeds are no different. When you have people blowing up abortion clinics because they disagree with the concept, I don't see that as being different. The Islamist extremists are just doing it on a bigger scale. They are Islamist, but they're not really practicing Islam when they do those things. So, real kindness and gentleness and respectful dialogue across differences, those are things I'd like to see us change toward.

Then the economy is a mess. Personally, it hasn't hurt me. I'm in a very small minority of lucky people—for the moment. That could certainly change. On paper things do look different, but day to day, my life is still pretty plum—pretty much in a fat bowl of cream.

There's all the conversation about the problem being mortgages, or this or that. The real root of the problem is greed and self-centeredness—worship of the almighty dollar. The path to happiness is not more money and more stuff—bigger houses, newer cars. That kind of motive has bred a psyche of greed in our country and really has to change.

As for health care, that's a tricky one. Again, the problem goes back to greed. When health care costs started spiraling out of control, the first place they attempted correction was with regulating physicians' fees. That was fair because physicians had gotten greedy. Lots and lots of people were going to medical school so they could be rich. That's not the right reason to be a doctor. Those people created the environment that caused the problem, so some of the regulation was deserved and needed to happen.

Of course, it gets more complicated when you have circumstances where non-medical laypeople—insurance people, HMO people—are dictating what medical care is acceptable and not acceptable for various conditions. That doesn't work. A hernia operation on an 18-year-old is totally different than on a 78-year-old. They're not apples and apples. It's difficult to quantify a lot of the conditions they're trying to quantify.

There's also the problem of distribution of care. You have cities like Dallas with 50 jillion hospitals. If you have a heart attack, there are that many places to go. Of course every hospital wants the latest and greatest diagnostic equipment because they generate income doing tests. In concentrated urban areas we don't need that duplication, but they might really need that equipment out in the sticks. Distribution is wildly uneven. And then you have so many hospitals delivering the same kind of care and competing with each other. In the past, hospitals were always non-profits. Now the primary concern is often in the bottom line instead of the best health care. That's a problem. I don't know how to solve it, but it's a problem.

A significant variable driving up healthcare costs is people who don't get any. When they finally get into the system they bring much bigger, more extensive problems. I hear people questioning whether access to some kind of health care is a right that everyone should have. I don't know. What is basic health care? Does it mean every 89 or 98-year-old person should get to have their heart reconstructed? Is that basic health care? It's awfully expensive.

I do know we need a lot more family practice doctors, pediatricians, and general practitioners so the need for specialists can be decreased. But then, going back to the greed problem, specialists make more money. Maybe we could set up the system so that general practitioners are reimbursed more attractively to encourage more physicians to stay in the general practices.

I've gone back to work—started back a couple of years ago after a good 17 years.

That's significant change–to put myself in a place that's not focused around my children and their school. I was surprised at how much I was out of practice talking about or doing things that weren't centered on my children. I've also started doing volunteer work at a clinic called the North Dallas Shared Ministries. Their mission is to provide help for the working poor. They provide financial assistance if the family needs help with rent or an electric bill or whatever. They help with job placement and finding ESL classes. They have a health clinic, and that's where I come in. I help with immunization.

My mother always told me that optimism was the key to longevity. I pretty much let things roll off my back, so I'm pretty hopeful. I'll be OK. I've even thought if things really, really got bad in the economy, I'd dig up my grass and plant a garden. I could get chickens. It would take a lot for my life to get turned so upside down that I felt hopeless. If something tragic happened to somebody I love, that would be bad. If somebody dropped a bomb on my house, that would be bad, too. But I think it would take something of that magnitude to really upend my world.

As a country we've gone through some major ups and downs and we've come through to the other side. Considering it from a historical standpoint, are we the Roman Empire in decay and crumbling? Maybe so. Perhaps that's a natural cycle of a nation and is inevitable anyway. I don't stay up nights worrying about that one.

Road Note
Road note: At noon on February 21, I drove north into Sherman, Texas where Juliana and I had gone to college. My little car shuddered with every gust of wind. Strong west winds are a familiar symptom of the shift into spring in North Texas. I lived there for thirteen years during the seventies and eighties, earning a degree in Psychology and English at Austin College. Later I met my husband when he joined the faculty, I pursued advanced degrees, and I gave birth to my daughter. After twenty-one years away, I was back.

Mayme Porter, the angel-fairy-godmother-mentor-sage of a woman I would visit today in a nursing home has been a source of wisdom and comfort, a guiding light for me since I was nineteen and a student in one of her classes. Late one summer afternoon when I was newly in my twenties, Mayme and I sat together in her shaded backyard, talking about family and happiness and learning. Mayme said, "Mary, you ought to consider going into journalism – some kind of work where you can interview people, listen to their stories and give them back to the world." I ended up choosing to be a psychology professor.

044 Mayme L. Porter
Sherman, TX

I contacted Margie Morris, Mayme's daughter and a business leader in Sherman. Margie helped me make sure I came at a time that would be easy for Mayme. There was no denying that this was a big moment for me. The timing was perfect. Just before lunch and for about half an hour, Mayme Porter came out of the fog of the Alzheimers Disease that had laid siege to her daytime thoughts of late. Within minutes she said, "I think I

Mayme L. Porter *Sherman, Texas*

have some things I'd like to say about change."

Mayme: Change is taking everything we have and listening to it so we can know where to go next. It means looking at things a bit differently to see what needs to be added to or subtracted from. It's an investigation. There may be previous points of change we haven't thought about before that go into the investigation. The question is, "What needs to be changed?" Investigating that is as important as changing itself. Your goal may be change, but if you start out investigating then you bring about the right kind of change.

Sometimes when people are asked about change they jump to the political. My thought is more about continual growth both personal and spiritual. That reveals a solid base that can change as it needs some change or as it becomes better with change. All the while it is never about changing just for the sake of change[11].

When more people feel better about change, that is good. When more people are involved in helping, encouraging or accepting change, society comes to have a more confident and permanent view. Still, change is constant and will continue to be that way. Small changes are just as important as the bigger changes. Personal changes are just as important as the political or financial ones.

Part of my hope is that people will change personally. It is interesting to watch the people in this organization. There are a lot of really good people here. I look at them and work with them just a little bit. I interact with them. So many of them feel a need for something they're not getting. It's hard not to see that because it is so sadly common.

It's also interesting to pick up from people their different reactions to me or what I do. For the most part, people are a little bit puzzled when they interact with me for the first time. They don't really know what it is they're feeling from me. They hesitate to begin to ask questions or move with that feeling because most of them have not had any experience with somebody like me. That's really strange, but it's like they are accustomed to this rather traditional notion of how they ought to be.

I appreciate the staff here. They've been trying to do things like a yoga class and a spiritual breathing class. I think that's really good and I'm sure such things are not happening in a lot of places like this. I want to encourage the people who are doing that.

N.B   In social science research there is the concept of morbidity. It is a detached and technical way of making room for research participants who drop out. On March 4, 2010 – (March forth!) – Mayme Lou Porter died. I miss her. All my thanks, Mayme.

MARSHALL, AR to MONTGOMERY, AL
—
2.23 to 2.25.2009

- When you say the word change what do you mean?
- Alongside change, what is important to have remain the same?
- What would be signs that positive change is occurring?

MARSHALL, AR to MONTGOMERY, AL
2.23 to 2.25.2009

Life in the United States rolled on like both the weather and the wheels of the Mini Cooper. Until now, the voices had carried optimism or at least hopeful willingness to wait and see what positive change would take root and spread after the result of the November election. Even people like Tommy (037), David (038), Shelly (039) and the guy in the Roseburg, Oregon coffee shop who had not voted for Barack Obama wished only good things for both him and for the country.

As I traveled into Arkansas and on into the deep South, the tenor shifted a bit. I could not be sure if this had more to do with the current events of the day or with regional mannerisms that are specific to this part of the country. Headlines that day read:

- Owner of Philadelphia Inquirer Declares Bankruptcy
- Freed Gitmo Prisoner Alleges Torture in US Captivity
- Admin: Healthcare Reform Top Fiscal Priority
- Many Elderly are Joining the Unemployed Ranks
- Treasury Advisors Preparing "The Largest Bankruptcy Loan Ever" in Case GM and Chrysler Declare Need

Each news story was reflected in the public mood. Things were changing but not exactly in the way many had hoped. Simultaneously, I entered the American South where I would see again that regionally, different cultures employ unique kinds of candor when it comes to discussing politics.

I know the South. Throughout my young life, my family navigated the summer highways between Texas and Georgia to visit relatives. The journey became second nature. Over time it went from taking three days in the late sixties to just one very long day after the interstate was finally finished through Birmingham, Alabama. Driving across the South this time, I continued to hear about the essential interest Americans from all backgrounds had in the wellbeing of families, communities and the planet. Closer to the surface, however, I sensed the tension of disparate beliefs mirroring the fundamental mistrust of the red/blue divisions that had come to pervade discourse in politics and media over recent decades.

Some theories of learning suggest that if you practice an idea long enough within a social group, it will begin to be accepted as reality. What gathered momentum as I traveled across Mississippi and Georgia, was not specifically the red or blue ideals by themselves, but the strength and practice of the division between them. People in general seemed to accept that division as immediate and real, and were wary of expressing their beliefs in mixed company lest they be dismissed or harshly criticized.

In retrospect, I realized that there were already shades of this tension while I was in Texas. Fred's (036) words were strong and clear. "The primary change I'm looking for," he said, "is to be able to trust my president. Right alongside that, I want to be able to disagree with my president or other elected officials without having my patriotism called into question." Rudy's (025) sentiments in San Diego indicated similar expectations.

The problem arises when discussion is neither happening nor possible. If the learning theories are right and the media continued to tell us how polarized we are, our behavior will follow suit. More of us will give public voice to the vitriol or worse, we will further separate ourselves by only speaking of our criticisms behind each other's backs. The unworkable and prevailing truth is that at some level and across all political ideologies most of us come to believe extreme versions of each other due to lack of information and communication.

The Southern states may be more vulnerable to such polarized tension because of the history and generational trauma of the Civil War. Perhaps related to these ancestral echoes is the skepticism that can arise in response to "political correctness." Conservative Southerners who see such posturing as a thin varnish can read political correctness as dangerously inauthentic and thus untrustworthy. Whatever its source, this civic stress reflects what happens in Congress when rigid party lines determine policy through votes that can so often hold us socially paralyzed. So far the voices of *EX:Change* call for listening and legislating outside the noise of this red/blue rift. At the same time, most of us unwittingly participate, actively keeping it alive by not taking time to talk with and listen to people who we see as on the other side of the line.

Here in the deep South, I don't know if people avoid talking with each other because of hatred or fear or both. I do know, however, what we say about one another when we are not talking is usually wrong. The voices up to now offer 44 reminders. Our versions of each other are wrong when they default to the absolute and rigid notion of "the other" as being of ill will and bad heart. Ironically, condemning and dismissing another for being intractable and rigid can only happen when we are being closed minded and inflexible ourselves.

As I return to the land of my childhood, I find again that I cannot extract the filters of my personality or of my character from my observations of the project thus far. A good deal of that character formed here in the South. Odd as it sounds, I actually appreciate the tension that this more overt regional division and candor provide. The truth of the matter is that we are and have always been a country divided. Many of us choose to gloss over this fact. The division embarrasses us. But the voices of the *EX:Change* suggest that we can be strengthened by our different viewpoints

The embarrassment and the ideal of our unity are not wrong or even the least bit inappropriate. And still, our vote this presidential election was split 47% - 53%. The fact of more overt tension here in the South may provide an opportunity. Listening across strong feelings and words gives any of us a chance to learn in spite of our embarrassment from our most dearly held and explosive differences.

Road Note: In Atoka, OK unleaded plus was selling for $1.89 a gallon. A bit farther down the road in Savanna, an exit off OK65 read US Army Ammunition Plant followed immediately by a sign for the Indian Nation Turnpike. In McAlester, Oklahoma the main roads are named Peaceable and Electric.

The highway leaving Oklahoma dropped me into Arkansas. I made my way into the Ozark hills around the Buffalo River and the rural county of Searcy. The land of Oklahoma continues to be known as Indian Country as their standard car license plates attest. In other regions throughout the United States, Native Americans continue to be quite present, at least on tribal lands and in urban centers. Searcy County, Arkansas was a different story. The Osage Tribe had been a primary presence there until 1808. Now the population here is 97.26 percent white. One local mentioned, "There are lots of people with Indian ancestors here – Osage, Choctaw, Cherokee. Most don't claim it. I guess that there is a sign of change."

Later in our conversation the same man told me "This used to be a place of farms, ranches and timber. Now our major industry is Medicaid." As in much of rural America, the population of Searcy County is aging and the infrastructure is suffering from a shrinking tax base. Roads remain unpaved, schools are underfunded, and there is little cushion for responding to the effects of destructive weather.

045 Randy Vincent
Marshall, AR

A high school teacher turned librarian, Randy Vincent agreed to an interview. He was raised in a family that has farmed the Arkansas Ozarks for generations. Politically, Randy often supports Libertarian candidates. As we sat to talk in a clapboard library outbuilding, Randy repeatedly emphasized what he sees as the obvious solution for his rural community. "We have to learn how to sustain ourselves on this land again – right here," he said, "With the families in this community." He went on, "Our hope is in planting and eating with the seasons; turning off our TVs and looking around to see what our kids and neighbors need."

Randy: The first thing I'll mention is globalism. It's something politicians use to justify their actions. But when you look at what economic globalization actually does, you see it takes us away from our families, our communities, our little tribes. It treats us like homogeneous nonsense that human beings cannot be. We need ethnic and cultural connections to survive.

My pet area, of course, is agriculture. My father was a crop duster. My grandfather and my uncle on my mother's side were farmers. Back in 1980 there was a huge drought, here in Arkansas and across a large part of the south. The crops failed to a large degree and a lot of people lost their farms. That was the start of it. By the end of the eighties the American farm–the small American farm–was cooked. My uncle farmed probably less than 200 acres. He didn't go bankrupt because he didn't go way in debt to do his farming but his farm failed.

The death of the small farm coincided with one of the greatest travesties in modern American agriculture, the depletion of gigantic water aquifers across the west and the south, through the bread basket where all the corn and wheat are grown all the way up into Canada. When aquifers go, what typically winds up happening is the soil gets so much salt in it that the growers abandon it. They stop producing crops that need water; specifically corn, and soy beans, and rice. Those are a lot of our staples and most of what we export. Put that with the fact that one tractor these farmers use nowadays costs a half a million to a million dollars. Well, do you know of a small farm that can afford that kind of stuff? I don't.

Another large part of the cost to farmers is chemicals. My dad was a crop duster–an aerial applicator–as they preferred to call themselves. He sprayed insecticide, fungicide, herbicide on crops to promote growth. It's been done since World War II and it's a huge problem for lots of reasons including how spraying put the small farmer in debt to the chemical companies.

There's two branches of science on this. One branch goes with commercial agriculture, and the other goes with organic type growing. You can grow amazing crops with the chemical stuff but it poisons people and animals. There are other ways of doing it. If you grow organically with cover crops, using animal manure or whatever organic matter, you may not have quite as high a yield, but your food quality is a lot better.

One of the things people have lost touch with is that food is seasonal. Certain things grow at certain times of the year. Right now in late February, unless you've got a green house, you should never be able to eat an orange. But with modern transportation being what it is, we can. To a degree that's ok, but it may be healthier to eat with the seasons.

A lot of children don't have any concept about where food comes from. In my opinion that should be against the law. If you're teaching children science in school, they should know where food comes from. They should know that nourishment, especially from fruits and vegetables, is seasonal. Part of being able to sustain our communities is having this knowledge–all of us having it.

There are places all over the world practicing sustainability already. India is a huge producer of Vermi-composting–dealing with their waste by using red worms. I've used red worms for a number of years. That's something we could be using in this country on a massive scale. What interferes with our doing that? It has to do with the same thing as our failure to develop high speed trains across the United States. (*whispering*) It might be the petroleum industry. All these agri-chemicals we were just talking about–every one of them is produced from petroleum.

Petroleum is a major issue. Petroleum and multinational corporations; they're killing us. I'm so disgusted to have to talk about it, but unfortunately it's all tied in with perpetual war. It's taking the heart out of this country. It takes away entrepreneurial spirit. It does away with everything we believe in and have worked for, now for 200 plus years. It's a money pit, and the pit is their pockets. The wars don't accomplish anything. They waste trillions of dollars. And our soldiers aren't even provided with what they need to carry on their day to day activities.

We have to move away from that and toward a more sustainable country and world. To do that, we must work on the large scale with families and small communities. If we get communities going strong, families going strong, working with other families then we can have everything from cleaner water to less pollution. We can recycle better, we can reuse things. We can start making good use of the American innovation that has gone so far off track to the point where we've just about lost control of it. I believe that one of the key things is to focus on innovative projects where people grow their own food. That way we all become less dependent on multinational agriculture.

One of the few places we can make real change is in our own families by educating ourselves to the highest degree. We have to educate people even though that doesn't always work out perfectly either. One of the things we see here in this rural community is that when young people who are fortunate enough to get a college education, or even go to a technical school and learn a trade, they are often pulled out of their local towns and communities. The jobs are not here to pay a decent wage. So they move out of state, often to an urban area, and we lose all of that youth, innovation and skill. I wish it weren't such a sacrifice for people to live here and try to earn a living.

You hear the politicians speak about it, the American spirit. Building families and communities is what I think of with those words. I'd like to see the American spirit across cultures–Christians, Muslims, Buddhists, and even people who are atheists working together to make their communities stronger, more independent, healthier, more vibrant in the arts. You always have those areas where there's strife, and rage, and violence–whether it's domestic, or one gang after another, or drugs. But the American spirit of people working together can decrease all that.

046 Ed H. Kemp, Jr.
Jackson, MS

Ed Kemp, Jr. is my 86-year-old uncle and my grandparents' oldest son. All my life I've gone to visit him, my aunt and three cousins in Jackson, Mississippi. Eighty years ago when he was six and my uncle Abbott was two, my grandparents left Georgia to try their hand at cotton farming in what turned out to be the West Texas Dust Bowl. Before long they returned to Acworth, GA to recover a more modest farming life there. My uncle, Ed Kemp is a WW II veteran and retired insurance man who has lived in Jackson since he married in his mid 20's. He is not a fan of the new president, a man he refers to as *"Obana."* At the same time and given his age, my uncle knows change as a close and certain companion.

Ed Kemp, Jr.: Some of us are scared of change. Obana. He's the one that put it out in everybody's mind. Now, here he comes. What's he going to do to us? We conservatives and Republicans are scared of him.

Down at our coffee club at Kroger, we're about 90 percent against Obana. We got a couple there–one 92 year old–he's been a Democrat since Methusala. He was certainly voting that way. And then there was another one–he was just tickled to death to come in there and say, "We're straightening you people out." But I said, "Don't come in here talking like that."

I don't know if you saw one of my e-mails. I said, "I love Sarah Palin, Vana White and Sis (his wife)." My nephew got a charge out of that, I reckon. Anyway. I don't know if I'm telling you anything, but that's been my thinking, alright.

I had a conversation with my high school classmate. He lives in San Diego, California. He was a naval aviator like I was. He grew up about a mile from us on the other side of Mars Hill Church. It was his dad's yard that I plowed up when I had that airplane crash–it had $46 worth of cotton in it. September 3, 1947.

I called him the other day and we got around to a little bit of politics. "Well I don't know now about you, Edward. I love your mother and all your family." He ended up sending an e-mail later on, "And I even like you, Edward." Obviously he was thinking Obana and change as many of you are.

The main thing is not to get going too far in the wrong way, I reckon. I don't know. The Lord's in charge.

Just like that situation I reported last night. The man that got to heaven and St. Peter said, "It's going to take you 100 points to get in."

"Well, I was a good man and I stayed married to the same person 50 years."

"That's one point."

"Well I always went to all the church services."

"Well, that's another good point. You get one point for that."

"I don't know another attribute. I helped in boy scouts and all that."

"That's two points."

Then the man said, "Well, good gracious. The only way I'm going to get to heaven is by the grace of God."

"One hundred points. You're in."

We're all sinners except for Jesus Christ who came and saved us from all our sins. All of us. But we have to believe that.

I started out over in that little community nestled in the foothills of the Appalachian Mountains over near Atlanta, Georgia. That's where I was born, Acworth, GA. I related this to our Pioneer Insurance Club when they decided they'd like to hear about some of us. We just meet three times a year. We're all old retired insurance people. We know about our insurance careers with each other, but we don't know about where we came from. I happened to be the first one to speak.

My parents were devout Presbyterians. I grew up in a little church organized in 1841 by ancestors. I believe I'm a direct descendent of seven out of the eight charter members of that church. Anyway, then I went in the navy. Flew an airplane in World War II. Made 20 take offs and landings on carriers. Spent time all over the United States–part of that time in Astoria, Oregon and Klamath Falls, Oregon. The Japanese saw me coming and quit. (*laughs*)

My three sons, my three siblings, I pray for them. God bless them and their families. God bless Sis and me. God bless my brother and sisters and all their extended family. Those are my regular prayers.

I know I haven't been perfect. Nobody is.

You know I think they say nations eventually fold up. Rome did. I haven't got a lot of thinking on those subjects. I just can't zero in on what would make me feel like everything's going all right. I hope we don't go downhill like history says every nation does eventually. I'm fairly sure I'll be gone by the time we do. I hesitate now buying these 5-year light bulbs. I even hesitate buying green bananas. (*laughs*) We never know when we're going. We've got to face that.

I'm wearing down I think.

047 Kim Wade
Jackson, MS

I made my way to a coffee shop to do the trip-maintenance tasks that required internet access. President Obama had given his first speech to Congress the night before. I sat working next to an African American man who was reading the Wall Street Journal. After we commented to one another about the weather, I asked if he had listened to the speech. Kim Wade had a lot to say in response. At the earliest break in his narrative I described to him what I was doing and asked if he would consent to an interview. Mr.Wade, local talk radio host[12], agreed.

Kim Wade: I am a conservative who has voted Republican. I spent 15 years in the Nation of Islam under Minister Farrakhan. I attended Morehouse College. My credentials as far as the whole black issue are strong. I've dined at the banquet table of hate in the tribalism I see surrounding the supporters of Obama. I've been there. I know it only takes you so far.

If what you believe in doesn't have a universal aspect, it's all gonna collapse. While many Obamakins, as I call them – African Americans in particular – are excited to support anything Obama says – at the end of the day we cannot be estranged from reality and be successful. There's too much history to show that the characteristics he displays, irrespective of his skin color, are precursors to the type death and destruction that was visited upon countries like Germany, Cambodia, Uganda, etcetera. It's a strong personality type that doesn't seem to have a moral compass. He's willing to do some good, but he doesn't seem to be willing to do right. Change is happening, but I don't think it's going to be good.

Our standards are so low in terms of what we expect of our leaders. Mississippi has the most black elected officials and they are the sorriest bunch of knuckleheads I've ever encountered. White Republicans on a national level and black politicians on a state level are just alike; they don't know how to pull the levers of power. You can put them in any position, the tip-top position, and they still won't make a decision that's beneficial to their people or to America.

The people who run this country, in terms of the political apparatus, are old, white Democrats – the Ted Kennedys, the Joe Bidens, the Chuck Schumers – that vile Chuck Schumer. They're the ones who actually pull the political strings and run the system, not necessarily for righteousness' sake, but they know how to get things done.

I submit to you, and you write this in blood, African Americans in particular will never prosper in this country as long as we have a scornful heart and this bitterness that we harbor. There were a lot of white folks who came down here in the '60s and stood shoulder to shoulders with us. When the worst thing you could be called in the South was a "nigga lova" they took the slings and arrows. Viola Liuzzo, who died over

---

12   *Stream access to archived programs* http://www.archive.org/details/KimWadeRadioShow110608. *Wade's radio program on WJNT Newstalk 1180 was canceled in October of 2010 after over 10 years of broadcast. Kim Wade's professional website* www.kimwadenoexcuses.com *printed the following notice, "The new Kim Wade show starts Jan 10th @ 5pm M-F on 103.9 FM WYAB. It will expand to 4-6 pm when we move into the new studios in Madison Ms."*

in Alabama, was a Michigan housewife who came down here and put it all on the line. She earned no distinction for what she did. Those whites who came down and stood shoulder to shoulder don't ask for credit. They don't say "Hey, you know, we did this with you". But, they've got to be sitting back saying, "What, what is it all for?"

Tyranny can run in the heart of any man and we're seeing that with black leadership today. We're more than willing to go in and tear down a man's house just like the Night Riders and the White Citizen's Council did 40, 50 years ago. We justify it because they are dealing drugs there. Well, you know what? That goes back to my complaint with the NAACP, the NEA and ACLU blocking charter schools that would allow our kids to get a good education. If these kids get a good education, the option of selling drugs may not be the only option they have. The ACLU, the NAACP and the NEA will sue on behalf of the prisoners up in Parchman, our state prison here, to provide them an extra 3 or 4 square feet of exercise room. But those people might not be in prison if they were allowed to get a good education in the first through third grade.

This is racism being perpetrated by blacks. This is criminal and I submit to you just as Elijah Muhammad said when I was in the Nation of Islam, "Blacks are going to be destroyed in this country". I had no idea that it would be at the hands of other blacks. The black on black crime that we see here in the city of Jackson; just the black on black murders here in the State over the last ten years dwarf the number of blacks who were lynched the entire time of Jim Crow. But, we don't care.

I have a theory. It's called the "One Degree of Jesse Jackson". When Dr. King was killed, Jesse Jackson did all the things Dr. King was attempting to do, but without the spiritual component. Jesse Jackson's role, in my opinion was defined by the marching orders J. Edgar Hoover gave him. Jesse Jackson willingly or unwillingly, in my opinion, was a part of the reason why Dr. King got killed. Jesse's role was to remove the spiritual underpinning from the civil right's movement. Every year since Dr. King's been gone we've been moved off center spiritually by one degree. That's why I call it the "One Degree of Jesse Jackson." Yeah, 45 degrees. We're pointed in the total opposite direction, spiritually. King wasn't a perfect man, but God has always worked through imperfect people. We as African Americans have abandoned our spiritual underpinnings and we're just drifting.

I will tell anyone who will listen that I returned home to Christianity about 10 years ago. I left the Nation of Islam; got tired of fooling with Farrakhan. Farrakhan was taking all that money from Saudi Arabia and Lybia. You could have read in one of his newspapers or in Ebony or Jet, that he was planning to write huge checks directly to the black community. He's never done it. He spent all that money on himself. I'm telling you this, we're in perilous times. What Obama is doing is just perpetuating more of the same.

When Obama leaves the Whitehouse in four years, because he won't be a two-termer – in four years, a black man won't be able to get a job washing dishes in Washington, DC. He's going to be just that bad. This is not against him as a black man; this is against him because his policies will not work. If deficit spending worked, the city of Jackson wouldn't be in the red right now. If pumping money into government was the solution, Detroit wouldn't be in the red; Michigan wouldn't be in the red. Economic realities won't be suspended simply because we have a black president. I don't wish for Obama to be destroyed or for him to be harmed personally. I want him to change his heart. He has a secular heart.

Right now, he's paying off constituent groups of the Party. Those actions will be to the detriment of the country's economic, political and spiritual health. But I believe there will be a group of individuals who stand resolute. As a matter of fact we're meeting tomorrow here in Mississippi; a like-minded nucleus of individuals who intend peacefully to make changes in 2010 through the ballot box.

My whole point is that there are Americans out here who don't want the government to do everything for them. They want limited government that only does things to protect the opportunities we all should be enjoying. When I hear Obama, I say "I'm just not looking for that level of care from my government". I agree with what Joe the Plumber was saying, "Hey man, just let me be free to fail."

Our founding father's guaranteed us freedoms that I intend to pass on to my kids at whatever expense. As Malcom X says, "By any means necessary." Our founding fathers gave us three votes in this country: the ballot box, the jury box and the rooftop. My position is one rifle, one rooftop. I don't want to go to that level, or the third level, the fourth level, but our Declaration of Independence gives that to us. This Administration can blow their trumpet like Gabriel, they can blow it like Dizzy Gillespie, I'm still not going bow down to those people. What I learned at the dinner table at my mom and dad's house doesn't coincide with what Obama's pushing. I still believe in do-for-self, I believed in do-for-self before I joined the Nation of Islam, I believed in do-for-self before I got to Morehouse.

What needs to change is to recognize that we've got it good here in this country. It's not a perfect country, it never was, but God has honored our imperfections through the prosperity that we've enjoyed individually and collectively. We need to keep things in perspective and refute those who constantly want to tear down America and tell America what she's not. You've got a lot of good people in America who want to do right. You've got a lot of whites in this country who want to do right. As a matter of fact, if most African Americans would be honest, were it not for a white person giving them a break they wouldn't have gotten anywhere. Instead we sit out here with this rapper's scowl on our face like everybody's against us. In actual fact, we're against ourselves as evidenced in the charter public school situation.

This is what gets me about the NAACP and others who are against charter schools. They say they were born into segregation. They say that whites don't want to go to school with black folks. They say whites have hated black folks. The bottom line is that we're sacrificing our kids' lives. We're full of crap. Blacks are the majority stockholders in the Democratic party. If they want to make a change, they can. Most of the change that is not happening in America is because blacks won't stand up and be mean. Let me make this clear, I can't stand a weak man and I can't stand a weak black man.

I lived in Atlanta when Maynard Jackson was mayor. Our professors over at Morehouse would always point to Maynard and say, "If you want to become a politician, do like Maynard did." They'd say "Every time Maynard steps in front of a camera his position's grounded in facts and/or the law. He's a man of integrity". They'd say, "You do those two things and you'll never get knocked off center." Maynard left there unscathed, no scandals. Blacks and whites worked together in the city.

The thing about Maynard Jackson is that he didn't come from a poor family. As a result, he didn't come into office with a chip on his shoulder. Obama has a chip on his shoulder and he doesn't even need to. He's had the best that America has to offer. We don't need him pushing that poison on our kids. I'm 53 years old. He and I are part of that generation the dollars fell on. Blessings have come to us in every direction possible.

Our young kids' issues are not our issues. They're new. We want to stake a flag and say, "I took a stand against racism". You didn't do anything and now you're making our kids confused. In the face of all this opportunity our young men are standing in the doorway of opportunity in their gangster clothes and our young ladies looking like hookers. All they need to do is turn their caps around, straighten their backs up, be a man or a woman and walk through the door. This is not rocket science.

I walked the sidewalks of Morehouse College listening to Dr. Mays and Howard Thurman and Mordecai Johnson. These were men who implored you to be the best that you could be. Now we have folks that say, "We understand you can't do it." Uh-uh. My girls don't know what limitations are. That's what I want them to understand. There aren't any limitations. Nobody has a monopoly on success. It's God that grants success.

So, this is what I would say to Obama, and Eric Holder and Michelle: "Cut the crap. Tell people what's good about America. You've had the best that America can offer. You're riding around on Air Force One, negro. Cut the crap."

Road Note

With both the candor and concerns of Kim Wade and Ed Kemp (046), the issue of political difference has come more into the foreground. The shared values on family, personal faith and education remain, but the differences have increased. I couldn't have known it the day we talked, but as I read over the Kim Wade's words today, they stand out as a harbinger of particular circumstances that have unfolded over in the years since. "As a matter of fact we're meeting tomorrow here in Mississippi; a like-minded nucleus of individuals who intend peacefully to make changes in 2010 through the ballot box." I can't know for certain, but it appears likely that Mr. Wade was on his way to a meeting for an early version of the Tea Party.

During our conversation, two local political leaders, a white man and woman, greeted Mr. Wade and paused to chat briefly about fundraising to support a woman who had wanted to attend the inauguration the month before. They described her as a wheelchair user and bemoaned the greed of the liberals who "would not help this woman with her dream." In the end, the woman been able to go thanks partly to the actions of these three conservative leaders.

Maybe the reason we don't talk across difference is because it's just easier to demonize one another. Oddly, to do that requires a strange interdependency. For one group of people to define itself as right, they must emphasize the ideals of the other, even when they are minimal or perhaps nonexistent. With this kind of opposition, each faction needs the other to define themselves. We are not them! I continued to marvel as the irony of this social phenomenon.

048 Marsha Cuyjet
Jackson, MS

Mr. Wade left for his radio broadcast. In the meantime, two more people in the coffee shop had become curious. They had not heard the specifics of my conversation with Mr. Wade but liked the idea of talking about change. Marsha Cuyjet, a barista at the shop, stopped between customers to speak with me.

Marsha: Being that I am an African American Baby Boomer, I think of the changes that I've seen in my lifetime. I'm 55 plus, not quite 60. (*laughs*) So, I saw the 60's, the 70's, the cocaine rage of the 80's. The 90's were sort of no change at all. I just coasted. This millennium, well, obviously that's a change.

When I say change I mean the big picture, not so much politically. For years now I've read the J.D. Rob series. The author is Nora Roberts. Her books are set in New York later in this century, like 2059, 2060. In terms of the change coming in the programs, structures and systems in our country, reading those books has been very interesting to me. I think we're going to arrive at that place where there is no real black or white – a time when our country is multiracial, and multisexual.

As for personal change, I'm looking for a big one. My only bird in the nest is about to leave. He's 18 in April and hopefully he will move on. I see my life changing in a positive way. I should be able to get back to myself. This whole mama thing was nice but it got old. (*laughs*) No, I'm just joking. I'm guessing he's an average teenager. But right now as a young black male, he just gets the stereotype. I'm very fearful of that. I pray for change daily for him. I pray that his mind gets right; that he pulls his pants up and decides not to start work right after graduation but to go to college or the military. There are not a whole lot of options for a 17-year-old black male in this day and time unless he's an honor roll student with some goals. Mine doesn't seem to have any. So, I pray for him.

To me the recent election was a hopeful sign. It's a great indication that the country is about to change. I don't think we need to discuss what the outgoing administration paid attention to anymore. The fact of the willingness to elect an African American president indicates a vast change. For pretty much an entire nation to be ready for this kind of change indicates not only a great need but a desire and willingness to make it happen.

049 Robert (Russell) Hewes
Jackson, MS

Russell Hewes, a regular at the coffee shop, is friends with Marsha. Russell is a father of infant twins and a tradesman in carpentry. Born and raised in Jackson, he tends toward an eco-friendly, cooperative lifestyle and lives by a simple observation: The challenge for all of us remains finding the way forward.

Russell: People spend way too much time focusing on things they don't want. They focus on their fears. Since 911 it's been instilled in us – this fear. I don't believe the war we're in right now has a lot to do with terrorism. I think it has a whole lot to do with oil. I wish somebody would stand up and say that.

When I think of change, I think people need to realize that fear is the worst thing you can hold on to. Fear stifles all aspects of your life. It interrupts your relationships with others. If we could put down our fears and see the good in life, we'd have a lot better world to live in. Living without fear would translate into people treating people better. That's the basic premise of change from my perspective. I don't care what anybody says, I think that's a good thing all the way around.

I hear some of that in what Obama is talking about. I watched a little bit of his address last night. He was talking about trying to rebuild confidence. People want to put all their faith into a leader. Everything. We're all wanting to let him do it. But I think people can act on their own. It actually really starts with individuals taking responsibility. He talks about that, too. He said, "We are going to do this." Not, "I am going to do it," but "We're going to do this together." I think that's a key element.

A good example of what I'm talking about is the media. People like to blame the media because they show all this horrible stuff. It's not the news anymore, it's the bad news. But honestly, the news is just a reflection of what people want to watch. The media go on ratings, so they're giving people what they want to see. It all goes back to the people.

Is the cause outside with the effect in here (*points to his chest*)? Or is it opposite? Could this be the cause (*points to his chest*) with the effect evident out here? It matters what you put out there. That's the way I see it. When petty negative feelings get put aside, you come from a heart that's overflowing. That's starting to sound a little gushy, but I think that's the way it is.

So many people go to church and talk about this, but I don't think they really live it. It's like they expect to practice kindness one day a week and then it's back to the rush and craziness of things. You have to live it every day. It's easy to get caught up in petty things, but there are principles that are so much larger.

All these groups focus on differences rather than commonality. Here again it goes back to perspective and where you want to place your focus. I consider myself a Christian, but I don't think most Christians would think that I am because I don't believe the way they do. I don't believe Jesus is the only way. I think that he is a way. Buddha's out there. I mean, do you have to take Tylenol or can you take one that doesn't have the name "Tylenol" but has the same stuff in it? Is Tylenol the only way it's going to be? You have to open up a little. If you put down your ego and start looking at what Jesus and Buddha are talking about, you see they're actually talking about the same thing. More people are out there doing that.

If we're really going to bring change, it starts with the individual projecting hope. That's where it starts. You let hope override fear. You listen. You talk to people and you see where people are in agreement. It also goes both ways, because you learn something and so do they. It's an exchange, right? (*laughs*)

050 E. H. Kemp III
Jackson, MS

Ed Kemp, III and Clarke Kemp are brothers, two of my three boy cousins from Jackson, MS. It's a pretty safe bet that Eddie and Clarke rarely support the same political candidates. Where Ed III is the pragmatist, Clarke is the philosopher. Still they live in the same town and see one another all the time. They're brothers and they like one another. Under the new leaves and soft blue sky of Jackson's typically early spring, Eddie weighed in on change and the practicality that grounds his guarded optimism.

Ed III: Well, change to me means going in a different direction. You hear a lot about change these days. Change is good sometimes, but change for the sake of change; I'm not real impressed with that.

I'm more interested in the basics. Just do things the way they're supposed to be done, the way they've always been done. I'm not saying I'm resistant to change. Some people feel if they're not changing they're not doing anything, they're not effective, but to me the best thing you can do is not change. If you get things where you want them to be you don't have to change.

I know most of the people wanting change are talking about politics. One side wants this. One side wants that. Neither side's ever happy with the other side. It doesn't matter what it is. "The sky's blue." "No, they're saying the sky's blue, but they're wrong. It's white." Really, it's kind of ridiculous to me. All the talk about "We're right all the time. They're wrong all the time." Both parties are that way. I get a little bent out of shape listening to that.

Everybody's different. Everybody's got different ideas about what's right, what's wrong; where we ought to be, where we ought not be. As big as this country is – not just the country, but the world. Everybody's got their own opinions. It gets especially monotonous listening to little bitty percentage segments with media exposure saying, "Everybody has to adapt to our way." There's also the wrongheaded, "You have to come on board with us AND everything has to be lovey-dovey perfect." We're just not born with that kind of guarantee. (*laughs*)

People ought to be able to choose how they want to live. I don't like the idea of forcing folks into one corner or the other. Everybody ought to have the right to believe what they want to believe and to do things, within reason, they want to do. An example would be how color TVs were an upgrade from black & white when I was a kid. I appreciate that. And HD TV is better still. But I don't see why it has to be forced on people. Maybe there's a reason. I just don't know. (*laughs*)

On all that, I think our country's getting smarter and dumber at the same step. (*laughs*) Part of it is because of progress. Progress is a great thing, but there's a point where just because you can do something doesn't mean you should do it. We can send something to the moon; let's go to the moon. We can probe for water on Mars; we've gotta go find it. If it's out there, fine, but we don't have to go find it. We've got a whole world to work with right here. We've got a place to live. We've got water. We've got air. We've got groceries. We don't need to go all over the universe to find those things. We need to worry about the home front before we worry about somebody else's house.

Still, I feel like America will succeed in spite of its government. It's a terrible thing to have to say, but if we could get all the government people out of the way, we'd be just fine. Congress is not high on my list. There's a lot of useless people in Washington, D.C. Most of them wear suits and ties and think they're pretty important. We out here don't think they're all that important.

The problem is they're all focused on their own interests and not what's best for the country. You've got representatives more interested in their district than the country. Senators are more interested in their state than the country. To me, they're supposed to work as one to provide what's best for all the people. I don't see them doing that. All I see is sniper attacks here, sniper attacks over there. "Let's take a shot at them. They're wrong about this or that." I can't believe I'm the only one who sees this. Surely you've got a whole bunch of people on tape saying the same thing.

Senators and Congressmen ought to all be farmers. They get up early in the morning. They work until dark. They work for nothing. They don't start a job that they're not going to finish. And they don't blow a lot of smoke. They get the job done. We need Congressmen like that. We've got a few I guess, but it's hard to tell. So, term limits, everybody! Two terms ought to do it. If they can't get the job done in that time, get them out – pat them on the back and then get them out.

Plenty of farmers out there.

051 Clarke Kemp
Jackson, MS

Clarke was on break from his work with film and media processing. We stood leaning on neighboring cars in the loading area behind his store and chatted about how he's been at this film processing gig for almost thirty years For Clarke, that's meant working directly with constant technological change. "I'm on break from all that tech stuff right now," he said and I listened as my cousin's thoughts turned to public governance.

Clarke: I tend to be a little pessimistic, but correcting for my own bias, I'm probably cautiously optimistic about our country and change. I said to a co-worker that I'd rather think the worst and be pleased with any moderate improvement. Then, if the worst comes along, it's no big deal. It may not be the best way to go through life.

The change I'd like to see would have our representatives actually represent people instead of moneyed interests and lobbyists. Change has its opposite in stasis. So, what's not going to change? There are going be two parties which too often seem to be two branches of the same party, or as Ralph Nader said, "the evil of two lessers." In my more cynical moments I refer to it as the politburo. That's probably a little bit harsh. There are some good people in Congress but they're trying to fight through a system that's been wallowing in corruption for ages.

Change begins with one person at a time. It begins with people and not the politicians. Politicians should lead a change that's already happened among the people. That's a valuable thing to me since I was a supporter of Obama.

Politically I think the Constitution is pretty good and we should be very careful to not go at it with scissors or executive-order it into irrelevance. I have seen one amendment offered by Senator Russell Feingold which would do away with gubernatorial nominations of senators when an office is vacated for one reason or another. I haven't examined it, but I tend to think Russ Feingold is a pretty smart guy. He's the type person that would be very careful not to do anything like that without serious consideration.

I did want to say something about Russ Feingold and John McCain and the way they got together on campaign finance reform. Here were two people from different parties doing something that both parties need – something that needed to be done for the sake of the people. Now it may be a wash in terms of the ways people have gotten around it but it was a bipartisan effort. I think we should strive for that.

We also need to keep our grounding in law. It beats the alternative of anarchy. Law is the only thing I can think of that's a universal social contract. It's often a last resort, but it gives people a standard of behavior.

One hopeful possibility for the fairly near future is the agreement by the Swiss Bank, UBS to pay a multi-million dollar fine to the US and reveal names of US citizens who have been squirreling away billions of dollars to avoid taxes. If those people are publicly brought to shame – it's kind of schaden freude, but in a way it would be a good negative model. It would demonstrate that you can't buy your way out. If that were to happen, it would help level the field between the income classes. Theoretically we don't have social classes, but we definitely have income classes. Your parents' income tends to determine what yours is going to be to a large extent.

I'd like to see another thing. I'd like to see science held outside politics with consensus given due respect. It's disturbing to watch media play with the science on the environment. Here are 99,000 scientists who say that global warming is most certainly happening. Balancing this on the other side is one scientist who might be sponsored by Exxon who doubts it all.

Based on science, the most helpful change would be for people to make every effort to be more energy efficient. That's the number one thing we have to address whether we want to or not. President Carter gave us a choice. When he was leaving office we were experiencing severe gas shortages. He said, "We can start dealing with energy issues now and, even though we don't like it, it will make for an easier transition. We can also wait and deal with it 30 years from now when it will be a lot more expensive and we may not be able to fix it." Here we are 30 years later.

That was a good message coming from our nation's leader. A president can tell us what we need to do. "Pay me now, pay me later." I hope we're going to be able to pay because we seem to be there.

I think of World War II when we were fighting two very fierce, capable enemies. Although I wouldn't normally want to have a Department of Propaganda, that department got the public making swift and vital changes in support of the country's wellbeing. Maybe it was World War I. The thing is; if the message gets through and people know what needs to be done, they'll do it particularly if it's very clear that the alternative is unpleasant.

People have children and put a lot of effort into raising and protecting them. That's one of the basic and most powerful motivators of human behavior. If people understand the threats to the environment are real and that making changes in the way we live can prevent future generations from having a worse time, then the change will happen.

I don't want a Department of Propaganda. That sounds just wrong. People don't want to be conned, especially for some ulterior purpose, like instilling crazy fear of religious or cultural groups. We've seen that. But, if the purpose is public – if it is honest and healthy and the science is there to show what is unavoidable without change, then we'll be willing to go for it. Reform is not out of the question just because there's a lot of opposition. There's always been opposition.

Now that I think of it, one of the best models for change might actually be breathing. You go through a moment of change from inhaling to exhaling. It's sort of like being at the top of a trampoline jump, hanging for an imperceptible instant in mid air. In between the two conditions there's movement – there's change; all of it leading to the next undeniable, and in the case of breath, necessary change.

Road Note

I hugged my cousins, got in the Mini and pulled out of Jackson. I was heading for Montgomery, Alabama. Over the few hours I had spent in Mississippi, I had spoken only with people in the capital. But still, in that time and space, I had heard a pretty remarkable array of opinions.

By now I had driven 3500 miles of the highways we all share. Through the windshield I witnessed remarkable changes in our nation's landscape. A week ago I was driving on roads in the desert of New Mexico. Today I rolled through the modest rise and fall of the land resting in the Alabama River Valley and leaving the Cumberland Plateau. I was also mapping the same road where as a child, I remember people driving horse-drawn wagons eastwards to be part of the Poor People's March on Washington. I was deep in the land of the Civil Rights Movement.

I stopped for gas in Selma. I noticed that all the neighborhoods I drove through there were full of people, which is not all that remarkable, except that it was the middle of the week. Many Americans say that the goals of the Civil Rights Movement, a presence I felt strongly on the historic road between Selma and Montgomery, have yet to be realized. Many of the people I saw in Selma live the truth of that assessment with far too little work and far too many families living below the poverty line.

052 Buena V. Browder
Montgomery, AL

I pulled into Montgomery at sunset and watched the orange sky fade behind the low and uninterrupted curve of the western horizon – bayou land. My schedule was marked by the generosity of Michelle Browder, a woman in her late 30's who I met when she and her mother were volunteering for the Obama campaign in Austin. A year later, Michelle insisted that I stay a night with her in Montgomery. Perfect. Even though I arrived after dinner, Mrs. Browder and Michelle were both ready and willing to be interviewed. Mrs. Browder, who can count marching with Dr. King among her many contributions to activism, started the conversation.

Mrs. Browder: Going across the country campaigning for Obama, I saw change just months after he announced his candidacy. I saw people come together like never before. People from around the world came into Mississippi to campaign. I said, "Why are you here?" I mean, from France, from Italy, England. I said, "Why are you here?" The Sudanese. I said, "What's going on?" They said, "The world is watching." And I said, "Why Mississippi?" They said, "The world is watching Mississippi!"

So, here I am in Mississippi and Barack Obama is our nation's president. If I took you back to the way I was raised you'd see that I could be one of the most confused Americans in America. I had family members that looked like you. Beautiful. In fact my own son has beautiful hazel eyes (*laughs*). We are Irish, African, Choctaw and Cherokee. A conglomeration. Plus I was born and raised in Chicago.

I was one black child, in a classroom of about twenty-eight. I felt like I was the only black in Chicago. My father was the caretaker of the Jewish Synagogue. So I tell everybody I'm a black Jew. I was raised by the Jews (*laughs*). I knew more about the Hebrew people than about my own black people. It wasn't really until I came to the South that I got a handle on blackness. You could put it that way, Southern black.

Of course my family members had same story as many; you know, from Mississippi and Alabama and then migrating to Chicago. Chicago is where my mom and dad met. My grandparents on both sides were still in the South. Traveling in the South, I had occasion to get on a bus. My sister and I sat down in the front and talked to the bus driver in Mississippi (*laughs*). As the bus began to get crowded he told us we would have to go to the back of the bus. We didn't understand that. We were headed to visit my grandparents in Huntsville and stopped in Decatur, Alabama where the toilets were filthy and said Colored. We drank out of a Colored water faucet there. I didn't get that.

Except for visiting the south, I was never in a predominately black community all the time I was growing up. I went to one of the most prestigious technical high schools in Chicago. We learned everything at that high school. When we graduated, business people came to my school to recruit, like business people go to colleges now. So I am a mixture, not really fully understanding all the bitterness and hatred.

Growing up I couldn't understand what was wrong with people. Why you got to label me? So, I felt Obama's heart by him being from a Caucasian mother and an African father; going to see his sisters and traveling all around where his father had lived. I felt his heart. I'm an American. Why you keep labeling me?

It's the government that says if you're eighteen percent you have to say that you're black. If there is any black in your bloodline, you have to say that you are black. So he has to be our first black president, but he is our president. My daughter and I say, "That's my president!" We haven't said, "That's our black president."

I had occasion to present Michelle Obama with a cowgirl hat during the campaign in Texas. We got pictures. At that time I told Michelle, "I will see you in Washington!" She responded by saying, "You will?" I said, "Yes ma'am, I will!" I just knew this was our time. That it was time for America to stop labeling. If we look deep in the genes, God only made one man, one woman. So we're all related. It's exciting!

In the work of the Mission[13]13, we go into the prisons. Even the men in prison were campaigning. (*laughs*) They can't vote, but they were campaigning anyway. That's their

---

13   *Montgomery Rescue Mission and Faith Crusade http://montgomeryrescuemission.org/*

world, that's where they live. We go to death row; we call it "Life Row" because we bring life to these inmates. You should've seen some of the portraits and signs they had on life row for Obama. President Obama was the only candidate I heard mention the injustice in the American prison system. That's change.

If you do the crime, you do the time. Sure, you have to do that. But when these men come out they don't have any place to go. The Mission has come under fire because we have an aftercare program. One businessman said to me, "I don't want them around my business." Them. I said, "We've been here twelve years and you didn't even know until now." Then I said, "You know what? In Biblical times even the lepers had a place." People need to have some place to go. Where do the men and women who are ex-offenders go? These are some of the things that I would like to tell my president.

I do see change. Where people wouldn't talk before, they're speaking openly about things. Even if it's a negative view, people are more ready to state it instead of keeping it in the closet. I'm seeing that especially at our Mission stores. People are just opening up and talking. Communication is always good.

The most exciting change I see, though, is in the young people. I see inspiration and intelligence, especially in the young black men. Lately I've seen hair cuts in the black community. I've seen young men come in the Mission stores and begin to buy suits and ties. Instead of saying, "My lady!" they're saying, "My wife!" Obama's presence has an influence.

He's a people president. This is a good, good thing. They've opened up the White House and all. Isn't that a change? You can go through again and tour. I've been to Washington twice. I've been to the monuments and things, but I've never been in the White House. I'm going. (*laughs*) Lord's will, I'm gonna go! It's just exciting to know the White House is not beyond our reach. We can go hear a speech and our president can shake our hand. It's wonderful. He's accessible to the people. That's a good change.

053 Michelle Browder
Montgomery, AL

When we met back in Austin, Michelle was taking her first steps into a life as a public leader. Over the intervening months she was emerging as an increasingly vital force in the politics of Montgomery. Michelle was born and raised here by parents who are themselves profound conduits for maintaining the social well being of this city. In keeping with Laura Geduldig's (014) words from Walnut Creek, California, the Browder family's footsteps are pointed in a powerful direction. Michelle enriches her legacy with her own energy and flair.

Michelle: Change would be taking some of the attention off the big banks. Right now the people need that attention. I would love to see change where the government actually focused in on social services and the organizations that are providing things like shelters, meals, and hygiene products. We all know that economic recovery is not going to happen overnight. The recession is going to continue on for another two or three years. We need to pull that money from the banks and put it into service organizations like the Montgomery Rescue Mission and Faith Crusade[13]. The Rescue Mission has been providing services without any government funding. People donate but it's not enough. We also have the thrift stores to help with funding. People are in need. I am hoping that our people's president, Barack Obama will shift the focus here.

This is my first time voting in a presidential election. I'm sorry, Martin, Coretta, (*looking to the sky*) everybody, I'm sorry! I'm not proud of it, but my change has been to be so engaged in this presidential election that I not only voted, I campaigned vigorously! So I am hoping that we can correct the mistake that is the circumstance we've all put ourselves in today. Part of it is my fault and the fault of others who, like me, did not care who was president. We had resigned to the notion that no change could happen. As a result we had the past eight years. Especially when the Republicans managed to steal the 2004 election, it only made sense to think, "Why go vote?" That was my attitude.

My change has been to see that I count. Other people like me count. We matter and our voices were heard because President Barack Obama talked to us straight. That's what drew me. I was drawn by his willingness, to say, "I'm just like you. I love the people in the south–side of Chicago." I think Michelle said it better than God could have said it (*laughs*). She said, "The have-nots–what about those people?" The point is that today there are any number of humble everyday Americans who say, "People matter; people count." The youth today feel they have found their place because President Barack Obama has said, "You matter." Regardless of race or creed, we all matter.

Okay, I'm thirty-seven, so I'm going to talk to all you twenty-three and eighteen year olds on the campaign who treated me like I was an old lady. That wasn't right. (*laughs*) There were so many young folks fueling that campaign! And right there, that's the change. I want them to treat me with more respect, but I celebrate that our next generation cares enough about America to be involved–to make things progress.

There's also change in kids younger than that. One of my girlfriends works for the Atlanta Public School System. She overheard a colleague say something to a student about his homework a few days after the Inauguration. The teacher said something like, "You know you need to do better," and so on. His response was, "Well I'm not going to do better because you're telling me to do better. I'm going to do better because my president is black and I have to do better!" There is a renewed sense of pride–no not even renewed–there is new-found confidence.

I'm going to be honest. I am only 37, but did I ever think that I would see a black president? Never! Never! No man of color did I ever think would make it that far. But now the children are saying, "You know what? I don't have to settle for being a rapper, or a ball player." Not that there's anything wrong with those things, but they're also saying, "I can be a legislator, a senator, a community service provider."

Of course, you know Governor Palin and those folks tried to make it sound like it's a bad thing to care for people–to be of service. It's is amazing that to organize communities in support of people's wellbeing can be seen as a bad thing. It didn't stop us. The day of Martin Luther King's birthday when Obama proclaimed a day of service, I saw young people in Montgomery picking up trash, caring about the community and being engaged. That's change and that's pride.

I also like the dialogue–just being able to commune with people and not worry about color or preconceived notions about who I am. On the campaign it wasn't about

Michelle Browder *Montgomery, Alabama*

preconceptions. I slept in the same room with lesbians. I slept in the homes of Jewish people and Catholic people. I slept in cabins with Muslims. I want that to stay with us. We really can coexist and love one another and still have our differences. We can say, "It's okay to agree to disagree." I hold onto that. It is so great to say, "I love you because we are in this thing together. We're going to put aside differences and make change together." That's what needs to be done.

I'm hoping that the Senate and the House and everybody else will wake up the same way–put aside differences so we can get the job done. That's the change I want to see. Get it done! Quit the bickering and let's do what we need to do.

Road Note

Before I left Montgomery the next morning, Michelle and I went downtown to see Mia Lynn's Civil Rights Memorial in front of the headquarters of the Southern Poverty Law Center. On a massive conical disc of dark gray marble, the names and dates of Civil Rights heroes and their memorable actions rest beneath a constant and shimmering flow of water. Behind the disk is the convex curve of a wall, twelve feet or higher and also veiled with water. Twelve eternal words of Dr. Martin Luther King are carved into it and read, "...Until justice rolls down like waters and righteousness like a mighty stream."

During the last century, the developmental theorist Lawrence Kohlberg concluded that humans always reason at a level beyond our capability to behave. While this is somewhat of a bummer, Kohlberg and other developmental theorists don't intend it as entirely bad news. To them, the ability to articulate our aspirations helps us identify the change we want. Then we can start to take steps toward it. It's practical. Like what Tommy (037) suggested in Kerrville, TX as he and David (038) were considering the best program for Baptist youth and echoed with what Holly (041) offered from her matter-of-fact perspective as a senior at the Hockaday School in Dallas. If we want to know where to begin, we need to know what direction we want to go.

The Browders' legacy of placing the impulse of social compassion into action stands as living proof that our behaviors can coincide with our line of vision. As Kohlberg suggested, our aspirations are guides for integrity. Actions that walk the talk are both possible and happening in American change. Justice and righteousness roll on.

054,055,056,057 Merle Evans, Mary Alice Kemp, Elizabeth L. (B.J.) Morris, Mina S. Greer
Decatur, GA

Decatur, GA is an incorporated city fully within the Atlanta metropolitan area. I'd accepted an invitation to interview a book group at the Decatur home of Elizabeth (B.J.) Morris. B.J. greeted me at the door. Close behind were three other women in their 70's, Mina Greer, Merle Evans and my mother, Mary Alice Kemp. They had just finished their monthly book discussion. "Now we're ready to talk about change," B.J. said.

Mina: What I hope for is change in the way government is run; less corruption, more concern, compassion and interest in all people, not just the wealthy.

BJ: I've lived long enough to know that change is inevitable. Life is not stagnant. None of us really like it and sometimes it's difficult for us. From one stage of life to another, we're constantly in change and flux. For me, it's one of the exciting things about being alive.

Mary Alice: On the other hand I can think of times in my life when a situation that needed to be changed. Even though I was not conscious of doing it, I resisted change. It seemed safer where I knew what was happening than to risk a change to something entirely different. I think change means risk and uncertainty and that's what's got us all so upset. We don't know the outcome of the changes being presented to us.

Merle: I would like to see change in the negative attitudes some people have toward Obama and the things he's trying to do. I don't understand why people can't give him a chance instead of putting impediments in his way. You would think people would want him to succeed with his great ideas of how to make our country a better place to live. Some people are not for that. They just want to cause trouble. I don't know how we can get over that. It makes me sad and angry at the same time.

It's not just Republicans, but anyone with the attitude, "Our way is the right way. We're not going to bend or give you any opportunity to prove us wrong." They're like little kids. They clump together. They don't want to try anything new. I'm thrilled we have a change of leadership and I hope they don't prevent his success.

The Limbaughs and the hate groups–I worry about that. I worry about him, getting killed by one of these groups, and there are more and more of them. Of course the Ku Klux Klan is up in arms that we have a black president. Rush Limbaugh. I don't even understand why people listen to somebody like him. He's a hate monger. Why do they want to stir up hate? Why don't they stir up kindness and love and compassion and understanding? Why don't we work toward a common goal? It's discouraging to me, but maybe Obama can pull it off. I'm pulling for him.

Mary Alice: We've heard about change for 18 months and, of course, we heard about it from both parties. The party that did not win the election promoted change by having a woman vice presidential candidate. I'm not sure about all the other change that party advocated, but the idea got picked up on both sides and clearly was being responded to by everybody whatever the word change represented.

I think it represents change from the secrecy of the Bush administration, particularly Cheney. The government is the people. It's for the people. And if the people can't know what's going on, then there's something wrong with how government's being handled.

There for a few minutes, even people who didn't support Obama were pleased that he has chosen people from different areas or different belief systems as his advisers. He doesn't necessarily agree with them and they don't agree with him. Even with that, it hasn't taken long for the nay sayers to decide they want Obama to fail and that's that.

Still, he has made the effort. That is something different. I see it as something hopeful.

Mina: And he does not seem to be discouraged, thank goodness. He says to the opposition, "OK. You vote that way. OK, you can do that."

BJ: I've been concerned about the checks and balances of government. They are very important. I happen to think in the last eight years there has not been as much constitutional balance as was directed and created by the founding fathers. The Executive Branch got a little out of shape with too much power and there were not enough checks and balance from Congress or the Supreme Court. I want those checks and that balance clear, demarked and followed. That protects me.

Mary Alice: At the same time, when you think of transfers of leadership in governments in other parts of the world, we have had an unusual record. So far we've been able to change leadership 44 times without warfare–with our votes. Sometime they're not counted quite right, but that is something to be treasured.

Mina: Yes, I would love to see emphasis on the goodness of the country instead of on partisanship. I'm old enough to remember when there were lots and lots of crossover votes. You don't have to be too old to remember that. It seems to have disappeared recently and that's a sad day for our country. It means the good of the country is taking back seat to something else which is usually self-promotion on the part of the lawmakers.

Mary Alice: Party loyalty.

Mina: Um hum. Everybody wants collaboration, but somehow it's not being allowed. I know there are Congress people who want to vote one way and are not allowed to by their Party Whips or whatever. That's one huge change I'd like to see. It would have to be self-initiated. It would have to come from within the leader him- or herself. Unless it comes from us, the people. Maybe it will come there. It will be interesting to watch.

BJ: I'd like to see some integrity back in the government. I think it's important that we respect and trust the leaders that run this country. We elect them and then they turn around and stab us in the back. There is so little hope in that that I can hardly tolerate it. Our value system desperately needs to change. We need to be concerned about our country certainly, and we need to be concerned about our neighbor. Everybody seems to be out for themselves whether they're the President of the United States or a person on the street.

There was such excitement on Inauguration day. Two of my grandchildren were in DC, 14 and 17. They said it was electrifying–you could feel the wonderful vibrations going through the crowd. That for me is hope. We can live without a lot, but not without hope.

Merle: I hope that enthusiasm doesn't wane. That it wasn't just a short episode. That people will continue to support Barack Obama and remain more aware of helping others. I'm also looking for the economy to turn around, for people to start having positive feelings. To know their homes are safe. To see their investments go up. I want to see people pulling together.

BJ: I want to see unemployment down. In Georgia is absolutely devastating. There are more people losing work every week. When we get back to 4% unemployment instead of 9%, there will be a lot of people happy about that change who are personally suffering now. It's tragic.

We're not suffering. We are very lucky to be retired. We can look at the sadness. We can look at the unemployed. We can hear about people losing their jobs and single mothers wandering the streets with their children because they're homeless. But we live safe and secure lives where we are. In four years, I cannot imagine that the four of us will be impacted in any way, shape, or form unless maybe intellectually and politically, but that's because we think about things.

Mina: We may have fewer dollars in the bank. But we don't need a whole lot of dollars. We have our fixed income.

BJ: We're in our future. We're not looking to our future. We're in the middle of it. Our lives are pretty much like they're going to be for the next however many years we have left.

Mina: We hope.

BJ: We hope. Right. That's a concrete and specific hope.

I also have hope for my children. I don't give advice to them. That's against my religion. The world my children and my children's children are going to be living in is so different from mine. I can't even talk to you about the things those kids can do. I would not even think to keep up with where they are and what they're doing from day to day right now, much less four years down the road.

They live in a whole 'nother world–another dimension. It's like those little green people from other planets. The aliens. I don't know if my children and grandchildren are the aliens or if I am, but we live in two different worlds. (*laughter*) I don't keep up with all that electronic stuff. I can't talk about their music. I can love them and really enjoy who they are. But giving them advice would be impossible. Absolutely.

Mina: Giving them advice would be just

BJ: Stupid.

Mina: No, but it could only include what we know will continue. And that is love.

BJ: And encouragement.

Mina: Yeah. That's it. That would be our advice–my advice. The things that live on.

Mary Alice: As far as how things will be for them–well, if I choose to worry a little, and I probably will, I think my grandchildren are going to have to make adjustments that my children didn't have to make. They'll have to learn to live with less. That's not something anyone does easily. It's going to be a challenge. But they can do it.

Mina: Sure

Merle: It doesn't seem very likely right now, but I would hope my children and my grandchildren grow up in a world that's more peaceful. I hope the country won't be at war and the hate will be gone. It is not very pleasant to live in fear of what's going to happen next. Maybe it's an impossibility to live without some fear, but I hope it will be more peaceful.

Mary Alice, BJ, Mina: Amen. Amen.

DECATUR, GA to NEW YORK CITY, NY
—
3.5 to 3.13.2009

- When you say the word change what do you mean?
- Alongside change, what is important to have remain the same?
- What would be signs that positive change is occurring?

DECATUR, GA to NEW YORK CITY, NY
3.5 to 3.13.2009

Early March. I had now been on the road for a month and was six weeks deep into the *EX:Change* project. I returned to Portland for a break and to check my mail, pay bills, fill out tax forms, things like that. Back in Walnut Creek, I had called ahead to Georgia to schedule the bodywork on the wounded Mini Cooper. The garage in Atlanta promised six days at the most so I would be set to go again when I returned.

Portland's spring emerged with its usual subtle abundance. Even the gray skies and incessant mist could do nothing to mask the first cherry blossoms peeking out from their pink buds. Crocuses and daffodils bloomed everywhere. Red and pink camellia petals already blanketed lawns after falling from ridiculous heights. Both bushes and blooms were seriously in danger of suspicion for steroid use.

Although good to be home for a bit, my heart and mind were still on the road. I was in love. The project, the voices, and the American people had captured my heart. I think the first time I realized it was while on the road between Albuquerque and Kerrville. Almost out of nowhere I said out loud, "I'm totally in love! Every person I talk to is the coolest ever. How could I be so lucky to meet and listen to these people?" Even as I attended to business back home, I continued to ponder all that I was learning.

The interviews up to now had voiced shared themes such as kindness, practicality, respect and optimism. I'm sure you heard them, too. Ethnographers expect themes to show up over time, revealed through overlaps and commonalities. For me, this emergence of the values and meanings that many Americans share was at once expected and astonishing – much like after the long cold stretch of winter when spring always makes another comeback. If you wait long enough and the days start get longer, the cold will diminish and the flowers will bloom. Still, with both seasons and the common threads in the stories that human lives tell, something fresh and miraculous always happens alongside what is expected.

Here are some of the themes I heard most consistently from the fifty-seven Americans I talked with along the West Coast, across the continental Southwest and into the deep South.

- Change is unavoidable.
- We're all in this together.
- Kindness and relationships see us through.
- No one person alone can change our country.
- We all want to do our part and we are willing to work hard.
- We expect our leaders to act cooperatively, from maturity and wisdom and in the best interests of the people.
- Poverty and joblessness are difficult and both need to change.

- We must end the wars.
- We need to make more revenue available for addressing poverty, joblessness, education and healthcare.
- We want clean water and air for ourselves And for generations to come.
- We are heartened by doing what we thought was impossible in electing an African American president. At the same time, we are still living with oppressive systems based in race, gender, economic resources.
- We can do this.

A more subtle theme was also emerging. The Americans talking with me wanted two things that can be seen either as competitive or complementary- the comfort of structure and the dignity and freedom to direct their own lives. These shared desires reveal again that there is more similarity than difference across Americans who subscribe to specific political groups. We all know about the hype around dichotomies of red/blue, of conservative and liberal, Republican and Democrat, free-market and socially-progressive. Despite these tags, the words, hopes and goals of the *EX:Change* voices emerge without distinct boundaries. These Americans want the structure Nick Minnis (009) described in late January. "I'm ready," Nick said, "but I don't have any guidelines."

The voices of *EX:Change* also want to be free of external scripting. They want to have the freedom to determine how they wish to live what poet Mary Oliver calls our "one wild and precious life." In Jackson, Ed, III (050) said, "People ought to be able to choose how they want to live. I don't like the idea of forcing folks into one corner or the other."

Then there's this theme. Americans value wise governance. Governance based in knowledge and wisdom can strike the balance between our potentially competing expectations for structure and freedom. Drawing on the best of all ways of knowing can provide reliable guidelines for our lives together in society while at the same time safeguarding and extending trust, regard and dignity as people write their own American lives.

058,059 Kelvin Anderson & Tommie Lee Corbett
Decatur, GA

Back in Decatur, the car still in the repair process, I settled myself into yet another coffee shop, this time on the Decatur town square. I had an appointment with the city's mayor later in the morning so it made sense to perch nearby. A few tables over two young businessmen, Kelvin Anderson and Tommie Lee Corbett (TC) were deep in conversation about inspiration, motivation and aspiration. At one of their uplifting "can do" comments, I looked up and smiled. TC smiled back. He said, "It's magnetic isn't it?" Soon the three of us were in the next conversation about American change.

Kelvin: I see change as more of an internal thing. Changing my mind, changing the way I view the world, changing the way I view my brothers and sisters. The change I want to see is at the top. Now, African Americans like myself, and little black kids, can see what we can be. We have a real visual of a different path.

A while back I heard a guy call a radio program and say, "My son asked me could he be anything in the world?" His son wanted to be President of the United States. This guy said, "I told him, 'Boy, you can be anything in the world, but you can't be President of the United States.'" This was before Barack Obama became president. Just recently they found that same guy, put him on the radio again and asked him, "What do you think about it now?" Of course, he had changed his mind. So, to me change means internal change. We can achieve and be anything we want to be in life, but we first have to believe in ourselves

TC: When I say change I think of behavioral change. But that depends on changing your attitude. Your attitude determines your altitude. Once you spread a positive attitude throughout your soul, you can take a grim day and turn it bright.

We were just talking about happy transformation. Things will not make you happy; you have to make yourself happy. You have to wake up and say, "I'm going to be happy regardless of what happens." The world is going to throw things at you–good, bad, indifferent. You decide how you handle it. Your attitude directly affects the outcome.

At the same time, changing your behaviors doesn't change who you are. It just changes the way you do things. You stay true to yourself. I was brought up not-so-well-off, for lack of better words. I was born in the projects in Atlanta. But I made some decisions in my life that changed the way I live today. About 15 years ago I said, "I'm going to change the way I speak. I'm going to change the way I see and treat my fellow men. I'm going to change the way I treat my mother. I'm going to change the way I treat my friends. I'm going to change the way I treat my employers." I'm still me, but those changes brought a lot of blessings my way. I changed my attitude–the way I see life in the whole.

It makes every day much more rewarding. Like the way I met you just now. I've changed to where I can speak to anybody. I want to make everyone smile. I believe my attitude is contagious. Is it worth catching? Yes. Because I smiled at you, you smiled back. That's what it's all about. We have to learn that as a people–not African-American, not white, not German or Hispanic, but as a whole people. Years, decades, maybe centuries down the road when we all get on the same court, our offspring will live in that kind of world. I want to start the trend today (*puts a hand on his heart, the other palm in the air*). Every day.

Kelvin: There's a specific change I want to see. Or school systems are broken. It's ridiculous. Clayton County doesn't have enough books. This is a big county, one of the largest in Atlanta and those kids can't take books home. It's amazing.

Education in this country is based on tax dollars which reflects how much money you make and where you live. So we continue to educate people who are already educated while the people who aren't getting the benefit of a great education keep dropping further behind. The only way to improve education is to ship kids miles away to the school with good education. I don't understand why we don't provide good education everywhere. There is enough money to go around.

At the same time it's about kids deciding to make changes. If you never make a conscious decision to change, you sleepwalk through your life. Education wakes you up. It gives you exposure to possibilities. We know this. Why aren't we offering opportunities? If you're a lawyer, chances are your kids are going to be lawyers. If you're a drug dealer or work in an auto parts store, chances are, guess what's going to happen? We know this, but we never address it by helping each other out. It's like you're on you own.

Whether you're black, white, rich or poor, if nobody teaches you about change you end up sleepwalking. It's incumbent on us to help the kids instead of waiting until they're 18 or 19 and acting in ways we don't want anybody acting. We don't come out of the womb thinking negative thoughts, but there is so much negative going on in the world. If you don't inject your life with positive thoughts then the negative will be all you understand the world to be. Positive and negative can't occupy your mind at the same time, so you have to purposely practice the positive.

TC: One place to practice the positive is in the way the races relate. The way I work on that depends on the ethnic background of the people I'm speaking with. If I'm speaking with African Americans, the history of slavery and racism is first thing I address. That is in the past. Understand that it took place. Slavery, segregation; all of that took place, and right now we have opportunity to make decisions to form our lives into the future. If you're riding in a boat and look behind you, you see a trail of water. It tells you where you came from but it does not tell you where you're going. You decide where you're going. You cannot let what's behind you determine where you're going. Slavery and segregation are behind us. It happened to us. We are aware of this, but it does not have to determine where we're going today and where we're going tomorrow.

When I'm speaking with Caucasians about race, I have to flip things. Oftentimes they are in denial not admitting the impact that continues with those facts of history. A person in denial may not even be racist. There's the modern day Caucasian who really isn't involved in active hideous racism but is still in denial that it exists.

We're trying to get white people to understand that racism is there. For example, you may not understand that when I walk across the street in a white neighborhood, even dressed in a pressed shirt and slacks, the residents lock their doors. If I walk into a Gucci or a Prada shop, they immediately suspect and follow me. You don't understand what that feels like. It's not that I want you to carry that tension, but I would like for you to be able to say, "I understand where he's coming from. I haven't felt that, but I can sympathize and not act like it didn't happen."

We cannot heal as long as we have one side that wants to blame another side for what they've done to us. Until both parties are willing to admit their part of it, we're going to have racial tension, especially in the South. We still have the KKK in the South. It's strong and it's very prevalent.

Alone none of us totally controls going into the future, but together we've got a good path ahead of us. I do believe that our change in the White House will help mend a few extra lines. It's better than it was in the 70's. It's better than it was in the 30's. It's better than it was in the 1800's. It will be better in 2020. It will be. I'm hoping that having an African American President will be an extra catalyst for blacks to see and say, "It doesn't matter that I was born poor. That doesn't mean I can't be president or CEO of IBM or own my own company if I choose to make it happen."

At the same time, the Caucasian American has to be able to say, "You deserve the same rights. I'm willing to lose that position." That's hard. When affirmative action was strong a lot of my white colleagues would say, "I don't think it's fair such and such got a job because he's black." Playing devil's advocate I would ask, "Do you think it was fair a white person got a job just because he's white?" I'm not saying it's fair either way. All I'm saying is if it was OK for you don't complain when it's going the other way.

Kelvin: In my view; well, I feel like we're just lying. The country's lying; people are lying. Everyone's lying about who they really are, how they really feel. One of the biggest lies comes from white men failing to acknowledge their role. The inequality and tension in this country is an effect of what they've created. Not only the degradation to African Americans but to white women as well. I'm not sure white men understand how it feels to be a black person or a white woman going into corporate America and being the only one. White men are always the majority.

For white female, black female and black male to actually have equal opportunity, white male has to acknowledge his role in and responsibility for the messed up values of our country. His role is so large he can affect the rest of us through the policies he makes. Racism may have decreased, but the policies haven't changed. Policies can't see people being racist. They were set up to benefit certain people and continue to work that way.

Overall, the system of this country was brilliantly designed and obviously it worked. It's why America is what it is. That being said, the policies still fail most people. For example; education, hiring and advancement. As a black man, I know how it feels when I go into an office building where I'm the only one that looks like me. It's very tough mentally. You have nothing in common, nothing to talk about, nothing to share. I know white women and black women feel the same way.

I'll give you a story. Every year I go to a University of Georgia football game with one of the attorneys I work with. This year was the Georgia/Alabama game. It was a blackout game. The joke was, "Oh, I thought it was 'Bring a black friend to the game,' not blackout." (laughs) It was funny because it was a joke between me and him. But at the game I'm watching 60 athletes who are 70% black. I look around the stands and see probably 5 people that look like me in the 90,000. I think, "What is going on? This picture is distorted." I look at the coaches. There's probably one black coach who's there because he can recruit black kids to come to the school to play football. When you look carefully, you see our whole social system is set up this way.

I'm in corporate America but I have yet to learn how to integrate myself into conversations with white men. I haven't yet learned how to talk honestly across that gap. I'm actually studying this–trying to figure it out so I can teach my fellow people; and I'm saying this to mean white females, black females, and black men. We need to know how to integrate into the system that excludes us so much of the time. How do I open dialogue? How do I become more comfortable in conversation so I can get people to pay attention? How do I keep an open mind and understand where they're coming from? With no idea of his point of view I can't judge him. I can only go by what I experience and what I've learned. But I definitely want to understand why white men feel the way they feel so that we can start coming to some kind of understanding.

TC: The major part of that is confidence. It's attitude again. A positive attitude changes everything. Breaking down barriers depends on the attitudes of the individuals involved. It depends on having confidence that I am equal. Like Kelvin said before, because your father, your uncle, your family were in drugs or prostitution doesn't mean you have to go there. Going back to that boat ride–that trail of water behind you doesn't mean a thing about where you have to go. You get to make a decision today where you're headed. It's about stepping out there. Reading books. Practicing self-education. Educating yourself does wonders.

Kelvin: I just want to share a saying. "Too many people overvalue what they are not and undervalue what they are." If we focus on where we're going, that's where we're going to get. If we focus on what we're not, we're going to get what we're not. Very important.

TC: I'll end with this. I just appreciate you coming and speaking with us because that means you're going to put our ideas out there so they can be an asset to the process of change. People who see or read about this *EX:Change* project are going to get so many different opinions and points of view. They will have an extra bit of education and that will empower them. It can even create instantaneous behavior change by inspiring them to become more completely and confidently who they are.

060 William F. Floyd
Decatur, GA

Change is unavoidable in Decatur, GA. Race and income class remain urgent issues. Voting and public policy can perpetuate these problems or address them. Kelvin Anderson and Tommie Lee Corbett urge participation in civic dialogue and action. Their mayor joins the call. From where Decatur mayor Bill Floyd and I sat to talk we could see the courthouse and the band shell that have been at the center of community events for well over 100 years. Mayor Floyd is tall and bright eyed. His hair is silver and his voice modulated by the textures of Georgia – peaches, cotton, red clay.

Bill Floyd: I've thought about this. Today, in these times, change seems to mean a change in attitude – about a lot of things. First, people at all levels want to see their government officials being more cooperative, talking to each other. When the Republicans controlled, the Democrats stood up and screamed about how bad everything was and the Republicans said "We've got to work together." Now the Democrats are in control, the Republicans are screaming and the Democrats are saying, "Why won't they work with us?" The people want to see all of that stuff put aside. They want leadership to concentrate on what needs to be done.

Another attitude change is the connection between change and hope. I grew up in south Alabama in the 40's and 50's and 60's; segregated south Alabama. I can remember when black people weren't allowed to go downtown to shop except on Saturday afternoons. I remember working construction in Ozark, Alabama with black men in the summertime. That was in the 60's. Every day I would go to the Dairy Delight to buy all of our lunches because the sign in the window said "White Only."

Then I remember being at Auburn University. I remember getting in my car, driving to Montgomery and going up four floors in an office building to watch the end of the march from Selma to Montgomery. At some point in there I realized I had no idea the courage it took to be down on that street. Just last week I was in John Lewis's congressional office in Washington. I had a look at his photographs of his experiences in the 50's, 60's and 70's. Just incredible.

This election is changing the world. For the two of us to be sitting here today with an African American president is nothing short of a miracle from God. It gives us all hope. We're starting to understand we're all in this and need to work together. I think that's the change. Mothers and fathers today tell their kids they can be anything they want to be, that regardless of their color, shape, size they can do it, because it's happened. That's the change people have been looking for. We're looking to get away from all the useless crap that's gone on.

Nobody in the world, nobody thought we'd elect an African American president. But we did. Finally the majority of us looked for who we saw as the best candidate and voted for him. From small towns to the national level, this is change everyone wants. It's a change in attitude and it's bringing hope to the heart of America. We're a people now. We're taking a big giant step to get past the pain we've caused and experienced. We can talk. We can take care of our communities together.

But we must always remember that we are diverse. The differences between us are important; between individuals, between countries. When we let our differences dominate, we lose ourselves as a community. At the same time, there remain issues and differences in things that go on between us. We must respect our differences and build understanding in order to identify our shared vision and develop our shared voice.

This is a great country. It was built on the shoulders of incredible people. But we are not that old as a country and our history is not clean. There is no avoiding the fact there were slave owners and other people who did horrible things. They were also part of building a strong national foundation. A change that is overdue is to bring everybody into the conversation.

Here in Decatur, we are still tremendously segregated. We don't legislate it; it's just the way people are. The African Americans tend to congregate. We whites tend congregate. I think we're going to see that start to change. People consider a community based on whether it meets their needs. They look for other people who they want to be around. More and more we will make those decisions with less emphasis on color or nationality or any other group identity. We'll be asking "Is this a good place for my family? Do I want to be here?" I think it will take a while, but it is happening.

Politically, I'm seeing the middle of the road folks becoming the ones with the influence. Our elections here in Decatur are nonpartisan. I focus on doing what I think is right for the community. I don't have to introduce division based on party affiliation. We don't have to deal with all the rhetoric and condemnation we hear at other levels of government. People are tired of hearing the ranting and raving without any conversation. Obama is doing right saying, "If you just want to rant and rave, I'm not interested in talking to you. If you've got clear issues or ideas to bring to the table I'll be glad to hear them." He would also be the first to tell you that nobody knows whether what we are doing now will get us out of this mess. We've just got to try things.

One thing I've always heard is, "Never fail to take advantage of a good crisis." It makes you take a good hard look at yourself to see what and how to improve. That's what we will take away from this. It will not be easy, but as a country we will be stronger and better when we finally get through because we'll have done it together.

061,062 Scott Hoff & Jason
Decatur, GA

From the Decatur Square I left for a date with the auto body folk. Scott Hoff was the customer service manager who fielded my calls. With courtesy and competence befitting his position, Scott had kept me informed and reassured. Finally, a day late, we were ready. The last part was on its way and would be installed in less than half an hour. Jason, who requested I not use his last name, is a specialist contracted with the shop. He had done a good deal of the work on the Mini. When Scott and I walked into the service area, Jason was standing nearby throwing in random comments. He was funny – witty. We got into a chat about the indigenous people of Georgia, the Cherokee. Jason talked about the influence Cherokee intellectual and governmental traditions have on current policies and practices in Georgia.

When I arrived that day, Scott had agreed to an interview. While Scott and I talked, Jason stayed to oversee the last of the repairs. He told Scott to let him know when we were done. He'd go next.

Scott: I didn't say the word change that much throughout the campaign process. Everybody else did, but in my opinion, it was more the Democrats. Yeah, we need change. I just don't know if we've made the right change or not.

I don't understand one thing: Why government has to be so big? Why do we have so many people on payrolls doing nothing? We have a congress that works less than half a year. They make what, $250,000-300,000 a year? I don't think that sets a good example.

I would like to see government run like a business. If somebody could run the United States like a business, I think we'd be OK. No good business can spend more than it's taking in. In my opinion, the federal government shouldn't step in. When big businesses fail it allows little businesses to prosper. If you pump money into big businesses that continue to fail, where are you helping anyone?

The federal government should not bail out businesses like CitiGroup, Bank of America, GM. Why is GM in so much trouble when Ford's not? Ford's doing fine. They don't want money. They're making it work. Ford is a company that's trying to be a little more conservative. Then you've got GM. They've already been through over $10 billion of our money. And they want more. They need to fail.

The country has always practiced if it fails it fails. That makes room for other people to prosper and things to build again. Are they going to let it correct itself? I don't know. I watched a gentleman on TV last night. His company is the banking company that's talking about giving the money back to the government. They don't need it or want it because of all the stipulations that come with it. I understand that. It's as if the government has forced millions of dollars on banks that do not need or even want it.

And if we give billions of dollars to a company, we don't want them giving it out in bonuses to CEOs. That $700 billion was a joke. All I see is the rich people and politicians doing OK. Everybody else is maintaining or getting poorer.

I would also like to understand how a war costs so many millions. They talk about all these costs, but they already have everything they went to war with. I understand they have to replace things but that kind of money? I think a lot of money is wasted and that's going to hurt our kids because they are the ones who are going to be paying for it.

Me and my wife talked about moving to Canada. Yep, numerous times. I just don't see this country going forward. In fact, I see it taking a step back. I kinda thought when Obama started in there with the attitude he had that he would do alright, but now he does what everybody else wants him to do. If he's going to be president, he needs to step up and be president. Act on what you say you're going to do. Don't turn around and do something else because that's what your party wants.

At this point I don't see any hope. Not until they say No. No to the bailouts. When they finally say No, that's when we'll be OK. That's when the big companies will finally fail so the little companies can gather up that business and build back like the United States has always worked best. You just don't keep big businesses going by giving them taxpayers' money. We're never going to see none of that money back. Never.

Jason: Do we really need change? This country's been around for almost two hundred and thirty years. We've been doing things pretty much the same over that time period with some evolution here and there. I don't think change is something we need. We need reform, a little bit different plan. Reform is a way of changing things but it's more about keeping things the way they are and making sure they're done properly, using common sense. We've got plenty of common sense in this country it's just not necessarily in our government.

Middle, upper-middle class, working and blue collar people have to make day to day decisions on what's most important in their household – what takes precedence in spending decisions. Do you go out and buy the brand new car or do you make do with what you've got because your kids need new clothes? Our country needs to use that kind of common sense. Starting from the bottom and going all the way up to the top.

I'm talking city government all the way up to national government. I've not paid too much attention to the Stimulus Bill. It's something way over my head that I've rolled my eyes at because I don't see anything good happening from it. I did hear on the news that Atlanta Mayor Shirley Franklin proposed installing a trolley car system with Atlanta's portion of the money. What is that going to do to stimulate the economy? It could be used in better areas. Get the money to the people who need more money, who deserve more money for the jobs they do: firemen, police officers, teachers.

Coming from a military family and being a citizen of a world super power country, I also feel we need to have a veteran in the office of president. I would feel safer that way because of the power stance America has in the world. We start slipping in that aspect, we may be in danger of take over. I know it sounds far fetched, but anything's possible.

Going out on a limb again with something I don't usually talk about – from a religious standpoint and knowing what principles and religion this country was founded on and also knowing what religion is against this country, I really don't feel comfortable having a Muslim in that office. I know not all Muslims are that way, but the hard liners are – "Death to the infidels." There again, I've seen him picking out Christmas trees with his kids. Muslims don't celebrate Christmas. But in one of his books, I have heard from a radio talk show host, he made a statement similar to, if America ever came to conflict with an Arab or a Muslim nation, he would have to side with the Muslims. That makes me very uncomfortable.

I also don't trust the media to show us if reform is really happening. They don't tell the whole story. I have several friends who came back from Iraq. They say the media only show one side of things. They don't show the children coming up to soldiers hugging them because they built a school. They don't show the man being released from a prison cell hugging the people who held him prisoner for freeing him from Saddam Hussein's grasp – a grasp that three days prior killed his wife and children because he was a school teacher. You don't hear about these things. So, as far as the media, I don't believe what they have to say. I get my information through more obscure outlets – not necessarily eye witness, because those also can be tainted, but there are websites out there that show things how they're happening.

I'll also say I'm not looking for taxes to be lowered. That's pissin' in the wind, for lack of a better term. What I'm saying about the government is that our country needs to take a look at what we're actually spending money on. I can see spending 'x' amount of money per year to go to war if necessary. The price of copper has risen. The price of brass has risen. That's what bullets are made of. You've got gasoline to pay for, you've got diesel. You've got soldiers' salaries. A lot of people don't know they get paid almost double if not more than double for combat pay. That's where a lot of the money is going right there. They don't do the extra for free. It's like here. I get paid one rate for fixing a dent in a car. I get paid another rate for putting a radiator in because that's considered mechanical. It's almost twice as much. You put yourself in a more precarious situation, the government reimburses you for it.

We also have to remember the wounded soldiers coming back. They're care is not free. Somebody has to get paid to take care of them, build their prosthetics and things of that nature. These guys are protecting freedom. They deserve to get funded. That's why tax money is needed. Here again, though, we need to look at how much we're paying for it. If this guy over here with a military contract is selling us bullets for $10 a piece and this guy over here has them for $6 a piece, let's see if we can't re-negotiate a little bit – shop around. It's not going to hurt to buy generic now and then when Stoffer's is not on sale.

As everyday American people we probably wouldn't know if better financial decisions were being made in the war. The way the government is now without reform, any money being saved they either lose in the budget for the following year or find somewhere else to use it. Government probably needs an internal affairs department like police departments have. Internal affairs units in police departments investigate corruption – bad, dirty cops, things like that. They're unbiased and have brass. They're a watchdog unit for the police department.

We need to watch for corruption inside the government and we need to watch for it in corporate settings. I used to work for Winn Dixie grocery stores. They went out of business in this state 2002, 2003, because nobody was looking out for the little guy – the guy who was bagging the groceries, the guy who was cutting the steaks, the woman who was slicing the cheese. You had these people making $7 and hour. If McDonald's is paying $8, guess where I'm going?

If you don't look out for the people who are making your money and you just try to suck everything you can out of them, you're going to fold. The twelve years I worked for Winn Dixie, the company went through at least 7 different regional managers, or presidents of the state area. Every one of them retired a millionaire. You think they cared about the longevity of the company and how many people were out of jobs when they decided to close down? Nope.

Then there's outsourcing. I've got a big problem with that. I've had several phone calls from Bell South come in from India. I refuse to talk to them. That's part of the problem. We're outsourcing jobs to get them done cheaper. Here again, the big corporations make money by putting the little guy out of business. Granted Shirley Jones may only make $10 and hour answering the phones or doing surveys for Bell South, but when she's put out of a job that's money she's not spending here at the grocery store. It doesn't go into the tax pool.

Something else, I kind of semi-lean toward a national sales tax. How many people are in this country illegally who don't have social security numbers and are working for cash under the table and not paying income tax but still reaping the benefits of this society? If we had a national sales tax, everybody would have to pay.

I'm just hoping my kids will make career paths in areas that can be recession and depression proof. Whether it be military, medical, even the grocery field. People are always going to have to eat. They're always going to need medical help. My daughter wants to be a veterinarian. Kind of borderline from where I'd like for her to be. My son is leaning toward legal representation of the military. If I ever catch them buying screw drivers and wrenches, I'm going to break their arms. (laughs)

Truth is, we're in for a long bumpy ride in this country. I have had offers to move to Dominica. I'm keeping my options open. After the Civil War, quite a number of Confederates decided they didn't like how the South was being rebuilt. They moved to Brazil. I don't like Brazil. I don't speak Portuguese. (laughs) There are always options out there. I have stated that if things get too bad, I will move out of the country.

Road Note

Questioning practices of government is key in a democracy. Kim Wade (047) set one tone in Jackson when he said, "My whole point is that there are Americans out here who don't want the government to do everything for them. They want limited government that only does things to protect the opportunities we all should be enjoying." Scott and Jason also questioned whether we really need all our government programs and just how much the government should be involved with our lives.

At the same time, there are noticeable differences in the stances of these three men. Scott questions spending on war; Jason sees the value and necessity of taxation to support military security. These differences reveal what is often the case with groups in opposition. There's as much difference within the group as between opposing groups.

Listening to Mr. Wade and later to Scott and Jason I caught fleeting thoughts I didn't particularly welcome. I was seeing consistent and clear overlap in values and goals across varied American ideologies and across all other categories of experience. We shared our most deeply held goals. But in these three conversations I caught myself falling into fears and suspicions that are symptoms of our almost obsessive interest in and devotion to maintaining polarization. Fortunately, I listened trough those feelings and I am very glad I did. Nonetheless, these reflexes are frighteningly strong and even with the EX:Change evidence so powerfully countering these divisive categories, I found myself wondering if we could ever breech our disparate ways of seeing the world.

Mr. Wade's words were strong and forceful, his anger clear and resonant. He said things I agreed with and not. He spoke in ways that are inciting of argument and defense. Scott and Jason were more matter-of-fact, consistently anchoring their strong positions in everyday practicality. In all three voices I heard the evidence of a deep love for family, for country, for people.

From the beginning of this project, I have listened for the wisdom in the worldviews of people who align themselves with conservative moral and fiscal values. I have heard that wisdom before in the words of leaders like former Senator Bob Hatfield of Oregon and from stories of my grandmother-in-law, the Republican Chairwoman for Mason County, West Virginia. Grandma Stout opened her home every weekend to serve heaps of food and make available clothes and shoes for the people in the county who had less than she. "Our responsibility is to take care of our community, making sure everyone has what they need to live," she was known to say. "That's what being a Republican means."

063 "Anna"
Marietta, GA

I was very interested to hear for someone who specifically supported Sarah Palin's vice presidential candidacy. My cousin helped me connect with a business woman in her 60's from Cobb County. Out of respect for her wish to be kept anonymous, I call her Anna. Anna and I met at a family restaurant in Marietta, GA. The air was warm enough for us to sit outside. Anna was slow to let her guard down. She gracefully alluded to her caution about my motives. It made sense to me. In a similar situation I'd be cautious, too.

Anna: Change has become such a buzz word lately. I think most people mean better when they say change. The word reflects human optimism. We want change for the better and therefore keep striving. To me, true change would mean less strife, less meanness and more understanding of people's differences, communities' differences, countries' differences. That would be signified with less conflict of all kinds.

We have a fairly homogeneous and very conservative immediate community here. The main conflict is in reaction to what is seen as liberalism in Washington. Ours is a very private enterprise, capitalism community. That right there is Cobb County, State of Georgia thinking.

What gets misunderstood in the whole public debate are people's motives. People who want socialistic-type change suspect the motives of other people to be greed and all for themselves. People who want free enterprise and individual freedom think the other side wants to take from them and give to people who don't work for it. The pendulum swings. We're here on it. I sure hope it goes back to the center somewhere.

For a number of years I worked at a chamber of commerce. At first I didn't understand the importance to the community of business and commerce. If the wheels of commerce don't keep turning, there aren't taxes, there aren't sponsorships, there aren't donors, there aren't contributors. A lot of people don't see that. They don't understand when they're cutting off their nose to spite their face, or some other trite expression that explains shooting themselves in the foot economically.

With the new federal administration, we're spending money we don't have. That makes me worried for my little granddaughter. Taxation going up hinders vital business communities. In free economic development, a developer includes sidewalks and schools and nice landscaping, things that make a community pleasant. Nobody has to force it. In practice many developers haven't thought about community as they went. Afterwards they say, "Oh well. Now we've got to fix it." I would like the goodwill upfront – not just, "I'm going to get my project done my way," and then having to deal later with community considerations. The truth of the matter is, to get anything accomplished in commerce takes a great deal of ego, and strong egos don't listen well. One sign of change would be more listening. It might even be more women. (*laughs*)

I'm working right now on publicity for a women's conference. That's probably made me more aware again. It's called, Possible Woman. Each year for 12 years the conference has focused on empowerment and economic development for women. This year the keynote speaker is Stevie Meyers, the former White House Press Secretary. Her new book is Why Women Should Rule the World. The event tends to be on the liberal side. To some extent the liberal women have been better organizers and women who get out front publicly tend to have more liberal agendas. More conservative women tend to stand behind men. I think that's changing but there is more tradition in the conservative community.

I supported Palin. It was easier to identify with her because she's a younger, more glamorous figure than other women who have made progress with the same kind of thinking. You had to admire her bravery. She put herself out there knowing there were things people were going to shoot at. That right there energized a lot of people – seeing an attractive figure willing to speak out, step out knowing she would get heavily criticized. There haven't been a lot of conservative female figures – or liberal ones, for that matter – willing to do that. Those role models are easier to find in the liberal community. I guess that's because women are natural caretakers and that fits in the liberal arena better than among conservatives.

I still think Palin can work better with the establishment of the Republican Party. Let's face it; here's this young, attractive, glamorous woman and this old man running together. To me that said they were reaching out, working with. The community rallied around her because she was so attractive. Our world has gotten to where it wants attractive figures. (*laughs*) That helped Palin and I think it helped Obama. They're charismatic people and in this day and age everything's visual.

I would say her bravery, her fierceness, her confidence in her approach and her conservatism appealed to me. She is probably much further right than I am, but I would certainly be willing to support her on most issues. Free enterprise, in particular, because it must always be possible for someone to go out, start a business and succeed without too much restriction. If that is not the case we're undercutting ourselves.

I appreciate our sense of freedom and possibility – the attitude that you can do just about anything in this country. It's important that we don't nip that too much in the bud. In other countries they don't have the same attitude. America has a very strong "I can" attitude. The lack of optimism in other countries is probably due to being so taxed and regulated and restricted. Free enterprise is the reason our country's been such a huge success. If the pendulum goes too far in the direction of regulation we won't be that shining place of opportunity any more.

American values and our respect for one another are vital to our success. Sometimes that gets out of whack, but it usually comes back. Our support for beauty and art is probably not as great as I might like, but it's there and it is important to who we are as a country. And as we were saying earlier, it is good for the country that the path for women is more open than before.

One problem these days is that we tend only to talk with people we agree with. It would make a huge difference for leaders on either side to take dramatic steps to reach out. I've seen it happen. One of my favorite people in the universe is our state senator, Johnny Isakson. He's a moderate Republican. I have seen his skills with reaching out to garner support from both sides. The Republican Party forced him into a far-right position when he ran for governor and he didn't get elected. But, if you let Johnny be Johnny, there's almost no way anyone wouldn't support him. He's a logical, reasonable, compassionate man. He's got a huge background in business, but yet he's been an education supporter and served on the State Board of Education. He also understands global stuff and he speaks beautifully. Because of the system, he's been forced into positions that are more extreme. That's unfortunate because he's got the skills and courage to be a true leader.

Balance is so important. Maybe we were too far right before (*laughs*) but we need always to be sure there aren't too many restrictions. I want progress not undercutting of business or personal freedoms. That way my granddaughter can have a good climate to grow up in. And I don't want any more wars and strife and killing and dying.

We've also had huge issues with guarding and protecting our natural resources. The state of Georgia is fighting two other states on water that flows north from here. Protecting natural resources and using them wisely is another thing I want for my granddaughter. Having those issues in the forefront has been a good thing. People have become more aware. You don't have to run the water the whole time you're brushing your teeth. It's a little thing, but water scarcity makes you think.

That's the way it is with change at every level. There is day-to-day stuff we have to figure out, but we also need to remember to step back and take a broader look – to get a little bit outside ourselves and consider the community and the coming generations. That's why if I could I would go to school forever and I would never stop work. (*laughs*) My change would be just to keep learning.

064 Egan Short
Decatur, GA

You'd think a conservative businesswoman who voted for the McCain/Palin ticket would be in polar opposition to a teenage child of hippies who canvassed for Obama/Biden on MARTA trains. A few hours after visiting with Anna, I was back in downtown Decatur to meet Egan Short. Before the camera was on, Egan, a senior at Decatur High School said, "I just wish we'd stop demonizing each other. I wish we'd listen and cooperate. It can't be that hard." Wasn't that the way Anna had started? "True change would mean less strife, less meanness and more understanding," Anna had said. Anna and Egan are both women, both southerners. But there are two generations separating them and they are starkly different socio-economically and politically.

Dalai Lama has said that Western women will turn things around for the great healing needed in this world. The bit of whiplash I felt hearing the same core value voiced back-to-back by these Georgia women was trance-breaking in a way that draws in predictions like Dalai Lama's. I have no doubt these two women could speak and listen to one another. I have no doubt their interaction would be productive.

Egan: Well I'm thinking of a very specific case. I was at this Oxford Scholars' Weekend at Emory. They asked us what we think is the greatest threat to America. I said it's our self centeredness, both as individuals and a nation. I see that as the root of a lot of issues – environmental issues, economic crisis – the greed that lead to those situations. Then in foreign relations we've been thinking what is best for us is best for the whole world. Real change would be stepping away from that. Obama's been saying, "It's not about me, it's about you." That's nice rhetoric. It sounds good, but I also like what it embodies. It's always about everyone. I hope that awareness spreads like many little branches to give us a completely different national mindset.

It's strange. You'd think people my age easily believe the world can change. But in my class they say, "No one does anything unless it benefits them. It's just the human condition." I don't believe that. I think we are completely able to care about how we affect everyone around us. I'm 17 – I haven't lived that long. I haven't been hurt that much. I'm astounded by how many people my age are already cynical. They automatically assume positive change is impossible. It won't work, not going to happen. Some people feel that way because even in just 17 years they've lived horrid lives. I can understand that. But the people I'm talking about are like me. They've grown up middle class, they have complete families, everything's fine and they're cynical.

I didn't understand it for the longest time. Then I saw how it's probably a coping mechanism for saving face. In my generation, you seem naïve or silly if you're optimistic or idealistic. I feel like I'm a pretty well-reasoned person. I'm not a fool, you know. But I'll say something optimistic or make some "I think it's possible" sort of statement and everyone looks at me like I'm stupid. Like, "Egan, really. We know you're a smart girl. Now, why would you say that?" Like, "Don't be so naïve." A good change would be to see that fade. No longer would everyone assume optimism guarantees you're going to be let down. Instead, people would believe the possible could really happen.

One thing I want to stay the same is the Constitution – the things the country was founded on. I don't think we need to go back and undo any of that. This country is for the people and by the people. When I was in middle school and Bush declared war on Afghanistan I wrote him a letter. I also made a shirt that said "War is not the answer." I stopped saying the pledge. People started calling me unpatriotic. Not in a mean way, but it was, "Egan, you should be with the country." I already knew the Constitution protected my right to protest.

These days I protest because I would like to see our leaders thinking further ahead as we make policy decisions. I'd like for us to naturally think of our children, our grand children, our great grand children. Like with the economic crisis. It seems that instead of thinking of how we can have money right now we need to be thinking first of the economic circumstances our children are going to inherit. I'm more familiar with environmental issues so automatically I think of the word sustainability. It's a good word. Thinking ahead can make positive change sustainable. Lots of people think of change like progress. But we should only go after progress that is good for the long run. Change is good, but not just for the sake of change. It has to be sustainable.

Real connection with other people has a great deal to do thinking ahead and sustainability because it supports happiness, contentment and feeling better off. I don't think you always have to be jumping for joy. That seems artificial and like it would be tiring. But a great change would be to see more personal connections and deeper relationships. It's not something the president can mandate, "Hey everyone, have better friendships." But it is symptomatic of the health of the larger culture.

I'm trying to decide if this next statement only sounds good or if it's really true – that our lack of deep relationships is an outcome of the fear that has been encouraged over the last four years. I've listened to speeches by conservative candidates. They seem so centered around fear. That's good for people in power because citizens who are afraid follow like sheep. Fear of terrorists becomes fear of people unlike yourself and definitely has an impact on your personal, individual life. You're afraid to get close to people – afraid to have meaningful conversations.

In the future I hope I'll be saying to the children in my life that this was a time when the fear and cynicism of the Bush years was rejected. I'll say this was a time of youth empowerment and community building. I'll tell them about Inauguration Day on Auburn Avenue in the Martin Luther King Historic District. On one side is Ebenezer Baptist where he preached and on the other side is the MLK Center. I will for sure tell about the incredible energy I felt there. Everyone hugging. Complete strangers. Old people and young people. That's the connection I'm talking about.

I'm thinking about my dad. He's lived so much more life than I have. During the campaign I kept asking him, "Do you think he can win?" And he kept saying, "I don't know, Egan, I think we underestimate the racism that is still present in this country." My dad grew up in Meridian, Mississippi – 40 miles from where the Philadelphia murders happened. He's hardly ever wrong, but he was this time. I will tell about that in the future. I mean, oh my god, this man who in his whole life had never seen anything like this. In fact he'd seen the opposite. Then it happened. That will always be a big moment.

Road note: Decatur, Georgia provided the same richness of range as Jackson, Mississippi had, in terms of true American voices. The next morning, I finally started making my way north. As if to reward how far I had come, both physically and with the project, that day's route wound through North Georgia and into the Carolinas along the breathtaking Blue Ridge Highway. For hundreds of miles I watched the hills lift to roll away in every direction; in green hues nearby, and deep gray-blue toward the horizon. Down the road, I saw an odd cloud in an otherwise blue sky which grew as I approached. I stopped when I saw the flames.

Highway signs indicated I was near the town of Franklin, South Carolina, which was likely quite small judging from the few homes I saw tucked between the hills. One of those hills was engulfed in smoke – a tall billow of deceptive beauty above the rolling green and against the backdrop of bright blue.

Soon I heard sirens. The fire trucks approaching from all directions were small, local, and volunteer. The drought plaguing Georgia, the western Carolinas and eastern Tennessee had been underway for three years now, and as a result, these timbered hills had become quite combustible. The physics of the weather and the land had their way. But when needed, the community showed up and before long, the fire in the Blue Ridge would be calmed.

065 Asa Kaylor
Asheville, NC

I arrived in Asheville, NC in the mid-afternoon. My hosts for the night were my aunt and uncle, Dot and David Kaylor. I had not seen them for at least a decade. We went to dinner on the deck of a home in the woods that belongs to my cousin Will. Will and I figured it had been 30 years since he and I had seen one another. I met Will's wife, Jen and his two boys; Asa, 9 and Hanson, 6. I also met his best friend, Allen. The feeling of family was everywhere that afternoon and the next morning. So was the feeling of community.

Asa: Change means like not having too many cars. If you live in the middle of the city, you only need one car to get to work–or if you're going on a trip. Mostly, you can walk wherever you want so there's not as much pollution. Change means clean up the rivers. Don't litter. Have electric cars; those are cool, like the Smart cars. Don't get huge gigantic trucks that get 2 miles a gallon.

Have people close together. Don't have people where every house is a mile away from each other. Keep your next door neighbor close. Keep the grass green and keep people happy. Have a house that's big enough for the number of people and for everybody to have clothes.

066 Neil (Allen) Mulkey
Asheville, NC

Allen Mulkey sat on Will's deck railing. Allen was born and raised in Buncombe County. Now, in his 40s, he is a dad, a communications worker and a union leader. Behind his shoulder a full moon lifted into the fresh spring sky. "I guess we go through all kinds of changes," Allen said, "just like that Carolina moon."

Allen: It's sort of interesting to be on the spot like this. What do I mean by change? I have to think about it for a second.

I really did want the whole thing to change. The way the government sees its constituents, the way the constituents view their representatives; those things need to change. I want more of a relationship and not a top-down thing anymore.

But, what does change mean to me? It's a hard thing to say. We go through all kinds of changes. Like right now, the seasons are changing. It's a beautiful time of year. It's one of my most favorite times with all of the new plants popping out of the ground. I love it. I was born and raised here in western North Carolina and I have no desire to live anywhere else. I've been other places and this is Shangri-La. It really is.

I mentioned I'm in the union, Communications Workers of America. There's change in that. I worked for Bell South, a telephone company here in the Southeast. We were recently purchased by AT&T. That's huge. We are dealing with the changing corporate atmosphere and on top of that we're in the middle of negotiations because our current contract expires this year.

I am the Buncombe County Vice President for the Communication Workers Local 3601. As the area VP and I have responsibilities for dealing with grievances and responding when people get in trouble or need help in their work, their relationships with supervisors or even in their relationships with other workers. I'm there to help. That's my role.

That means there's a lot of change going on in and around my work life. My home experience is pretty constant. At least so far. I'm hoping it will be staying that way. The main thing I want is to stay employed. Number one. That's what allows my family to live where we want to live and do the things we want to do. I'm just hoping the economy doesn't crap out to where I'm out on the street. If I'm without work, that's going to effect my loved ones especially. That's a change I don't want.

Change happens in little bitty steps. It's like watching a child grow. You don't see the changes because you're seeing it every day. But if you go away from it and then come back, you go, "Oh wow." You can really see the change then. In a lot of ways, you don't notice change when you're right with it even though it's happening right in front of you.

One thing I have seen is more people in our little corner of the world willing to claim out loud that they're liberal Democrats. That's a big change. This area of the city is a little liberal island surrounded by a huge bunch of conservative hillbillies. I am born and raised here but I have a different world view. There are lots of hunters and real conservative Christians here that don't have any qualms saying they're Republican and claiming Obama is going to wreck the world. I work with them.

Half of our union membership is Republican. Still, they elected me. That's because

Allen Mulkey *Asheville, North Carolina*

of how we in our local union deal with that. For our work, the hot button issues are off the table. Abortion, gun control, those really fiery issues. All of our political decisions are focused on workers – especially when it comes to the political candidates we endorse. It's all based on how the candidates view workers and organized labor. We take all of the other stuff out of it. You can find common ground with a Republican when he's working with you and suffering the same thing you are. I have stewards under me that are Republicans. They fight just like they should for their fellow workers regardless of political party.

A lot of people view organized labor based on images of the AFL-CIO suits. Those folks are elected, but they're usually very detached from their constituents. At the local level we're elected by the folks we work with. You hear Rush Limbaugh talk about "union bosses." Man, there ain't no bosses in my local union. We're all co-workers. The bosses are the managers who tell us what to do. They're not in the union. They assign us work. They don't put on boots and climb polls.

Our local has maybe 210, 220 members – 50-60% of those are Republican. North Carolina is a right-to-work state. You have to join the union to get its benefit. I think there are 19 locals in North Carolina. And there are definitely arguments within the union membership. It's like a church group or a social club – like the Civitan or the JCs. I'm sure they have political conversations and they argue, yell and spit, too. The thing is, you can do that and still do your work. And, like I said before, in our local union positions are all based on workers.

Like I said, we're in negotiation right now. That's the reason I came over here to get my truck. I have to drive to work in the morning to take up our strike vote. We have to authorize our president – the president of the CWA – to declare a strike if it becomes necessary. So, I have to take up the vote in the morning.

I drive that big truck over there. Most of the time I leave it parked. I take the bus back and forth to work every morning. I like having the truck. And my neighbors like it that I have it so they can borrow it, but I've only put gas in it 5 time since last May. That's right. I've got my bus pass right here. (*pulls it out of his wallet to show*). Honestly, I'd like to see gas back up at $4-5 a gallon because that really impressed people who aren't as inclined to think of the environment. When gas was up at $4 a gallon, I saw so many hybrid cars. Even the Republicans I work with were more inclined to drive hybrids. That's real change.

I also wanted to mention what happened at a 22nd precinct meeting a week ago Saturday. For one thing, I was elected vice chair, but we passed this great resolution to impress upon President Obama the importance of using the stimulus package to make low-interest, no-interest loans for homeowners to install solar panels. Everybody in this dang neighborhood would have solar panels if we could afford them. That right there would create a whole industry.

067 David William Kaylor
Asheville, NC

The next morning the Flip camera and I took a hike with my cousin, Will into the North Carolina hills. Lots had changed for both of us in the past 30 years. For one thing, we were both adults now, citizens with experiences and opinions, with responsibilities and habits. Will is a musician, artist, carpenter, dad and now a student in accounting. He walks his populist talk by working on the board of a non-profit food co-op. Will and his compatriots on the board are putting into action ideas on community-supported and sustained agriculture like those Randy Vincent (045) spoke of back in Arkansas.

Will:I think when people say change these days it comes with hope. But, I'm skeptical about how great things can get.

There's this challenge. The further you are from the apex of power the more you want transparency. And the closer you get to the apex of power the less you want transparency, especially if you're operating from self interest. Then you want to limit it. It's a human reality. If Obama is going to change anything, it has to be at the top where they must understand they are accountable for what happens to people at the bottom. They are leaders and not rapists.

When you have a lot of money, your money is power. If you have currency, you can buy materials and you can buy labor. It's power. You make decisions about what people do. That's power. Right now, Obama is doing a lot to give power to people of lesser means. That is a huge change and it makes me feel positive.

A couple of years ago I was 42 and deciding whether to keep doing woodwork to make money. I was frustrated with my business. Financially, it was impossible to do the kind of woodwork I was happiest doing. My target client had become the very wealthy. Even with that client pool, anything I was happy making would be considered a luxury. I wanted to be an artist and do residential stuff – fire place mantels, counter tops, drawer facings. I found out that building green and doing architectural detail are incompatible goals.

I went to the Chamber of Commerce and UNC-Ashville and the Bureau of Labor Statistics. I looked at job descriptions. I hated the news on the radio and wanted to have some kind of effect on circumstances in this country. I wanted businesses actually to do business so I said, "Aw hell, I'll go be a CPA. I can do that."

I'm doing OK, but it's hard. (*laughs*) Younger minds work faster. The other thing is that I'm half dyslexic and I'm antsy, so I'm not the best student in the world. It's easier to be a student in my 40's – by far. Still, this is a big change for me. I'm making good grades. They drop off a little in the 400 level courses. That's all right.

In the last four months I joined the board of directors at the French Broad Food Co-op2. I don't know anything about local farming but it's something I've wanted to support. When you break America down into smaller regions, you can see we are food insecure. If anything interferes with transportation to take food from the Midwest or Southern California to the rest of the country, we're fried. We depend on dragging our food all over the country. It's silly. We should all be growing next door to each other. That's the kind of thing the French Broad Food Co-op promotes.

We're not really concerned about making profit. Still, we're struggling to stay afloat because Ashville is a community with a lot of natural food stores. I'm re-writing the ends-policy for the Co-op – translating broad, pretty, fluffy statements into something measurable. Now that I'm in business and management classes I'm getting very bullet pointy. The Co-op needs that. We want to be all cool about it, of course, so they have to be cool bullet points. I still have a lot to learn, but I'm the most financially literate person on the board and I still have a lot to learn.

Food security is a great phrase. It is good for the Co op and other grocery businesses to use. There's enough business for all of these stores if we're doing the right thing. There's huge demand for locally grown produce and we're not meeting it. We just need to organize this stuff. It can be done.

I'm really seeing that financial literacy has to increase in the country. There were no classes in economics when I was in high school. We didn't talk about money. Meanwhile, money has gotten very complicated. My accounting teachers can't fully describe credit default swaps and what happened with them. Finances have simply become too difficult for most people to understand. We need to build bridges between financial and political people, and artists and growers – between people with means and people without means.

Road Note

I left Asheville and drove "into the belly of the beast," according to Will. That leg of the journey stands out as the only stretch of the entire 10,000 mile odyssey where I struggled to stay awake. Lipton green tea (not my favorite) and serial NPR were my only salvation. Near sundown and entering the D.C. beltway, I found myself accidentally listening to a congressional confirmation hearing after surfing the dial. And not just any congressional confirmation hearing. This one happened to be for Ron Kirk, an old college friend and the first African American mayor of Dallas. Whoa, President Obama had appointed Ron to be United States Trade Representative? That woke me up! I immediately called Juliana Perkins (045) and exclaimed, "You're not going to believe what I just heard!" "That Ron!" she giggled and gave me his cell number and I left message for him. Ambassador Ron Kirk. Excellent.

I stayed overnight with my sister and her family, feeling grateful for the familiarity. In the morning I took the Metro Orange Line to the National Mall. A man in a suit stood on the train to take a picture of his nine-year-old son, also dressed in a suit and joyfully plugged-in to his iPod. I offered to take a photograph of the two of them and that led to one of those perfect on-the-train conversations. The pair was from Boulder, Colorado and his son attended the Bear Creek Elementary School.

Dad beamed as he described their day's plan. They were attending the ceremony at the Capitol where they would represent the school to accept the prestigious 2008 James L. Oberstar Award given annually by The National Center for Safe Routes to School. "Seventy percent of the kids at our school walk or bike every day," the man said. His son smiled. "It's all about reducing our dependency on cars," he informed me, "and about the kids teaching the whole community by example." Now the son smiled even more. "That's change," Dad said as we all stood to get off at the Smithsonian station. Then he winked at his son and said, "We're going to the Washington Monument first."

The father and son team turned left, both of them winding up the cords of their earphones and, in unison, tucking them into their pockets. I watched them disappear into the morning crowd. Like a giant push pin, the Washington Monument held down the west end of the National Mall's lawn and walkways. At the east end sat the Capitol building, looking more like a paperweight. I headed in that direction and walked up the hill to meet with Andy Walton, a Presbyterian minister.

068 Andy Walton
Washington, DC

Andy was raised in rural Georgia. Early in his adulthood, he spent a good deal of time directing the theater on a military base in Oklahoma. Then he went to seminary. Now well into that career, he's the pastor for the Capitol Hill Presbyterian Church of Washington D.C. – a church which formalized itself with an inaugural Sunday service just after President Lincoln was assassinated.

Andy: When I think of change, I think of inevitability. We're changing all the time. Sometimes we don't even know it's happening. When we do know, we usually resist it. Still, it happens whether we want it to or not. We change. Change doesn't have a moral value to it. It doesn't have any kind of value to it. We decide whether it's good change, bad change, but it's just there and it's going to continue.

When it comes down to it, I don't know that I want anything to stay the same. There was a time I would have said family, but I know it's not going to. (*laughs*) There are a lot of things I would like to have continue – my relationships, my marriage, my children. But I know it will all change, because it has. That will continue.

As signs of positive change I look for lightness of spirit, acceptance of where and who we are and of other people. Positive change brings contentment. That doesn't mean complacency. In fact change can be exhilarating; it brings wholeness, a sense of purpose.

With a church or a government, the real trick is how consciously to be involved in change? How much do we guide it, lead it – for what purpose? The church changes every time a new person walks in the front door. There was a time when I had routines and liked things done in certain ways. I didn't do well when things didn't go the way I expected. Through the years, I've learned how to roll with change. That flexibility and responsiveness is what I try to live and encourage people to be a part of.

That's what the compromise thing here in Washington is about. The wise people know how to read the political weather. They know when there's momentum in a certain direction even if they don't agree with it. They try to figure out, "How can I be a part of this so I can get some of the things I feel are important." They begin to play the game; holding back, saying, "I can't support that unless you support this." Compromise.

Out in most of America, which is where I've lived most of my life, compromise is a dirty word. You've got to stand your ground, hold your values. Politicians know this. That's why they talk that kind of language back home. But when you get here to

Washington, compromise is a way of life. It's the way you get things done. Without compromise, together with not taking things personally, nothing would ever get done.

Unfortunately, there isn't as much of that as there used to be. I've heard old timers saying, "Maybe we can get the spirit back." I don't know when it changed. I've tried to ask. Maybe it was pre-Nixon. The spirit of compromise is characterized with, "It's all business. We get on the floor of the Senate or the House. We stand our ground and push for what we believe and when it's all over we go to dinner together. We're still friends."

You still see that among older members of Congress. You saw it at Teddy Kennedy's birthday celebration with Oren Hatch's honoring of him. Those guys are good friends. That doesn't mean they can't get on the floor of the Senate and vehemently disagree. Sadly, the people who've been around a long time say that spirit has been scarce for awhile. Congressional relations have become very partisan. They don't even socialize across the aisle. It's a spirit that would be good to revive.

That's not to say it doesn't ever happen, though. One of the things I like about our congregation is the way we connect across party differences. This church was formed at the end of the Civil War. In the midst of all that destruction, the congregation met in the Capitol Building until they had their own space. Now, we're three blocks from the Capitol. Everything going on there has always had an influence on us. At the same time, it's a neighborhood church. People try not to bring politics into it. We have wonderful people in this congregation who have very different perspectives. We worship together. We have fellowship together. We're friends. There is difference and we certainly defend those differences, (*laughs*) but there's room for the conversation.

A good friend of mine here in this congregation, is a Senator from Wyoming – Mike Enzi. Mike's a very traditionally conservative guy. He's a typical Western conservative. If you did a political litmus test on issues of the day, he and I would probably differ on well into 90% of them. But we can always find something that we agree on. A lot of it has to do with this church community. Mike's always coming up to me after a sermon. He'll zero in on a point that he can agree with and that's what we'll talk about. He's told me that's how he tries to work in the Senate. He says, "I try to find the things that we can agree on." He's been pretty successful at it. Doesn't get a lot of publicity. Nobody wants to pick up the Washington Post with a headline that says, "Republicans and Democrats Agree." (*laughs*) That's no fun.

As you travel the country talking to people, I'm sure you rediscover that we're all human. There's security in that. When you get down to it that's all we're looking for. But it gets convoluted very quickly with fear and anxiety. We start closing down our circles, striking out at other people. Unfortunately there are people who for whatever reason take advantage of that fear. They build themselves up by inspiring anxiety. They profit from it. They gain power from it. It's another piece of the game, but it is not wisdom.

In my own experience and tradition, the most famous wisdom of the Christian Bible would be Ecclesiastes or Proverbs. Both of those books hold a great deal of wisdom. Change is inevitable. The preacher in Ecclesiastes says, "There's a season for everything." Another phrase in Ecclesiastes is, "There is nothing new under the sun." (*laughs*) That's just the way it is. The wise person knows that and tries to live in it instead of trying to buck it. Flexibility and openness are signs of wisdom. Obstinacy, resolution, and those kinds of things are signs of not much wisdom.

I am basically optimistic. What I try to share is that Creation is good. It is. It's amazing really, and it's abundant. We're called to ground ourselves in that goodness and to look at the whole – everybody and everything from that perspective. If we do, we start treating each other better.

That's a struggle now in Western Christianity because Western theology has at its core the depravity of man and sinfulness of the world. We just don't need that garbage. And I do call it garbage. I don't agree with it. I think there's another side that people experience and live that didn't get voted on over the ages as the main way. I get a lot of that perspective from Celtic spirituality and Sufi mysticism. I've been reading a lot of Hafiz and Rumi. I love that poetry. It's beautiful.

Recognizing the abundance and goodness of Creation has always been a significant part of Judaism, Islam and Christianity. For some reason it's taken as subversive and always gets pushed down. Maybe it's because there's no control in it. You control things in two ways. You create fear and you create scarcity, neither of which really exists (laughs) except in our imaginations. When you create those two things and exploit them, you can control people. That's what so many of contemporary systems do.

We really need to relax. It's so cool to see the Obamas here in Washington going to Ben's Chili Bowl for a hot dog, going to a Wizards game, putting a swing set on the White House lawn. There's a relaxed feeling. Sitting in the Oval Office with an open collar, you know? Some people nearly had heart attacks over it. But, those are little signs of broader relaxation that could be taking place.

069 Justin Leak
Tyson's Corner, VA

Still in the D.C. area, I met with Justin Leak at a Cheesecake Factory Restaurant in an upscale complex of shopping centers. The night came on fast and the DC traffic worked its bafflement. By the time I arrived, late, Justin was taking his last bites of burger and fries. "You found me," he grinned. "Catsup?" Justin was raised in Philadelphia. When he came to graduate school in Oregon I was a professor for a few of his classes. Now I had the unique privilege of seeing a student a few years out from completing his degree. Justin works with a nonprofit foundation. "When you make it through a childhood of economic and racial challenge and then get the opportunities I've had," Justin said, "it's just so great to be doing work that gives back."

Justin: Hope and change. I use those two words interchangeably. Hope is the beginning of change. The economy has hit this area really hard. People need hope. Having that hope is the first step. Where I work, for the Jack K. Cook Foundation[14], we love our jobs. It's because we're offering money and support to low-income families. Few people are in a position to do that–to offer financial support with no strings attached and the recipient's best interest truly at heart.

Our focus is on education for kids. It's expensive in this country. The public system

14   Jack K Cook Foundation http://www.jkcf.org/

is not where it needs to be. That's an area that must be changed. Some governmental agencies and school districts are trying to help students from the top. They're creating magnet programs to help learners focus their studies, but we're not there yet. In the meantime our foundation is helping in a significant way. Even if it's only 75 kids a year, we still help that many kids through boarding school, private school, summer school, whatever it takes to get them into a decent college. We know that 75 will give back to another 75. The change is small and gradual, but it is real change.

The fun and disappointing part at the same time, is that we won't see what all of them do in the next 10, 20, 30 years. At the age of 15 they have plans to start their own foundations and organizations to create all kinds of change. They are going to be leaders. With this job, I know I'm giving back to a community that gave to me.

With the resources we have in this country, there's no reason for us to be in this situation. This is my soapbox. I truly believe there is no reason anybody should be hungry, homeless, uneducated, jobless or without health care. With everything being so privatized and what not, we have a system where the wealthy have access to those things, the middle class might have access, and then 70% of the people who don't have jobs or qualify for some social program are just out of luck. There's no reason for it.

At the Foundation, we're trying to change that. The population we work with is very low-income and high-achieving. When I say low-income, I have students who are homeless. Those are youth who almost didn't get accepted into our program because we couldn't find them. They were in a shelter or on the street. It took us weeks to track them down to say, "Hey, you're one of our scholars. Congratulations."

And these kids are not only scholars they're also committed to community service. I walk into where they live–these kids on the verge of being without homes–and they're making stew to take to a homeless shelter. You know what I mean? They're doing things I never would have dreamt of doing as a kid. It's amazing. Despite all the family unrest that is going on–the divorces and all–these kids are pulling straight A's. They're so resilient. At the same time, they're completely humble when an organization like ours comes in and says, "We're going to send you a laptop to help you with school."

Once you have an experience with change like this it's hard to forget. As a kid, as a parent, or as a provider it is so positive. For example, part of our program brings the participants and families together for a conference. People who live in severe poverty don't get to have long weekends where they just talk about education, what their kids need and how they're going to get it. For them it's a huge exception to be treated well. We treat our families with the dignity and respect they deserve. The family may be in a low-income situation, but the focus of "Welcome Weekend" is on what we can do for these children. How can we help them get ready for college?

As time goes by, I would love to use the story of this time in our nation and my time with the foundation to show what optimism can mean for action–what change can mean if you just have faith things can get better. Regardless of the situation you were born into or have ended up in, things can change. Hope plays a big part in that. And commitment. Commitment to being part of it; to doing whatever it is you can do.

It's going to sound corny, but besides hope, I really count on my faith–faith that things will get better. I don't believe the circumstances of my life now are going to be my end result. I definitely know there's something bigger and better out there for me, too. Faith is going beyond just having hope because faith makes it possible to act.

Road Note

Driving out of D.C. towards New York City was a big deal for two reasons: The traffic and the energy. I expected the intensity of motoring to match the increased concentration of the other people on the road. Over the years, I have spent plenty of time in New England and New York. Since that had mostly involved air travel, East Coast traffic loomed in my imagination as a new challenge – but only of Herculean proportions.

Then there was the vibe. The distance between Atlanta and New York City is not only measured in miles, but also in culture. As passé or irrelevant as they may be, the storied impressions that southern people have of Yankees and the ones northerners have of the South persist as stubbornly and as steadfast as any rendition of red and blue.

I don't have any residual accent- in fact, I have come to realize that the effort I put into not sounding Southern is its own form of internalized oppression. Realizing the extent to which I had changed my accent was a lesson in the power of culture. Over my youth, and often without knowing it, I had absorbed certain judgments about superiority and inferiority that lead to my reasoning, "If I want to be taken seriously, I have to get rid of the accent."

Still deeper than accent, I carry socialization as a Southerner that makes for a level of anxiety at the doorstep of the North. So there it is; my very own participation in a polarity. Almost reflexively, I jump right into the South-North story. Even knowing better, I continue to experience an attitude of caution around Northerners. All I had to do was cross the state line into New Jeresy to see my guard rise from dormancy to a status of subtle-but-quite-present. I was on their turf, after all.

Wasn't I was past this sort of thing? I mean, there I was driving around the country – our country – to find out what we Americans think about change. I spent nearly twenty-two years married to a man from East Brunswick, just off Exit 9 in New Jersey. None of these thoughts quelled my low-level vigilance. I juggled toll payments, followed the signs for I-95N and drove into Manhattan. Navigating the narrow canyons between skyscrapers, I found my way to the brownstone on the East River where more people I'd never met were opening their home to me. I even found curbside parking.

I credit Peter Frishauf for this smooth transition. A medical policy analyst and entrepreneur in his sixties who was born and raised on Manhattan, Peter had initiated phone contact while I was still on the road in New Jersey. With spontaneous kindness, he talked me from the Lincoln Tunnel all the way to that great parking spot. Opening my car door and offering his hand, Peter then led me into the brownstone where his wife, the artist K.C. Rice and their two cats welcomed me like I was family.

I awoke to air that was generously laced with the scent of coffee and we sat at the kitchen table for a breakfast interview. Peter and K.C. were thoughtful, adventurous, profound and witty- all shared with a camera that was never turned on! We planned to try again the next morning, since by then I needed to be off to a scheduled visit with Rose O'Brien.

070 "Rose O'Brien"
New York City, NY

Rose in Manhattan. Rose at 26. Rose of an Irish/Cherokee mother and Mexicano father. Rose who I'd first met when she was a spindly little girl of 6 running through the summer fountains of Portland, OR's waterfront. The fact of her ancestry in the indigenous cultures of Mexico and the U.S. together with her considerable scholastic skill took Rose to Dartmouth's Native American Studies program for college. Now three years out, she is a New Yorker, a professional woman, and an already accomplished and respected champion of what she terms venture *philanthropy*.

Rose: When I think about change in my own life, both personally and professionally, I think of doing something better. It can be as incremental as changing apartments because I can afford $1300 a month instead of $300 a month in New York City. It can be changing positions because I've gotten a promotion. In particular for me, it is often changing the way I work to be more effective, efficient and productive. If you'd asked me ten years ago what change meant, it would not have conjured up positive thoughts. There is also a real difference in how the word is used in New York and in the United States as a whole.

In New York City we're going through a challenging time. New York has been so wealthy. That wealth has been fueled partly by personal lavishness, but also by public sector allocations. So here, change means we're contracting economically and are going to see increases in violence and in need. More people are going to food pantries and soup kitchens. In the schools, more kids are coming to class without jackets in the winter. I don't think we've bottomed out economically, yet. Public and private leaders are thinking about how we can pull everyone up.

There is something very unique about Americans in our veracity and tenaciousness. Those are inherent aspects of our national character that support change. At the same time, there is a sense that wasn't erased by the recent election or inauguration, that the generations post-60's, post-70's have been stagnant. There's a perception that we haven't been engaged. It's a little untrue since during the election we demonstrated the capacity to motivate for change. I hope that trend continues. I hope my sister who is just 9 years younger than me has a solid sense of responsibility for herself and her community, her city, her state and her country. I hope the generations hold onto that.

The broad indicators of change, you know 10 or 20 years out, will show up in the leadership in Washington, DC looking more like the rest of the country. The fabric of people going into politics and positions of leadership will more accurately represent the citizenry. Other big change 20 or 30 or 40 years down the road will be in access to health care. We'll see changes in who can afford to make sure they're not getting diabetes at the age of 40. In New York City we'll see changes in who can avoid having asthma at the age of ten. Those indications of change will show things are shifting in a positive way.

An economic downturn is never great because there are people on the fringe who fall off when things get tight. But one of the positive outcomes is that everything becomes a bit leaner. The underperformers get shed in both business and philanthropy. Both funders and supporting not-for-profit organizations will have to be fiscally sound, without a lot of overhead expenses or great intentions that aren't reflected in outcomes. The organizations that are power houses, the ones that are doing things effectively, will still be around and kicking in ten years. And they'll be affecting positive change in very real ways.

When I talk about venture philanthropy I'm thinking of philanthropy as a business investment. You look at the strength of a charity the way you would look at a small business you were thinking about investing a million or two million dollars in. What you want are dividends from that investment. The philanthropic dividends are evident in the strength of your community when people are actually being helped.

Our focus for public and private funding may shift or broaden. For example, in ten years I wonder what the discussion will be regarding access to water. In the U.S. we haven't really confronted large scale restrictions to our ability to get clean water for drinking, for cooking, for bathing, for watering our gardens. I wonder if in ten years we'll be affected by the fact that, right now there are significant water issues around the world. I wonder if that will be a discussion with the youth of 2020.

Someone said to me last year, "You're really idealistic." I was shocked because I don't think of myself as idealistic, but I am hopeful. I'm cautiously hopeful. It's not going to be a very easy road. The next couple of years are going to be challenging for New York City, for New York State and for the country at large. But I think that good things are going to come out of it. We'll figure out things we need to do differently and we'll come out of it.

Road Note:

I know, it's early to insert another road note, but ... well ... I was in New York City and Peter had offered to take me for a late afternoon bike ride through the streets of Manhattan. Three things combined to persuade me to take him up on the idea. First was the fact that I had actually accomplished driving those streets the day before. Then there was Peter's commitment to urban cycling as an alternative mode of transportation and his contagious enthusiasm for showing off the bike lanes he'd worked so diligently and long to support. Finally, there was the unbridled, even giddy pride Peter has for the city of his birth.

Cycling Manhattan. Who knew it was really possible, let alone so fun? New York's ubiquitous yellow taxis were out in force, but they were entirely polite and respectful to all the cyclists using the new bike lanes. We pedaled into Greenwich Village and then went by Ground Zero. A week before spring equinox the air and wind still felt piercingly arctic. Admittedly, I was fresh out of the South and in the cold I'm just a little prone to hyperbole. "Brrrrrrrr," I said for the umpteenth time. Peter motioned for me to stop in front of a neighborhood hardware store. A few minutes later he appeared with magic hot pads to put in my gloves and shoes. Toasty warm now, I continued following Peter through Battery Park where we stopped to admire a magnificent sunset over the Hudson River.

As if anything could surpass the delight of our Manhattan cycling tour, K.C.

met us at the brownstone and we went out for dinner at their favorite neighborhood East Indian restaurant. Under the combined effects of the inspiring interview
with Rose, the bike ride, and the exceptional food and conversation with K.C. and
Peter, I began to notice my own bit of change. The assumptions I'd been carrying
about the North were losing their grip on me. I was even beginning to catch some
of Peter's affection for his hometown.

071,072 Katharine (KC) Rice & Peter Frishoff
New York City, NY

The next morning was Sunday. I would leave for Long Island before noon. With the
renewed aroma of coffee and in the yawning presence of two goddesses of luxury
masquerading as cats, the three of us sat again for an interview on change. This time
the Flip camera worked.

KC: Really I don't mind change as long as it's interesting. I lament some of the changes
that have happened here. A lot of the negative change has come with what feels like the
suburbanization of Manhattan. I mean, you walk on a block that used to have ten or
twelve different storefronts. Now, you find a Bank of America stretching almost to the
middle of a block and a Duane Reed Drug Store coming almost into the middle of the
block from the other side. Between them is a little wireless store. That gets repeated
block after block. You used to have tailors, fabric stores and all sorts of things. I don't
know where to go to buy fabric anymore.

Then again, would I trade all that to prevent the parks reverting to being dangerous
and crummy again? The change in the parks has been a wonderful. It started when
running became a craze. More people were using the parks and they became safer, more
money went into them. I do wonder why the trade offs have to be so imbalanced.

Peter: It's all about the need human beings have to be amongst one another. The
suburbs are so isolated they had to invent the mall where people could be together.
It's part of what we mis-ascribe in America to the need to go shopping. It's really a need
to have social interaction. We created the mall out of that human need.

It is the concept of the piazza; the reason churches were the center of commerce in
medieval communities. They built big churches, and market places would form outside
in the plazas around them. They could extract money out of you because god's way
was a large part of the economy. Religion was very integrated with the state. But the
fundamental human need was for a meeting place, for interaction on a scale like that.
You find it in cities and you find it replicated in suburban malls.

If you think about it, the future of the mall might be to take the parking lots and
start building housing there. What would you have? You'd have the little town which
would become the little city. We'd be right back to where we started and, of course,
also be much more efficient. As long as people aren't killing each other, as long as they
are living in healthy relationship with one another they like living close together just
fine. If time passes and the community becomes destructive and decrepit, they'll say,

"This really sucks," and move to more isolated rural-like and thus suburban situations again. That of course requires something like cars to allow the separation and isolation.

The challenge seems to be in learning how to get along. As soon as people understand the joy of that they'll be able to get together to listen and learn from each other without blowing each other up.

KC: It's an interesting idea. Shopping has become such a prevalent activity. It's kind of the cause of the mess we're in now. Shopping becomes the placebo to soothe the need to get together and interact.

Peter: All market places are like that. In Viet Nam at the food market places.

KC: Scarborough Faire in Merry England. People think it's the shopping when it's really the need to get together and have interaction even if the interaction is only money changing hands. For interacting, shopping or not, New York is really a wonderful place. Change happens at such a rapid rate here. Peter, you grew up here from 5 years old. You must have seen so much that was part of your childhood just obliterated.

Peter: I think that's right. But in terms of being comfortable as an adult it was very helpful to experience the chaos that is this city.

KC: Is it really chaos or just a rapid rate of change? What about the rate at which things come and go? All the things disappearing that were part of your childhood. I guess that's why a lot of people leave New York in the end. It isn't just the noise or the crowding or the crime. It's the constant adaptation that must occur.

Peter: I've been thinking of this physician whose sister died of breast cancer. His main work has been on cures for different cancers. He described the cellular theory of apoptosis which is the Greek word for death. In biology it is the process of cellular death. Without apoptosis we get cancer and die. In order for us to live it is critical that cells die. If they don't die, they proliferate. They turn into tumors and eventually overwhelm the body and we die. So the notion that death as necessary for life is something he came to appreciate from the science of cellular death. He drew a lot of comfort from these lessons of science rather than religion.

Death is absolutely necessary for life. If humans lived forever we would starve the planet. It would be a completely irrational system. Even religious people who think in terms of eternal life would agree. Immortality is basically an absurd and inherently bizarre concept. Coming into touch with the reality that death is necessary for life is essential. It has to do with the reality that we have to eat in order to live. That means other things, plants and animals and water, have to be deprived of their otherwise uninterrupted existence. Our gains are always to some extent at the expense of someone else or some other being. It's really not useful to be in denial of that.

Change is certainly relative. Today's positive change could be tomorrow's negative change. We see that over and over. We talk about environmentally neutral building products, but we really have no idea. Is artificial turf more environmentally harmful than natural grass? Well, how natural is "natural" grass? The grass on the lawns in this country is completely non-native. It was an import from the United Kingdom hundreds of years ago. In most communities, our lawns require unbelievable amounts of water and chemicals to keep them looking like nice places for geese to shit on.

So, positive change is often about alleviating short term suffering. Positive change for some people is to get gas prices cheap again. Some long for an economy that restores the time we could buy endless amounts of cheap shit at Walmart. For other people Walmart is a catastrophe in terms of economic destruction to smaller enterprises that actually make and sell things locally. It's hard to know the consequences of change.

But death is not always the enemy. It's a balance. We try to live our lives as minimally piggy as we can, but all the time we could be wrong. You do your best, but recognize you just can't know. That doesn't mean you're not going to fight like hell for what you believe is positive today. You try as hard as you can to think about issues in broad context and to enrich your understanding.

That's where dialogue can happen. Listening is the key. You have a much better chance of getting it right if you really work at listening. That's why techniques like repeating back to someone what they have told you no matter how bizarre or ludicrous it may seem is often helpful. If people really believe that all life forms were salvaged in Noah's Ark and they tell you the story, it's important to repeat it back sincerely–to say, "Let me understand this. You believe this happened 4000 years ago. If you really believe this, I want to listen."

KC: You were lucky in that you didn't grow up with any sort of dogma. You don't have a lot of stuff to break down before you can listen.

Peter: That's true. My parents did me a huge favor. I'm very grateful to them for this. They came from families who were murdered by the Nazis or forced into suicide to escape being murdered. But there was something they didn't do. Unlike what happened with many friends whose families also survived World War II, my parents refused to pass on the fear and horror to my sister and me.

We were really quite unaware of the enormity of the tragedy. They didn't talk about it. Many of my friends also had parents who had either been in concentration camps or escaped by the skin of their teeth like my parents did. But they grew up in an atmosphere of fear that the brown shirts were going to break down the door and come into their apartments any second. They were paralyzed by this fear. My parents permitted us to grow up without that. As a result, we've been able to have reasonably happy lives while many of my peers have not because of all that fear.

Many of these same people considered my parents' choice to be a tremendous cop out; especially those who felt it was a betrayal of Jewish heritage. From their perspective we were part of the problem–assimilated Jews who thought we could get along in the larger society by escaping Jewish identity. They warned that when the racists and haters came in again even the assimilated would be told, "No, you're Jewish and we're going to kill you anyway."

That logic requires a very superficial interpretation of history. The fact is; people are going to hate one another for all kinds of reasons. Maybe they'll hate me because

I'm freckled and used to have red hair. It's hard to say that being Jewish is the only reason you'll be persecuted. In fact it's just plain stupid because the Nazis did a great job exterminating many more people than Jews. Jews were singled out as the largest population for extermination, but first came the political opponents, then came the mentally ill, 20 million Russians, and lots of economic and military exterminations. The scope of the tragedy was immense. All hatred works like that. Gays and lesbians, niggers and Jews, lazy Indians if you're from the Americas, smelly Indians if you're from Southeast Asia and on and on. It's an endless and stupid list, borne out of ignorance.

Maybe, positive change is trying to be a little bit more enlightened in terms of opening minds to the possibility that those things are wrong. Maybe there's a better way to raise children that empowers them to think rather than trying to intimidate them with fear. "You will do this, because we don't want you to burn in hell." "You will do that because you are one of the chosen people." Maybe the most empowered change is to work to be less ignorant. We're all ignorant and discerning wise action is a life long struggle. If we commit ourselves to doing our best to be wrong less frequently, well, that's about the best we can do.

KC: Yes. We don't want all those millions to have died for nothing.

LONG ISLAND, NY to SEATTLE, WA
—
3.14 to 3.31.2009

- When you say the word change what do you mean?
- Alongside change, what is important to have remain the same?
- What would be signs that positive change is occurring?

LONG ISLAND, NY to SEATTLE, WA
3.14 to 3.31.2009

In the Chinese language there is a word composed of two characters, one for danger and the other for opportunity. This combination was present in the conversations I had in New York concerning our country's current economic circumstances. What appears as danger may also be opportunity for positive changes like shifting the quality of life for people who have lived with little to nothing, enhancing the quality of education for the youth who have had less access, improving the quality of our air by reducing the use of petroleum-based transportation. Recognizing and pursuing these kinds of opportunity in times of economic unrest requires some level of public coordination.

Although it may not be at the center of attention in the course of everyday living, the seventy-two voices up to now do agree that our government continues to matter. So does responsible citizenship. Both are needed to maintain the well being of this place we call home. We vary in our beliefs about the role and reach of government. We want connection, compromise and collaboration, but we also become frustrated in the face of a system that feels distant, inaccessible, and impossible to influence. Cohesive mobilization is tricky when it spans hundreds of millions of people – 309 million according to the 2010 count. And then there is the challenge of knowing where to begin.

Abraham Maslow developed a theory of human need and motivation in the 1940's that has withstood the test of time. Human beings, it seems, focus on the needs that match our level of satiety. Basically, if our circumstances include a scarcity of essentials like food, water and shelter, we naturally will give all of our attention to that. If those needs are met, we then can attend to community and belonging. And if we are fortunate to experience reliable social connection, we try to understand life itself in ways that give the whole experience meaning. When our survival and social needs are met, we then seek explanations for our existence like those of science and spirituality.

A democratic government acts as the guardian of citizens' fundamental needs. To understand and assess the daily interests and concerns of the people democratically we must have public conversations. The initiatives of activists and elected leadership have thus far driven these conversations in order to stimulate positive change. Momentum can get derailed however, because it is not easy to remain on the highest level on Maslow's hierarchy long enough to become grounded there. Even when our social connections and basic survival needs are not truly at risk, we can become fearful in the face of a perceived threat and, instead of remaining motivated by wisdom we become motivated by fear of losing access to basic sustenance – a fear that, at its base, is the fear of death.

Unknowingly, each of the *EX:Change* voices offered guidance for how we as individuals, families, communities and a nation have the ability, when necessary, to draw on our shared wisdom to change in order to meet our needs. Since the landscape of personal and social requirements for living in the United States is as varied as its 309 million inhabitants, we can also benefit from wise guidance. Ideally, our system of electing governmental leaders is set up to provide that guidance. The distance between current reality and that ideal is one territory of American change.

The actual territory of our country also and literally provides us with common ground. From the Pacific Coast, across the southern tier states and up along the Atlantic, I had watched the land shift back and forth from forest to marine coast, to concrete and steel, to flat-world desert, into the soft hills on either side of the Mississippi and through the mountains of the Blue Ridge. The *EX:Change* journey was about to turn again toward the west. The tangles of asphalt I had found as I drove up the East Coast would begin slowly to unwind into single strands of highway. But first, I would venture just a little farther east.

With Peter's precise directions, I made my way out of Manhattan and onto Long Island. This would be my first time ever to set foot on the stretch of land I associate mostly with suburbanization or with legendary comedians like Rodney Dangerfield and Billy Crystal. I was pleasantly surprised by its agrarian feel. In about an hour I came upon the small town where Emilia Lopez lives with her husband, parents and two children.

073 Emilia Lopez
Long Island, NY

Emily emigrated with her parents from Cuba. She was a teenager at the time. Now she's a professor in Queen's, NY. Her scholarly and practical attention is on English language learners and their families. For 25 years, Emily and I have been friends through our scholarship. It is good to know someone a long time and even better to learn new things about them. The words she gave to the topic of change drew forward threads from every aspect of her life. This is completely consistent with what I know of her as a scholar. She researches, writes and practices based on what she's lived and known.

Emily: The first thing that comes to my mind is changing the way we think about each other, the way we get along. But, I'm not very optimistic; my voice is not going to be an optimistic voice. Certainly there has been a wave of good feeling as, even though many of us were skeptical, Obama was able to win. I still wake up in the morning and think, "I never thought it would happen in my lifetime!" So there is a change. It's significant because as a nation we move collectively to say, "We choose this person to be our president."

That change came out of a lot of frustration. People were feeling very discouraged and wanting something different. I could see it in people I never thought would make that kind of choice. I have Cuban family members who live in Florida and are very Republican folks. My aunt said to me, "Well he's an African American man and it's time to give him an opportunity. Maybe he can fix it because he comes from a place that all these other people don't come from." I remember listening to her and thinking, "Wow." She was taking this chance because she thought it would make a difference.

That's all great, but I fear there is an undercurrent our expectations can't touch. We want lots of changes but we've been doing things the same way for so long. Our politics are so engrained. The way we talk to each other, the way we don't listen to each other and the way we tend to go to our own corners–all of those are hard to change. When I look at the politicians and I see we live in a country where we have two parties, the Republican and the Democratic. We don't get along very well. We don't talk to each other. Our elected leaders reflect the values and beliefs of the people. I am having trouble seeing how that will change.

We live in a nation that is so rich, and still we are constantly complaining that we don't have enough. I think about that lot. I had a totally different experience as a kid in Cuba having so much less than I have now. I hear this complaining and think Americans don't know how to live any other way because there has always been such abundance. That leads to the hysteria behind the economic situation, the comparisons to the Great Depression. We fear we will have much less. For us as a country that thought is more devastating than in other places on earth because we are so used to having it all. God forbid we can't have our 50 inch flat television screens or our fancy cars or whatever it is we think we need in order to feel okay.

We all want safety. We want well being and happiness. I've been reading some stuff by the Dalai Lama and it has influenced my thinking. Those things–safety and happiness–really have to come from within. Feeling content and full doesn't come from things you have but from the people around you–people taking care of each other and connecting. We have to get better at that. A sign of change would be to sit down and talk to each other. Bottom up and top down. When there is a way to talk about differences; that will be a change. Ultimately we all want the same things, but we get lost on the way. Maybe it has to start small, like in the family, and grow from there.

There are huge differences that make it hard to talk about what we all want. Not everyone believes they can get what they want. Because wants are often defined in terms of things, the conversation can get stuck in the materialistic. Then we don't hear the huge differences in how people feel about their ability to achieve fundamental things. Things like education or the well being that comes from knowing you have a good job and can live in a community where you and your family will be okay.

There are many people whose experience is they can't get those things. There are others who feel they can easily get them. Those are very different paths. It is difficult to talk honestly across those differences. I don't think it's an impossible gap to bridge, but it's pretty darn hard. It would be a start if people of privilege even wanted to talk about it. That would mean really opening to listen carefully to what the people who have had limited access have to say. Too often the attribution is, "It's your fault. You haven't worked hard enough. You're not committed."

The everyday realities of race and class just don't go away. Within weeks of the election we had a terrible episode out here on Long Island. A Latino man was stabbed to death by an African American. It was intentional and hideous. At the time there was such a sense of excitement in New York. You could feel it in the streets. I'd never seen anything like it. People who didn't know each other were talking about the election. They were buying buttons and tee shirts. It was electrifying. Here on Long Island and in the city. Then that killing happened and I remember my sense of, "Oh yes. This is reality."

I think of the world I live in. I want to see real change in schools for children who are culturally and language diverse, and for children who are poor. When the people in charge make good policy decisions, the trickle-down still comes to the individual educator. It trickles down to each and every one of us. It will always come down to that. It is an individual responsibility to say, "Here I am at this moment, in this place with this person or group of people. What is the right thing to do?" I see that at times and it's a great thing. But, I want more of it. That may explains my sense of disappointment. Maybe I want it to happen too quickly. I guess I have the American impatience, too.

The last thing about change; it has to be maintained. Making it happen is sometimes hard, but maintaining it is harder because people must be committed to whatever gets rolling. That requires long-term attention and deciding over and over to keep it going. Part of my pessimism comes from watching how quickly we retreat to our corners. I keep thinking, "Oh boy, I sure hope we have the courage and endurance to do this."

074 Daniela Plunkett
Long Island, NY

Daniela Plunkett is Emily's oldest child. She is at the end of her 8th grade year in middle school. Daniela had hung around to help us clean the table from dinner, but gone to her room to listen to music while Emily and I talked. Before too long, she re-emerged and sat nearby listening in. When Emily and I finished I turned off the camera and looked toward Daniela. I smiled and lifted my eyebrows. "OK," she said, "I'll do it, too."

Daniela: To me change is to get up in the morning and decide, "I'm going to do something to better other people–my community," and then to do it. There are those days where you don't want to get up out of bed but you say, "I have to get up, because I can change something." Change benefits everyone, change for the better.

I want to see communities change. We're so isolated into different groups. You go into a school and you see certain types. In the cafeteria, there's a group of girls with the same likes and interests who sit together. Then there's a separate group of boys that sit someplace else. You look around and go, "Why can't all of this change?" But they're stuck in their ways. They don't want to change. They feel change is bad.

But, you don't call a bad change, change. I think of change as a positive thing because you're moving toward something for the greater good. I want to see change in the grouping at my school because now the minute people step outside the classroom they want nothing to do with each other. Then they get the wrong ideas about other people. One group will look at another group and go, "They're freaks. They're outsiders. We can't talk to them because they're different from us." But once you talk to each other you realize, "These people aren't that different from me."

We have people who are very sports oriented. We have people with scholarly aspirations. Then we have people who are very much into their art; that's a large group in our school. People don't mingle with each other because they feel they have totally different likes or wants or needs. But, they're humans. They need food, shelter, water, and most of them have lots of the same ideas as the person who's sitting across the room

Daniela Plunkett *Long Island, NY*

from them. The negative stories that come out of that splitting are hurting people. t

All you need is a catalyst. One person can be a catalyst and change everything. On occasion I will see someone walk over to another table, sit down and act as if there wasn't a difference at all. That's what we need to work towards–to walk across the room or across the street. You can walk across the street anywhere. You can drive across the country like you're doing. You can go anywhere and find connections with people.

Change means to feel more at ease–to feel more comfortable. Definitely it does. I've seen people experience the uncomfortable part and it's not fun. It's degrading. No one wants to experience being pushed away or ignored. By getting to know other people you realize "Oh. What I said or did to this person hurt them. They're a human being, too."

We're working towards it. People as a group–as one group, not several different groups. All ages, all races, all height, all weight. It's a movement. It's not an occurrence, it's a movement. The biggest sign of the movement is that we elected a new president. It has shocked people. It's amazing what we as American people can do. It's amazing what we as a world can do–not just Americans.

I want is to be able to look to the person next to me and say, "Let's do something that can make a difference." To get up in the morning and say, "I'm going to change something." To walk across the room. There are many different ways of changing things. Just little random acts of kindness can help. I've been blessed enough to experience that.

Road Note

Every place I laid my head down to sleep on this trip put me on the receiving end of those acts of kindness that Daniela mentioned. Between stops were all the stretches of highway; themselves the kindness, so to speak, of tax dollars allotted to the U.S. transportation systems. Of course, in the whirl of traffic I didn't always remember the kindness part.

From Long Island, I navigated a dizzying mass of parkways disguised as interstates and finally made it to the George Washington Bridge. I drove into New Jersey again, and had a moment of near euphoria when I saw the letters "W – E – S – T" beneath the numbers on the highway sign. Aaaahhhh. Headed home.

The traffic thinned as I came to the mountain ranges, starting with the Delaware Water Gap – a stunning rise in the landscape at the beginning of what I later figured out to be the Pocono Mountains. On the other side of the Gap lay the farmlands of New Jersey and Pennsylvania dotted with comfortingly enormous red barns on the way to the forested hills of the Allegheny.

I stopped for gas and a short walk in Ridgeway, Pennsylvania, where I took one of my favorite photos from the trip. A small front porch caught the afternoon sun. On it were samples of what looked to be the most popular local art form, chainsaw sculpted hardwood. Two figures dominated. The first was about my height (5'6"), a smooth faced monk of East Asian traditions and the other being at least two feet taller, appeared to be the Sasquatch!

075,076 Susan Stout & David Snyder
Warren, PA

An hour later, I arrived in Warren, PA with the promise of interviews with an Allegheny forester and with an information tech professional. Susan Stout, the forest researcher and David Snyder, the computer specialist, are my former sister- and brother-in-law. We'd not seen one another for many years, but even with all the water that had passed under it, the bridge between us was still sturdy. Thirty years earlier, I'd danced at their wedding and now this couple had offered not just to host, but to share their thoughts on America with me.

Susan: I have two answers. One is very explicitly about race.

I was a freshman in college in 1967-68. The college I attended had recruited its highest proportion of African American students. From when we arrived until spring break, there were the beginnings of a conversation about race. There's that quote in the Bible about don't talk about the speck in your friend's eye until you can address the log in your own. I think people appreciated that and were really present to the discussion. Then, over spring break, Martin Luther King was assassinated. We came back to campus and black people were eating at black tables and white people were eating at white tables. If that conversation could resume–well, that's of what change means to me. We came so far in the Civil Rights Movement. Now, if we could actually talk about of race and its role in American life that would be real change.

Then the second answer. I think the correct reading of history is that we've never had dialogue across political differences. If you read about the Adams and Jefferson elections, it was the same kind of crap we see today. People on both sides of the issue had really smart ideas. I work in forestry. The ideas of Republicans that people can improve livelihood by good stewardship are really smart. The government can't do it all. The government can't own enough land. If we make it profitable for the people who do own the land to be good stewards, that's smart. Why can't we have that conversation?

So, I would like change to mean we look at the log in our own eye and start to have real conversation about race. As long as we're doing that, why not extend it to include dialogues between people on opposite ends of ideology on social issues–education, energy, environment and finance? Having conversation can bring the best of the whole spectrum forward and build better ideas.

In subsets of the American universe, people know how to do this–to be respectful of one another, to trust that some of their neighbors are doing the best they can. It would be nice if we could sustain that respect. I think the two dialogues I've already mentioned could make a huge difference for respect and dignity in our country.

Eric Holder, the new Attorney General, just gave a speech in which he talked about the cowardice of the American people in the conversation about race.[15] That's a sign that change is occurring. Here's a man whose voice we have marginalized for well over two hundred years. Even though he pissed a lot of people off, he is in a position

---

15   Eric Holder, Full Text: U.S. Attorney General Eric Holder Remarks on Black History Month, 'Nation of Cowards' http://www.clipsandcomment.com/2009/02/18/full-text-us-attorney-general-eric-holder-remarks-on-black-history-month-nation-of-cowards/

of authority and had to be taken seriously. Two or three days later, there was a piece by this black columnist for the New York Times, Charles Blow.[16] He said, "'Cowards?' That's probably a little harsh." He showed data about how afraid white people are to be perceived as racist. It's incredibly stressful, physiologically stressful for white people to be in situations with black people because they're so afraid of that perception. Blow wrote this in a constructive way that carried forward the dialogue.

Blow also mentioned the website, Implicit[17], a Harvard-based project to collect data and allow people to measure their biases. I took two of their tests. On racism, I actually scored OK. But on women in science I scored strongly associating men with being good at science. Since I am a woman research scientist, I thought that was really funny. (laughs) Anyway, I took Holder's speech and Blow's article, and sent them to everybody who works for me. I also suggested they take the Implicit test.

One of the women I work with is a white woman married to a black man with children who visually present as black. Incredibly courageously, she replied to everybody describing her life reality. She wrote about windows that have opened for her to understand the broader American experience. She gave the example of all the times people in grocery stores have seen her, this white woman with a black child, and followed her around telling her she shouldn't be afraid to apply for food stamps. She's a highly successful scientist. Her husband is a highly successful teacher. But the assumption is that a white woman with black children needs food stamps.

So, Holder's talk filtered through Blow's article became an opportunity for communication on race among my co-workers. That makes me hopeful.

Overall, I would have to say I'm cautiously optimistic. The financial challenges are overwhelming–to revive an economy that's built on consumerism with the paradoxical need to create an economy that is more conservative, responsible, and saving. So I'm cautious and terrified, but optimistic. It feels like if we fail, the failure is bigger than we can grasp–so that's the "terrified." "Cautious" is knowing the problems are terribly complex. "Optimistic" is a little bit mystical.

The ideal that all human beings are created equal is right. I don't believe the United States is better than anybody else or that we have some special mission or relationship with God. Still, at critical moments in our history we have been blessed with leaders who somehow saved that ideal of our equality. Obama may be another such leader. And this time remembering "All people are created equal" includes Muslims and Animists and Atheists and Asians and Arabs and Africans and Russians and South Americans and North Americans.

If we salvage that ideal from this mess, it will be salvaged for good. Lincoln salvaged "All people are created equal" to include black and white, South and North. Roosevelt salvaged it to included working people. Maybe Obama's task is to salvage the ideal that "All people" is Kenyans and United States citizens, Indonesians, Hawaiians, and all the people of the world.

David: I guess I haven't given a lot of thought to what change really means. Of course,

16   16Charles Blow, New York Times. http://www.nytimes.com/2009/02/21/opinion/21blow.html?_r=1&ref=opinion

17   Implicit. https://implicit.harvard.edu/implicit/demo/

it depends on the context and if the context is the past 18 months, it's about ideas of political and social change. In that, I think I've bought the possibility of change to more transparent government. I'm not sure it's really going to happen, though.

In general, I like the concept of change but I'm not as adaptable as I wish I was. Every evening I come out, I sit down and I have my cigar. I have a cigar in the morning and one in the evening. Don't get in my way. (*laughs*) I like stability, like knowing I can count on people and they can count on me. Knowing that if they call me and say, "Hey, can you take my brother to the airport?" ten minutes before I'm going to leave for work that I can say, "That really screws up whatever, but yes." I like to be able to count on reciprocal relationship.

I'm very cynical about government and politics. While a real sign of political change would be transparency, I'm afraid I would suspect the motive. I'd think, "There's a reason they're doing this and it's not necessarily a good reason." I even feel that about the current Administration. I think I'm discouraged a little bit right now.

When I consider that we are in the early 50 days of the first 100, that's a huge mountain. It's an absurd mountain. Early on I felt, "You know, I don't expect anything to happen quickly." But still there's the feeling, "How can this happen?" or, "Why hasn't that happened?" Like with the recent national budget. Obama basically said, "That's not really my budget. We're just taking care of what was left and it's not the fault of my Administration." That's valid. He didn't create the situation, but I felt disappointed.

That's part of the reason change is so difficult, at least for me. I'm the first one to admit that I don't have any idea how all the pieces fit together in this puzzle. Think about how many pieces there are in any one national issue. It's beyond me. I say that real deliberately. It is beyond me to imagine all the pieces.

Like the whole stock market thing has had effects that never occurred to me. I don't want to know anything about my 401K. When it's time for me to tap it, then I'll be disappointed or whatever. But there have been other effects. For example, I'm on the library board. I never considered all the pieces involved in a library. Suddenly we're looking at $1 million less than we had last year. How is that possible? It's a stock market thing. Then there's my dad who's retired and living on money he has in the market. It's not good. I always think of the stock market as these gambling fat cats; if they lose it's their problem. Now I see there are huge effects I had not thought about.

It's a puzzle. It's hard to figure. I will say one thing I appreciate is the fact that Obama has been honest. He's said, "Look, I don't necessarily know how to fix all these things." I appreciate that. If he'd said he can fix all these things I would have said, "That's bullshit. You can't." I wish he did know how to fix everything, but he can't. When he talked of all of us playing a part I even felt optimism, but that is sort of melting now. With all my cynicism, though, I'm cautiously optimistic. I think I was very pessimistic up to right before the election. Maybe a week before, I started saying, "This is really going to happen." I'm glad the things I was most worried about didn't materialize. My optimism was boosted because of so many people who really want things to happen—including lots of people who traditionally don't want to see change. That was good.

People have been saying they want to be a part of the change. I would like to be a part of the change, but I'd like to be a part of it in a way that doesn't intrude on the rest of my world. That's a disappointing part I see in myself. I've thought, "OK. How would

I like to be a part of it?" and I haven't come up with a very good idea about it. Right now it's vague and amorphous. It would be very helpful to have a list of things I could look to. "Yeah, I could do that. I would feel good about doing that." To my knowledge there's no such thing but that would be really helpful for a person like me.

Some people identify contributions that can be made or actions that can be helpful. What you're doing right now is an example. I'm not nearly that creative. Or perhaps I'm too lazy. Maybe that's what it boils down to.

Road Note

The good news: Seventy-six voices were in and I was three-quarters of the way around the country. The not so good news: I had been forced to skip New England, because things weren't quite right with my little steed. Auto professionals in service stations north of Georgia and Safeco officials via the Internet had advised me to get back to Oregon sooner than I would have liked. For time, I was now on fast-forward, moving across the northern states in giant leaps (*as you'll see from more frequent road notes over the next couple of pages*).

Highway time stretched out and EX:Change conversations became more sparse, but no less real. Sparse and real. The description fits in many ways the pattern of the Midwestern cities that marked the sprawling land west of the Mississippi – Cincinnati, Gary, Chicago, Ames, Omaha. The smaller towns scattered across the plains, mountain ranges, deserts and plateaus between those cities were also sparse and real. The states lining the northern part of our country sustain the American magic of blending our history and culture with the abundant beauty left here by countless eons of geology and Nature.

077 Police Sergeant George McMurray
Chicago, IL

I arrived in Chicago in time for St. Patrick's Day – a day my internalization of American lore has somehow always associated with Chicago. That serendipity was cool all by itself, but imagine my delight when a Chicago police officer walked into the coffee shop where I sat preparing for an interview later in the morning. And not only that, Police Sergeant George McMurry agreed to talk with me about change.

Officer McMurray: Change means hope. Change means progress. I think most hope for changes in the way things are being done in our government. We were unhappy with what was happening.

Especially in this time and place, change is fraught with so many expectations. Still, you need basic underlying institutions that bring stability and order. The turmoil in the economic markets reveals the problems that result when those structures are not constant. Fear has fostered many of our economic problems. Fear fosters actions by people to protect themselves–to take money out of banks causing runs on banks, etc. So, we need basic structures of law and order that bring stability to our daily lives. Things like what I do, you know. That needs to remain constant, because if it doesn't, you have chaos. One would hope we can avoid chaos at all costs.

Shifting to recent events, there are big signs of change. The election of President Obama is a sign that people had reached a point where the status quo was unacceptable. Together we decided we need to head in a new direction because the times called for major change. The old methods for dealing with things–be it the climate or business regulation–had proven ineffective. We're fighting two wars which is costing us a zillion dollars. We've got an economy that's in shambles. People have a lot of uncertainty. It's not good. They've said, "We want something different. We want things to be better for our children."

One of my great disappointments as a baby boomer is the short sightedness of my generation. They want things to be good for them but there's never any thought of future generations. All of the hippies turned out to be narcissists. I've never quite understood how that transition took place. Maybe it was too much dope. Maybe we can blame it on cocaine. Everybody stopped smoking reefer and started snorting cocaine back in the 70s. Disco. We can blame it on disco. We can blame it on a lot of things. But that altruism that was so evident in the 60's and early 70's has disappeared from society today.

I was in a restaurant the other night and heard a few people who looked to be boomers having a discussion. One said, "Well isn't this great. Finally we're going to get some answers on climate change." Another person was arguing against climate change because he had to sacrifice. "Why should I sacrifice when these other people don't have to? Why should I be called upon?" Anyone who takes that narcissistic attitude, well guess what, we're all going to be on the same sinking ship.

Luckily in Chicago and the Midwest, although things are bad, they aren't as bad as they are on the coasts. The real estate bubble didn't get as large here. Less of our economy was dependent on things that were real estate related. Times are tough and tax revenues are down but I think we're situated to not go down as far down and to come back up quicker. We'll see.

I'm very hopeful. I'm optimistic. I mean, I think we're into some tough times. The next year to year and a half is going to be tough. We need to see a complete revamping of the things that brought us here like the lack of regulation in the financial sector where greed was allowed to run rampant. Lots of people got very rich and the rest of us got screwed and handed the check at the end of the day. Part of me still holds on to a little bit of that hippie-ish socialist idealism from my youth. Of course entrepreneurial efforts should be rewarded, but there needs to be some sort of balance. Do you really need two yachts and eight houses? When is enough enough? Does Bill Gates really need 43 billion dollars?

I think perhaps in our aging, when all of the great social narcissists of the baby boom generation start to face their mortality, we'll start to see the state of things we're leaving for our children. Then there will be changes. Either that or they better buy all their kids a lot of sun block–buy stock in something like that.

It's a funny thing. What I see, not just in my job, but in my friends and across society as I view it on a daily basis is that some people are very hard hit by this and other people seem oblivious. Things are really bad. People's retirement incomes have been wiped out. I find it strange. I don't find that there's any universal sense of doom. I don't find that there's social unrest at the edges of society. At least not yet. Hopefully there won't be with the government taking steps to ensure that those most affected will be helped. We'll see. I think this thing is far from over.

078 Glenna A. Reyes
Chicago, IL

Glenna Reyes was 20 when we talked. From her vantage point on the threshold of adulthood, she was appropriately astonished. To be 20 in America is to be change-on-legs. The particulars for Glenna included her first experience grappling with being seen by the world as bicultural. Very recently, a journalist had pegged her as mixed-race and interviewed her regarding her response to Obama's election. The result was an article in the Chicago Tribune.

Glenna: Well, change...I guess for me it's not losing sight of the beginning, but moving in a different direction, on different path. I always say, "I want to be a different Glenna. This is the new Glenna." But in essential ways there'll never be a different Glenna. I'll still be me even as I change. So, I don't want to compromise what and who I am, and at the same time as I grow up, I need to change.

Everyone's different and everything's different. When change is necessary, we need to do it without compromising people's dignity. That means being respectful. My opinion is never the only one even if lots of people feel the way I do. Respecting other peoples' opinions is important.

What I love about America is that there's so much opportunity. Obama was on the radio a few weeks ago saying, "Now we have this opportunity to really do something new. Take a chance and do something that you would never have thought of before." He was reminding us that we have opportunity and that's what America was based upon. Like, I can go to whatever school I want—almost. And yes it is hard to find a job, but luckily I've found something that makes me happy and I don't have to be concerned about money as much. I also have a lot of support from the friends and family in my life so I have the choice to get help when I need it. At the same time I can choose to go off and do my own thing. I like that I can go wherever I want and know I have my brain and my heart and that's all I need to get around.

I guess I'm cautiously optimistic. I almost lost my job a few weeks ago, but we were saved by the bell. When it was uncertain, I was like, Wow! This is happening to me, and my group of friends, not just to the people on TV. What if I did lose my job? What if I looked and looked and kept on even when I thought it was never going to happen? To have that hope? At least I'm trying, and lots of people are going through the same thing, so we will help each other out. That's my optimism about it. We're all going through the same thing. Everybody understands this is hard. There's comfort in knowing that.

I went out on Saturday for the St. Patrick's Day Parade. I had to take the bus because my car was in the shop. There was this energy in the crowds. Like these drunk Irish people dressed in green were lost and everyone was just like trying to help them find what bus to take, which direction to go. There was a fun, generous feeling on the bus. That was nice.

What I enjoyed about the whole election process was that intelligent conversation was in the media and everywhere. Everyone was trying to learn about this stuff. Now I feel like that has kinda slowed down. It would be nice to have it pick up again—to be hearing about important issues and opportunities on cool radio stations, on youtube and everywhere. If we could get everyone back into wanting to get involved that would be one of the best social changes I could think of.

This is a time when Americans don't have as much security as we had hoped for. We have to rely on ourselves more. It is a time for trying hard; not a time to be lazy, sitting on your butt watching TV. Like the situation with the environment; that's changing the way we think about living, not just the way we vote. Maybe people are starting to realize we have to stop taking things for granted. The environment is not just America's problem. It's a world's problem. We have to work together. Twenty years from now, the environment will be the first problem affecting everybody. Whether we believe in global warming or not, people are seeing effects, and we have to do something about it.

A more personal change for me was being in an article in the Tribune18 about Obama being elected. First, it was strange being asked. I haven't really thought of myself as biracial. For the first time I am realizing that is how people look at me–as if that makes me have a certain viewpoint–as if my skin color has something to do with my viewpoint. I'm Glenna. This is Glenna. But maybe I need to embrace the different parts of myself that make me Glenna. I'm still trying to figure that out.

Before I was like, I'm not white and I'm not black. Like, I hang out with everybody. I talk with everybody. I studied Chinese and I'm not Chinese. Now I'm thinking I am a mix. I guess I would like to be comfortable with the mix. It makes me want to learn more about myself and my culture. I want to understand what parts of my beliefs and my upbringing have formed my morals and my opinions. I know I'm Puerto Rican and Jewish. I want to know how that difference matters.

I just had a random thought that one of my problems growing up was people assuming I was something. Like in high school, people thought I was African American. "Why weren't you in African American Club? Where were you?" I'm like, "I'm not African American!" And then people thinking I'm Cuban or something. My problem was telling them, "I'm Jewish and Puerto Rican." And they're like, "Jewish?" You know like, "You're Jewish?" Now people are like, "Oh, cool!" That's a change. People are less likely to say, "So, you are this, right?" They ask, "What are you?" So, that's something.

So there's all of that to think about. These days I mainly hope I choose the right major. I won't be happy if I haven't. I'm ready to immerse my brain in knowledge–to suck everything in and learn as much as possible so, hopefully, I can know more about myself. I've never challenged myself to 110% in school. I want to be able to hold my own and find the point where my power ends. Luck, fate, government, weather, will all have their effects. But I want to make sure I get to the point of fulfilling my own power.

18 "Nov 28, 2008 ... Glenna Reyes, 20, grew up on the North Side, the daughter of a Jewish mother and a Puerto Rican father. Glenna calls herself a 'Jewican.'" www.chicagotribune.com › News › Chicagoland

Road Note

St. Patrick's day in Chicago. Perfect. Now I was back on the road. I managed to get pretty lost in South Chicago until I saw the signs to Indianapolis. Wasn't I in Indianapolis yesterday? With a slight course correction I headed for Nebraska.

Here was another late arrival, this time in Omaha, Nebraska, my body none too pleased with the long driving hours I'd been keeping. Michael and Gretchen were waiting, taking advantage of this rare child- and work-free moment to sit and chat with one another. They welcomed me, handed me a warm mug of tea and offered a cushy place on the sofa. Michael and Gretchen are miracles.

Sitting in their den on the other side of midnight, they asked quiet, comforting questions about the *EX:Change* journey. Yes, I had come a long distance. I had listened to American lives. Knowing some of the acute trials these two had faced, I felt their peacefulness as we talked–a quality that can only come in the wake of many near-brushes with destruction.

This whole experience was showing me how, beyond any cliché or wishful thinking, every single one of us is a miracle. Think of it. We wake up to greet each day and year as it comes, somehow finding our way through. If nothing else, *EX:Change* provides data that is consistent enough to support the idea that our country is a collection of champions. We are definitely not perfect. We are not done. But in our joys and our sorrows we forge on.

079,080,081 Michael, Zachary & Hanna Bishop
Omaha, NE

Over the past years, Michael and Gretchen have sustained a marriage and a family through some of the toughest curves life can throw. Theirs have been the challenges to sanity and courage demanded for dealing with the fallout of addiction. Several years ago, Michael hit a bottom none of us would want to visit. It cost his job, but it gave him back his life. The next morning, Gretchen had left early for work. I awoke to the sounds of Zachary (8) and Hanna (4) playing before school. Over breakfast, Michael who these days is a stay-at-home dad, talked about change. Then I heard from the two young ones.

Michael: Change is a constant. Even when we think things are the same, they're changing. There was a period in my life where I thought I was stable, not changing. It turns out I was really changing; going further down the path of living each day more fearfully than the day before. The kind of change we're not very good at detecting is the subtle change. Since you were here last, you can see the change in my kids. I don't see it as well.

It's like the Tai Chi metaphor Master Frank talks about. Our stress level pokes us in the ribs. We say, "Ouch." We adjust ourselves, get used to it. Sometimes the poke comes back. We only notice if it comes back harder. Pretty soon, you arrive in Omaha and your chest is all tight, *(laughs)* and it's because of not noticing the little changes that occurred from the time you left Chicago.

Zachary and Hanna Bishop *Omaha, Nebraska*

In terms of change in America, I think there are ideals, principles we want to have stay the same. "We the people," democracy. But even our concept of democracy has changed and we haven't realized it because the changes have been incremental. We're now more of a corporate colony. We're driven by that power base. It's different from the monarchy we fought against in Revolutionary times. It's also different from the divided union we fought to prevent in the Civil War. It's even different from the aggressive world dominator we feared during the Cold War. We are not fighting now. Instead, we bow to special interests and corporate welfare. We don't see it that way. We see it as incentives and economic expansion. So, when I think about the founding principles, as much as I'd like to say integrity and freedom and those kinds of things stay the same, they probably change. Our conceptions of them change anyway.

Things always happen to put any period of time and its associated ideas in a different context. A classic example is what happened to me on March 3, 2005. If you'd asked me about it on March 31, I would have said it was the end of what I considered to be my life. Now, I look back and see it as the birth of a whole new life. I don't dread or fear the fact of that moment anymore. I'm at the place you were when I talked to you about it. You said, "Oh, thank goodness; now you can move on. It's over." Conceptually I understood that. I didn't have a chance to feel it or understand it back then. Now I do have that chance. I live the change that occurred as a result of that moment.

Was that a big moment (*claps his hands once*) of change? Yes. Then there is sitting here today and talking to you about it. What is more important, that big powerful moment or all the little evolutionary things that have occurred since? It's hard to separate that stuff out. Even getting to that big moment involved a series of evolutionary changes. Navigating the change is the key. Finding how to do that is my new task in life. For example, I'm trying to be more sensitive to the daily changes in my kids, not to overreact or insisting they arrive at some developmental point when they need time to progress. For myself, I'm doing the same thing.

I'm reminded of the Taoist story of the farmer who has a son. The son breaks his leg while plowing the field and the neighbors say, "Oh, that's awful." The father says, "It may be awful, it may be good. Who knows?" Then an army of recruiters comes and can't take his son because his leg is broken. The neighbors say, "Oh, that's so fortunate," and the father says, "It may be good and it may be bad." The story goes on. The whole point is to teach us. We react to a change in plans or an outcome. We can say, "Oh, that's awful." But we don't really know, yet. We may not ever know. It may not reveal itself until we're long gone from this earth.

So, as our country has gone from a democracy of the people to a democracy of corporate boards, is that good or bad? At what point do we sense that change? At what point do we evaluate it and say, "Is this really what we want?" There has to be some way to answer. It may be in our ability to plan. We get up each day with a plan. Then things change and we either adapt or get frustrated. We still have to deal with it.

The question is how? Do we deal with it through anger, resentment or retribution or with a stronger commitment to enact the plan the next day? More force? Less force? Or do we go back to the planning process and say, "OK. We're here now. What does that say about any future plan?" It's critical that we know when to stop, get quiet and take stock, and we're terrible at that in this society. Just look outside at the trucks going by. We can hardly sit still let alone be still. And it's the everyday kinds of stillness that we need.

I read something in USA Today. "Was the war in Afghanistan a mistake?" In 2001 hardly anybody thought it was a mistake. Today, a lot of people think it was a mistake. I looked at that and I was astounded. I think about all the changes our country has gone through and how we abandoned our commitment, right or wrong, to helping that country change. Whether what we were doing was mostly in our interest is a separate issue. I do think women and children in Afghanistan are better off because of our initial efforts, but we couldn't stay quiet enough to focus on our original motive to help.

Part of being quiet is recognizing we are really only capable of doing one thing at a time. As individuals, as a society, as a collective. Any time we're trying to do more, we get ourselves in trouble. (*big laugh*) Master Frank talks about that all the time. I'm here talking to you and then in my head I'm remembering back three years. That means I'm no longer here talking to you anymore. I'm mentally three years ago. I can't do both.

We pride ourselves on doing more than one thing at a time. The better multitasker you are the more admirable it is. That's a change that we need to assess–a pinch that is getting to us in an evolutionary way. We don't even notice it anymore. It's a scary thing to have a society of little waterbugs that skit, skit, skit, skit.

It goes back to the question, "What remains the same?" You have to focus on the moment and you have to focus on the big picture. We have to have some ability to see linkages. If I take this step, what direction will I go? What's the developmental trajectory? If I'm off now, I could be a lot further off in the future. It's like teaching these guys to ride bikes. They want to look down at the wheel. I keep having to coach them, "See where you're going and your wheel will follow." As individuals and communities and a globe we need to do more of that.

MC: I've been driving around the country talking to people, American people. I ask them what the word "change" means. So, when I say the word "change" what do you think?

Zachary: Like different things and

Hanna: I think something. That things are changing.

MC: How do you know when things are changing, Zachary?

Zachary: Because it looks different a little bit and it feels different.

MC: What have you noticed that changed?

Zachary: That we have a black president.

Hanna: And we have fish instead of two cats. We used to have no flowers and now we do.

Zachary: Like changing clothes.

Hanna: Or changing a light bulb.

MC: What about the words "the same." When I say, "the same" what does that mean to you?

Zachary: It means never different, never apart. Before Barack Obama got elected, we had all white presidents.

MC: So that was always the same. Is there something that you like to have stay the same?

Hanna: The same meatballs.

Zachary: I want my school to be the same instead of changing to another school because right now I like my school and I don't want to move to a different one. I might have to and I might not have to.

MC: What about you, Hanna, what do you like having stay the same?

Hanna: Our house. My animals.

Zachary: Stuffed or real?

Hanna: Stuffed. And my pictures.

082,083 Two Starbucks Baristas
York, NE

The Bishops were off to school, and I was back on the road to Denver. Michael had poured coffee at the breakfast table, but now that I was behind the wheel I was ready for another cup. Keen as a turkey vulture, I scanned the roadways through Lincoln and another hour further onto the plains. Finally, several miles outside of York, NE – barely a blip on the prairie's flat screen – I spied an obelisk the height of a satellite tower. On top, way up high, was a giant green disc. "A mirage?" I wondered out loud. Providence was on my side. Starbucks. Two sunlit baristas tended, in that very Starbucks way, to tasks behind the counter. The first was an immigrant from Eastern Europe, probably in her thirties. The second was younger and local. "Born and raised in York, Nebraska" she said.

Barista I: The media have a very bad habit of exaggerating the negative. We get the wrong picture and start thinking no one can be trusted and that the country is doomed.

Barista II: Yeah. Really good luck with your trip. We need it. We need to know what Americans are really thinking.

Road Note

Since the 1950's the abundance of gasoline and the establishment of the highway system in America have made it possible to maintain friendships across thousands of miles. Things are changing. Limitations both physical and political may soon render road trips a thing of our past. I remember first having this thought in the 1970's when, as Clarke Kemp (051) mentioned back in Jackson, we were warned about oil and other energy shortages by President Carter. I had logged a lot of miles during the years since. I became friends with our country, its National Parks and cities, and visited people I hoped to know forever. This time I was much more aware of the precious privilege of taking such a journey.

Down I-80, just east of Kearny, Nebraska, a highway sign in official green-with-white lettering read, "Road built with 47,000 recycled tires." Who knew? Then just outside Lexington, another official sign announced the opportunity to visit the Heartland Museum of Military Vehicles. I did stop, but not to visit the museum. My interest was pulled instead towards the Sandhill cranes resting in the neighboring farm pond. Michael (079) had told me of these incredible birds. "It really is amazing luck to be on I-80 now," he said. "They're right in the middle of spring migration." I had begun to see these Cranes hundreds of miles earlier – feeding in fields or perfectly synchronized in high flight. Their migration seemed definitely worth the time to stop and give a few minutes outside the car to watching these beings. They too were in the middle of change.

I looked toward the pond. Hundreds of lanky birds rested there. In the background sat the irregular shapes of military tanks and transports. Spurred by a breeze or simply on a whim, small clusters of cranes would take flight. They rose up out of the water, stretched their wings in achingly delicate arcs, glided a few moments on the afternoon air and surrendered again to the surface of the pond. There is something to be said for rest stops.

Back in the car, the road moved easily now. Soon I was snaking into foothills of the Colorado Rockies. Snow covered peaks burst sporadically into view. Just that quickly, I was done with another day's drive and safe in the Conifer, Colorado, home of yet another friend of a friend, Rachel, who works as an obstetrician. We visited over a late dinner.

Rachel awoke and left very early the next morning to usher another batch of babies into the world. That left me with a cat warm and purring on my lap. Both of us sat gazing out the south wall of windows watching a contagion of purple shadows rise into the blush of sky. I contemplated the Rocky Mountains – their courage and endurance in igneous relief. The tallest I could see from that morning was Pike's Peak.

084 Janice Gould
Colorado Springs, CO (via Tucson)

My friend Janice Gould lives at the base of that mountain. Janice is a professor and a poet. She is a musician. She is a descendant of the Konkow band of the Maidu Tribe of Northern California. She is life partners with Mimi another poet who is also a teacher and librarian. Janice had agreed to an interview back in Tucson, much earlier on the trip. I place her words here, because when we talked in Arizona she was just days from moving to take a position in Colorado.

Janice: I have to bring it back to the personal because I don't know the big picture, yet. My partner and I are changing right now because we're moving out to Colorado. I've been thinking about how change is not just what happens to you, it's also about the way your change affects other people.

Being hired at University of Colorado–Colorado Springs is change for me and it's change for them. They were wanting to change. Hiring a Native American faculty person is part of that change. Already I have brought some change to them and they've brought change to me. It's not a one-way street when you change. There are always reciprocal things going on.

I went back to school for two and a half years after my doctorate and started to really understand what I like and what I want to do. Making it real is the hard part–finding the ideal teaching situation. Getting a job is a big sign of positive change for me. As a person who's been underemployed for more than ten years, it is a huge change to have a full-time tenure-track job and the sense of security that that will bring. It's a sign for me that I've changed, too.

In many ways, things have fallen in line. There's going to be a reality that sets in. That may be where the real nuts and bolts of change happen. I will have to figure out if I have the resources inside myself to deal with these changes. I'll need to work with what's demanded by new circumstances–especially the things that are hard to deal with. Confrontations arise with people that you don't wish for, ever. But they happen. Then there's dealing with a whole institution. All of that stuff is hard to do. Like a lot of people, I'd just as soon insulate myself and not ever have to deal with those kinds of things. I'd like to protect myself, protect my heart. But, it's not going to be possible.

I'll make it with the things I rely on like the sense that I can depend on my friends for emotional sustenance, for reality checks. And I can always go back to the sources that enrich me like poetry or music or the outdoors. I would say my relationships with other people are my most valuable constant but all of these things are continuances in my life. Even if each of those things changes in its own incremental ways, it remains part of the fabric of my world and the way I live my life.

There's a part of me that's into reading the paper every day. I think about the difficulties in the kinds of changes we really need politically, economically, and culturally. As a nation we have been starved for true enrichment. People want to feel spiritually enriched. Not religiously enriched necessarily, but spiritually enriched so that they can face each day with some sense of hope that there is a way to move through and to be there for your loved ones, for your kids, your family, your community.

Janice Gould *Colorado Springs, Colorado*

We're going to face some hard years with all of that. If we want to make the shift to hopefulness in this country we will have to do more than ride the wave of the change that we started with the 2008 presidential election. We will need to have the commitment to go to the really hard places where it's not going to feel that easy to get through. And we will have to do it as a people.

We've had a lot of entrenched negativity. The Hopi people say that you have to wake up every day and feel cheerful, feel happy and have some gratitude for the day. When it's hard times for people, that is very hard to do. We have to reach inside somewhere and find cheer and gratitude. Maybe it must come from building it first inside yourself, but it's also from building gratitude with other people so that we can do the hard work together.

I think that's it.

085 Sharon Wright
Las Vegas, NV (via Washington, D.C.)

My route took me to Salt Lake City and on to Portland. Well north of Las Vegas. Nonetheless I'm placing Las Vegas resident Sharon Wright's interview here. Sharon and I met in the lobby of a Washington, D.C. Marriot earlier in the month. She was on her way home that afternoon and looking forward to seeing the kids she helps with reading in a local elementary school. Sharon was raised in the San Francisco Bay Area. She and her husband have now been in Las Vegas several decades. There, she has a successful business and her husband is a professor. The couple was in D.C. for an event associated with new administrative appointments.

Sharon: I'm very interested in the Holocaust. I read The Diary of Anne Frank twice. There are so many movies depicting what happened to the Jewish people. My friend, she's Caucasian plus we're really close, she kept saying, "Sharon you've got to go see the Holocaust Museum." I said, "OK, but Deb, I'm really disappointed the Smithsonian doesn't have anything to show the experiences of slaves." I said, "This country was built on slaves." She said, "They're going to suppress that." And I said, "You know what, they don't have to anymore. We're going to make it happen." It's important that there is a museum where you could go in and see how slavery actually was. Right? That would be a change.

The first time I saw slave chains was when my best college friend, Tony, took me to an African museum this black guy in LA owned. He had part of a slave ship. He had slave chains. He had whips. He had everything. It actually brought you to a realization of what really happened. If you would have seen those. So, here we are in the nation's capital. We have all these museums about how our founding fathers established America. Let's come on and tell the truth about slavery, too. We're changing so let's bring out the truth.

This change means we're coming full circle almost. We're coming to a point where we all know what's happened–where it's time to build the country over and do the right thing.

I don't mind helping. We have money. I pay my taxes. In fact, I owe my check when I get home. I don't mind. Don't be so greedy, because what you do with greed is you hurt people. There are people homeless, people losing their jobs. It doesn't matter what color they are. They need help.

I go to little communities where there are black children whose parents are in prison, jail. The stories they tell me, I can't believe it. But I always talk to them about hope and change. I talk to them about Obama. I'm going to show them this when I go back (*reaches for picture of herself w/ Harry Ried*). I'm going to tell them about Harry Reid. A lot of people say, "Why is Obama talking about education?" He's talking about education because you've got to educate the poor so we can all live together.

My husband is a commissioner on the Juvenile Justice Board. I didn't want him to do that. He was appointed the last eight years to do studies and help people get jobs. I was scared. I said, "You're going in and out of these prisons. I don't want you to do that. Will these people know where we live?" I was raised in San Francisco and now I've lived in Las Vegas for 30 years. I was born upper middle class in San Francisco. I had ballet, piano, all the little lessons; debutant, whatever, college. So to me, when he said he was going to go to these prisons, I was scared to death.

After he started and I went with him, I found myself talking to people just like I'm talking to you. Because my husband's a professor he said, "We have to educate these kids so they don't come back out on the streets." They have a choice to get educated in the prison. Those that don't choose that are the ones that don't want to be helped.

I don't know if you ever saw Jeff Henderson[18] on Oprah. He is a black chef that went to prison and he's famous now. My husband asked Mr. Henderson to help him with his work on the Juvenile Justice Board. They helped each other and started culinary arts and other programs with at-risk youth in the community.

Now, the big huge change is that Obama is the president. I never thought a black man would be president. We were masked for eight years. Now, everybody wants change and they want to know the truth. Obama keeps telling us more truth, more truth. But nobody really wants to hear the truth because, "Oh, we're in this mess?" We've been in this shape for a long time, people. It didn't happen overnight. It didn't happen yesterday. It didn't even happen a year ago. This has been going on and on. And the last Administration didn't suppress just one race. They suppressed the whole country. The whole country was prostituted. That's how I feel about it.

Just the fact that we voted for Obama, that tops it all. Think about it. It wasn't just black people; it was also white people that voted him in. Everybody was like, "You know what, we're tired. Sorry. Sorry Sarah Palin." She wasn't for us and she'll never be for us. Never. Because she has the old way of thinking.

We all have new ways. I mean, look at you traveling around. Look what you're doing. It's wonderful. It's great.

Road Note

I didn't make it all the way into Nevada, but the road west continued to weave the EX:Change together in ways that were both awe inspiring and quite practical at the same time. The first 150 miles past Denver relentlessly shifted their breathtaking vistas. The front range of the towering Rockies eventually yielded to the red rock of the Maroon Formation which in turn gave way to Glenwood Canyon. Tucked

---

18   Jeff Henderson. *http://www.foodnetwork.com/the-chef-jeff-project/index.html*

among these giants of topography lay every Colorado ski resort you could ever long for.

I got lost again, this time in the desert of Western Colorado. I pulled off the highway at a weather-beaten frame building behind a faded Sinclair sign. I looked out at a single gas pump with four dusty Harleys parked nearby. It was my first sign of people in awhile. I walked in the shadowy entry around the corner to find an odd pod of family and friends – in all sizes, with few teeth, but generous smiles and expert travel directions. It turns out I was in Mack, Colorado, the last stop for services on I-70.

Like too many others in rural America, the folks gathered at the gas station were working people who were out of work. In the filtered light of the last day of winter, I stood watching the unique choreography of overused hands holding mugs or gesturing into the air above the Formica tabletop. Besides giving instructions for getting me to the right road, the Americans at the Sinclair station in Mack shared their unified desire for change. They want work. "It's good to know we've always got coffee and our friends here," the tall woman said, filling the pot for another round. "It would sure be good for work and income to be that reliable again."

Thanks to the citizens of Mack, I was back on course. with a trio of highway signs narrating the miles: *Leaving Colorful Colorado*, *Entering Utah*, and my all time favorite use of tax dollars, *Eagles on the Highway*.

086 Paris Mullen
Seattle, WA

By the end of March, I was back in the Pacific Northwest and on a midweek trip to Seattle. Between meetings, I sat in yet another coffee shop. That afternoon, *EX:Change* serendipity and the otherwise empty store brought Paris Mullen. Paris is, by my assessment, the quintessence of new millennium scholar and gentleman. He is an inspirational speaker, a teacher and an environmental activist. Paris is a gay African American man with enthusiasm and vision that radiate from his deep commitment to what it means to be related to every being on the planet.

Paris: I say, "Life. New life." My associations are all good. Obviously there's bad change in light of where we are in the world, in this nation, and in my community. But I say, "Life." Change means letting go the old ways in our government–the old way of looking at the world.

I'm very involved with sustainable living, so when I think of change I think of old ways that have put our communities and consequently our globe in a disadvantaged place. It's so cliché but I think of living green. How can we be better stewards of our natural resources? Politically, change is just a big overhaul. I don't want to throw out the baby with the bath water, but there were a few big ticket things that need to go. The Iraq war, for example. Another thing would be how we define marriage in this country, insurance rights and partner rights and all those things.

I was rooting for change, but I don't think I knew what it would do to me. I'm seeing how I've got to change. Just because I want something doesn't mean I'm ripe for it when it actually happens. My ways of thinking are having to evolve, change and maybe even being inconvenienced so that I can contribute to what is greater. Sustainable living is a good example. How much do I drive or do I drive? Where do I buy my produce? From how far away is my food shipped? How can I affect carbon in the air? In the past it's been, "Oh yeah, that's great change. I want it." But actually being in it, you realize there's some skin you've got to put in the game. Before, it was more of a theory. Now it's "OK. The work's coming, too."

In all of it, I want the U.S. to remain united as a democratic system with due process and electing our officials. We may need some additional checks and balances but I'm for a country for the people, by the people where we have basic regard for one another. Most important is our human connection. That really came through with 9/11. We had to get down to what was really essential. What do you really have? In the end of the day all we have is each other. We're realizing that. We've got to stick together.

Looking at where the economy is today, we're back to, "OK. What really matters?" Is it our things or our people? You have yourself. We have one another and we have the planet we're on. These connections are priceless. It's funny how a lot of people want to change, but it always takes that few to stand up for it. When the leaders show up, the people come out of the woodwork. My point is that as far as change is concerned, it is helpful to know there are others who want it and are doing something about it. Strength in numbers, I guess.

Keeping connection in mind, I'm for stem cell research. It will help so many people. A good sign of change would be overturning bans on that science. There are certainly both sides of the debate, and I'm for going with the science of it. Next I support same-sex marriage. There was a law passed to protect same-sex partnership rights. That small change is helpful. Then, as I said, I'm very active and interested in environmental policy. We need to change what is happening with large industry, with manufacturing.

Other than that, I'm going to say something funny. I really think the approach to policy and politics is becoming much more accessible for everyday citizens. I can see it in the way the first family carries themselves. Like Michelle Obama. She's obviously a very intelligent woman, still there's an approachability about her. Even in her dress. And the president was just on Jay Leno and he's on the covers of Vogue, of GQ, Esquire. That's where the people are. He's become a pop culture icon in that way. There are two sides to that, but the point is we can see the regular person in that position who is more like us.

The resounding theme of this time? Anything (*laughs*)–have faith that anything is possible! Regardless of longstanding laws, spoken or unspoken, written or unwritten, anything is possible. You may not see the change you want in your lifetime, but I'm telling you it is completely possible. I can't, I can't, I can't say that enough. Many said we would never have an African American president. Look what happened. Around him there are a lot of other firsts. In his Cabinet, in the White House there are ethnic and gender firsts. Everything is turned upside down right now, and in good ways.

Change is messy. It's kind of like birthing a child. I've never birthed a child, but I can't imagine the process is ever neat. Still it's a beautiful thing. It takes lots of concentration and faith. Things happen that I'm sure a woman doesn't expect. There's science to it and there's art. It's flawless. It does its own thing and there's always that, "We didn't know" factor–that spirit in it all. That's what we have now in this country. A lot of birthing–a lot of, "We didn't know" factor–a lot of spirit. Yeah, it's messy, but the product is new life.

So when it comes down to it, there's no certain script. It's all improvisation and faith. What we know for sure is that we were tired of the way things were being done. We have an idea where we want to go. We're not sure what's around the corner, but we know this–we don't want to go back. What we want is life.

BACK IN NORTHWEST OREGON
—
4.1 to 4.30.2009

- When you say the word change what do you mean?
- Alongside change, what is important to have remain the same?
- What would be signs that positive change is occurring?

BACK IN NORTHWEST OREGON
4.1 to 4.30.2009

I was back in Portland at last- eighty-six voices, seventy days and 10,000 miles later. I had traversed changes in landscape in all kinds of weather and I was still vibrating from barreling down I-80 through Iowa and across I-70 out of Denver amidst the constant giganto-truck traffic. The Mini made it the whole way home and was now in the shop... for four weeks. No matter. I was back safe and sound and ready to look for the final fourteen interviews.

There exists a common misconception to think you know someone when you really don't. What I do know is the story I have in my mind about a person, whether or not it is entirely accurate. The truth is that we all have stories of each other. When we first meet we apply conscious and unconscious ways of assessing this new person so we can begin our story of them. This is a very natural social impulse that most often contributes to building relationships.

For instance, I may be in the checkout line at the supermarket and glance toward the cashier. Without any bad intentions or judgments, I find myself developing a story about that person. Maybe it's only based on an observation like, "That guy has enormous earrings." Other things, including visual and cultural references or vague impressions contribute to the story I wrap around him. These impressions may or may not be right, but they occur without any particular motive or bias.

Over time, if I enter into more substantial interaction with the cashier and our regular contact develops into a friendship, my inner story grows. I gain new information with each interaction, but sometimes I may find that I'm not willing to change the story I've started in my mind. In those instances, I can end up disrespecting him by refusing to change my original version of who I think he is. This can happen with anyone -- my work colleague, my next-door neighbor, the president, my daughter. When I insist on keeping my story, what began as innocent observation can develop into judgment. New information can be difficult to accept, because there are things we don't want to be true about the person across from us. Whether it is with close friends or relatives who share news that concerns us or with strangers who behave in ways that challenge our stereotypes, we can run into difficulty when we refuse to modify our stories.

For example, Anna (063) and I both came to her interview knowing that my cousin, a conservative Republican, had talked to each of us about both the project and our political leanings. She had agreed to the interview and was willing to talk candidly about her affinity for Sarah Palin regardless of the fact that we tend to vote differently. That takes courage and openness. Anna's interest in promoting dialogue, her devotion to the dignity of women, and her concern for the environment surprised me as significant components of her value system. These things didn't "match" the story I had in my mind about her. Again and again, the unique range of ideas and perspectives in many of the

EX:Change voices both astonished me and called me out on my own biases.

Back in Washington, DC, Andy Walton (069) illustrated this kind of listening-in-practice when he described his congregation at Capitol Hill Presbyterian; "We connect across party differences." This ability to relate is an interest so many of the *EX:Change* voices have emphasized. Connect is one word used to describe this sense of collaboration and the idea that no matter our differences, we are fundamentally all on this trip together. Everyday Americans can be compelled by political structures and dominance. But even as we participate in those systems, the practical concerns and experiences of our daily lives continue to reveal the inescapable magnificence and the ruthless trials of just being human on this planet together.

Tara (012) and Brett (013) in Walnut Creek, CA delivered the first model of what putting action behind the words (*connect, compromise, collaborate*) could look like. Without thought to political and social divisions, Tara and Brett live a friendship of speaking and listening across their differences.

Across the country, I have spoken with a mix of familiar faces and complete strangers. All continue to teach me about the art of listening. People are so hungry to talk with someone who is actually paying attention. Time and again, being listened to set them at ease and they quickly shifted to speaking with candor and untroubled openness. Maybe this is universal. We want to tell our truth. Not necessarily defend it, just tell it.

In many of these voices there is evidence for a willingness, or even a longing just to *relax*, most clearly in terms of faith, mystery, and spirit. Justin Leak (070), my mentor Mayme Porter (044), Mrs. Laura Gamble (034), and Se-ah-dom Edmo (005) are just four of the voices who speak to the respite and courage available in the ineffable constant that resides silently, even invisibly in all place and time. By whatever name, the calm this presence allows makes many of the Americans I've talked with more capable of responding to the challenges and complexities of change. They draw on and trust their faith in the face of the unexpected, assured that they will at least take some sort of initial action and then they will go from there.

This courage is reflected in the inner sense of resolve and perseverance so prevalent in the American character. Russell Hewes (049) and Colleen Suwara (026) expressed concern with what they see as diminished optimism and purpose. Russell said, "People spend way too much time focusing on things they don't want." Similarly, Colleen's wish for change was to see more optimism in people, "more of the positive." "When you're fearful," she said, "you can't change. When you're fearful, you can't move. You can't breathe." These two hardworking citizens give a clear illustration to the hypotheses of happiness that psychologists Jane (020) and Collie Conoley (021) described in Santa Barbara. American optimism is real – even when it is optimism for a future of renewed optimism.

Change can be quite frightening. It reminds us of the vulnerability that is a fact of being human. Change is relentless, challenging us in all facets of our lives – at work, in our families, with friendships, and in immediate circumstances of health or safety. In all of this, there are small echoes of that most profound, evasive and unavoidable change – death.

At their kitchen table with its sweeping view of the Santa Barbara hills, I relished the banter and humor of Marshall (018) and Carol Ackerman (019) as they shared their observations of American culture. For these octogenarians, every day holds death as a close companion. Their years of wisdom give them a gracious tenderness when it comes to the topic of change, but age does not diminish their passion for justice, for the health and happiness of every person sharing this globe. Marshall and Carol affected me like Elders can, and I found myself inspired and heartened for my own aging.

Whether we admit it to ourselves or not, death is a constant. It does not discriminate according to race, political party, religion, class or gender. The only guarantee with being born is that death will follow. As they speak of change, the *EX:Change* voices describe all manner of human annoyances, challenges, and disagreements. In their words I am also hearing a quiet awareness that it all boils down to fear. We are afraid of difference, afraid of one another. We polarize, we isolate, and we judge each other- partly as a way to avoid our fear of the biggest change of all, death.

Americans vote Republican and Democrat. Some vote in other parties. Americans are elderly and young, working and unemployed. Many of us have discernable accents. We have different shades of skin and textures of hair, and because bodies are vulnerable we experience various degrees of physical challenge. Naturally, we like some people better than others and allow them to come closer as friends and companions. The 86 people who have spoken up to now as part of the *EX:Change* seem weary with the antagonism that comes with separation and polarity.

They also have the fundamental impulse toward kindness and affiliation that we all have. It is the kindness that shows up in the way we are forever telling ourselves stories about who other people are. *EX:Change* is showing me that most Americans really want to know more in answer to that curiosity. We want to know each other, to move past the fear and separation that too often we can't see because it has become so habitual. We'd rather be affiliated and cooperative than hostile, divided and unnecessarily at cross-purposes. Maybe we're changing. Maybe a sign of this change is that we Americans are learning to listen.

087 Mohammad Bader
Portland, OR/SE Belmont Street

Mohammad Bader is a counselor in Portland, OR. He works mostly with geriatric clients. Mohammad was raised in Jerusalem. He is Palestinian. He is married to and U.S. citizen who is also a Presbyterian. They are raising their young children with both Christianity and Islam. Mohammad and I have been friends for almost a decade. I remember first hearing his stories of unexpected visits by the FBI in the months following 9/11. "They said they were randomly contacting American families, but I never heard about it from anyone outside the Middle Eastern community."

Mohammad: When I think of change, well unfortunately the word that comes to my mind is disappointing. I was thinking that change would equal hope. But as you ask me about this today I'm thinking there are a whole bunch of unknowns and uncertainties. At this point we are in a holding pattern with a lot of difficult things coming.

I'm optimistic by nature so I keep thinking, like a Pollyanna, that it's going to get better. But, you wake up every day and you hear of one tragedy after another with layoffs and things like that. The ironic thing is that 22-25 years ago, before I came to this country, I was not attached to material things. Now, these things provide me a sense of security, cushion, and predictability. If I were younger I would not be as concerned with good health care or having a crappy car.

The other thing I see about change regardless of the economy, is the polarization of going to extremes one way or the other. You see people getting more religious, more fanatic. Especially as a Palestinian. Going back into the homeland, there's a progression toward more conservative, more orthodox ways of thinking. Even some of my friends are returning to religious thinking, feeling they need that kind of security. When I talk with my family back in Jerusalem, a lot of them speak of returning to that kind of life.

When I grew up in the 70's my sisters were not as religious. They did not worry about rituals. They did not worry about certain customs or how they got dressed. Now they've changed their attire, the way they get dressed, the way they think about things. My sister now tells me, "I didn't understand my religion when I was young." The younger kids, her children and grandchildren are more religious, too. They feel religion provides the answer. In some instances it helps them feel more fulfilled. Since there's not enough control and the economy there is so bad, it gives them a sense of community.

It is important to have things that keep you stable but it's different for everybody. I want to have some control over my healthcare and my assets. I want to be able to have the basic freedom of expressing my opinion and practicing my religion. The safety aspect is important–to make sure I and my family are not subjected to crimes. I want my friends to be around because it takes a long time to develop a friendship. I hope to keep my job because that gives me a sense of accomplishment and identity. For some of us men–well, for me, my job is everything. I'm learning to spend time with the family and to enjoy other things but my work is my security blanket–I want it to be there.

It's very different than what I grew up with. I grew up under occupation, so at least we had some healthcare. Even when I lived for awhile in Amman, Jordan I could go to a clinic that would at least prescribe something. You'd pay a symbolic fee for diagnosis and medicine. They did not kill you. Here, it's a concern for lots of people.

Still, coming here in 1987 was a very hopeful change. I found the ability to be lifted out of semi-poverty. I wouldn't say we lived in abject poverty, but I was raised in a type of poverty. My family probably wouldn't like for me to say that, but when you look at the pictures of my house, it does not look like a rich person's home. My parents were custodians for a school in the Old City of Jerusalem2. We lived in a small house on the school grounds–one bedroom, a very small kitchen and a common bathroom that all the neighbors used. We had one spigot of water for all of us to use. We had to carry propane tanks to fire the stove in our house. Technically, our house didn't have a bathroom or running water. My dad brought in water and electricity in the 70's. We didn't have TV until the mid 70's.

We were not a rich family, but education was important for my dad. He wanted to make sure I got educated. So the opportunity for me to come to the United States was a big thing. I say that to people. I say, "Regardless of all the bad stuff here, all the problems, I think this is still a great place to live." Where I lived as a little kid it was a struggle to do lots of things. You had to carry papers and, as a Palestinian in Jerusalem, you had them checked all the time. Here you have law and order to abide by. There are some corruption problems, for example with cops, but I've seen problems with cops in other countries that are so much worse. Here there is law in place against corruption. Corruption happens, but there are controls and criteria.

I work in social services. These days when I ask people, "What do you want to do?" they say, "I want a place to live. I want to learn. I want to work." Live, learn and work. These are three things that give people satisfaction. Good signs of change would be people having places to live, learn and prosper. I want this generally and also as a dad expecting my kids to go to college. I even sometimes think it would be good for me to go back to college.

Unfortunately in all of this, money is a sad and serious thing. I want to have happiness as my highest value—joy and fun, (*laughs*) respectfulness, caring. If I were to choose, these would be on the top of the list for me. Then you find out you need money to have joy—to maintain a living environment, to secure education. But what I want is hope, happiness, to play and have fun, and enjoy the scenery.

After all these years, I've gotten into kayaking. It is easy to forget, even in the metropolitan area of Portland, that there are a lot of wonderful places nearby. I don't know what got me kayaking, but that's a positive. It does not cost a lot or damage the environment. That's something joyous—something I'd like to remain the same.

088 David F. Jones
Palatine Hill Road/Portland, OR

To be an American man is to be acutely aware of purpose. Purpose, in turn is intimately related in our culture with work. Mohammad spoke of this experience. David Jones speaks of it as well. David and I met on the steps outside his seasonal workplace at a college in Portland, OR. David, an African American man in his early 50's, works for a paycheck and benefits in food service. He is also an entrepreneur – an independent small-business person.

David: When I first started hearing the word change I was thinking "Democrats and not more Republicans. No more Bush. Time for a change." Of course change can mean good and bad. George Bush was change. That don't mean it's good. I wasn't even a fan of his dad, so I knew I wasn't going to be a big fan of the next one.

It's early still to know about this new administration. I haven't seen anything negative. You've got to give Obama time. He walked into a big mess. You don't just go clean up a mess like that in a couple of months. He can probably stay in office for eight years and never clean it all up. So far, I think he's going to do ok.

I've never been big on politics to be honest, but I know I don't want it to stay the same. I would like to see people get back to work. There's so many people out there without jobs. More and more. When I was a boy and you were a girl, there was always that old random guy—the random bum who wanted some change. Now, it's high school kids, people from all walks of life asking for change. You can't walk the sidewalks without someone stepping to you asking. It wasn't like that 10 years ago. I notice that. And a lot more people are sleeping outside.

There was a time when you could open up the newspaper and there were job listings all the way down. "I'll go get that job right there. I may not like it, but at least it's there." But now you open up the paper and there's not even that job. So, change. I guess I really don't know what he meant when he said that. I think we're already in a recession, we just don't admit it.

I don't know what it was like back in 1933, back in the Great Depression, but I think we're there. We're in debt. Like my hometown in Las Vegas. They went and built all those homes five, six years ago. Big City. Now all of them are empty. All I know is the booming came to a halt. There are foreclosures, people can't afford their mortgage, and there are no jobs.

I grew up in Las Vegas. I could see booming and busting almost any time. Like 9/11 when they took all the airplanes down out of the sky; that turned Vegas into a ghost town. You need the airplanes to land in Vegas every 5 minutes in order for the city to work. It's a different kind of city. It's dropping in Vegas now, too because people don't take vacations like they did 10-15 years ago. My kids both live there. They're doing OK, though. Just like me.

I don't go looking for jobs. I create jobs for myself. If there's no job to be had then you have to create your own. I did that 10 years ago on my 40th birthday. That's the day I got my very first e-mail account. I work on line. Eventually I will do that full-time. I don't care what they say about a home-based business, it's hard to stay home all day every day.

Still, since 2000–1999 I haven't worked food service in the summer. This job is hourly and keeps me going, but eventually I'll quit and be my own person. I never had any faith in the economy anyway, so I started my own thing. I'm self-employed. I would love to see everybody get a job and start buying stuff again. I need people to buy product from me. See what I'm saying? Last summer was OK, but I know people don't have money.

One way I know it will be different for me is because I lived to see a black president. Not only that, they guy's younger than me. (*laughs*) It's been kind of a shock. I still half way don't believe it. I thought something big was going to happen after the election. I didn't know what. I was afraid someone was going to get things riled up, but everyone kept pretty regular. You never know. Like after the Rodney King thing–oh, people had to go nuts. But the Obama thing went smooth just like every other president.

The second time George Bush got elected–this was after 911–I wouldn't want to be president after that either. He had started the war, though, so I kind of was hoping, "Dude, you gotta get reelected. You've got to go finish that off." You know, really. You can't just start a war and then step. I was glad he got reelected so he had to deal with it.

But really, no matter who's president, as a person I'm better off every year. I get wiser as I get older. When I was younger I was much dumber. I guess everyone is. And it has nothing to do with who's the president or the economy or anything else. The more white hairs come out the wiser I get. (*laughs*) I don't have as much money as I did. Life isn't all about money. In fact back in the 70's when I was making minimum wage, I was better off than I am now. Back then I was able to save, but I can't save anything anymore. Every dime I make goes out on something. You just have to ride it out.

I will say I liked that big poster with "Hope." We definitely need a change in a good direction. Maybe we can get going that way. And yeah, I get wiser every day. I really do.

089 Avishan Saberian
NE Broadway Street/Portland, OR

Avishan Saberian is of a bridge generation, born in the U.S. to parents who emmigrated from Iran. In her early 20's, she is also a biology major, a big sister, a swim instructor for infants and a bit of a sage.

Avishan: Change doesn't have just one meaning. I see it in multiple ways. I see the scientific side because I study biology and work in a research lab. I see change with the way that organisms behave and evolve. And I see it in a physical way–in the way humans change physically. That's something we can see and evaluate–something that changes. Then, emotionally there's change and also culturally.

In biology change occurs as organisms evolve. They're born and they adapt to their environment. They learn to survive. So, change to me is a way of survival. Organisms acquire traits and pass them down to their offspring from generation to generation. If they are able to survive by changing they continue. The environment, the planet changes all the time. In that change the skills and traits an organism has acquired may no longer be necessary or adaptable. In those cases, the organism will die become extinct. That's how I see change, scientifically.

Physically, the cells of our bodies are constantly changing, eating each other and creating new cells. Change on the inside is reflected as our appearance. Like, I cut my hand the other day. It was an open wound. All of a sudden the neutrophils that take care of cuts came together. They were like, "OK. We're in action now and we've got to change this situation to heal this." No one tells the body to do that. It just changes by itself. It's amazing. And we humans like seeing things like that. We can measure change better when we see it. We can understand and accept it a little better.

When I think of emotional change, I think of maturation. A child doesn't have knowledge. It has innocence. It is influenced by its parents, other people and the things it sees. That's how it learns and grows. We learn values, morals, the right, and the wrong. Each of us then uses the skills and knowledge taken in early on to get through life later. I'm a swim instructor. I teach little kids. Even though they're just 6 months old I see the importance of how I connect with them emotionally. I teach them how to trust, and that can influence how they interact with people later on in life.

As small children, we never really know all of this is happening. For example, parents tell us, "This is right. This is wrong." But they have their own perspectives. They've come through their own influences to arrive at definitions of right and wrong. Definitions of right and wrong are where the most miscommunication happens. Meaning changes over time, over generations. People sometimes have a hard time understanding each other because even though we may go through similar situations we never have the same exact experiences.

So, emotionally, change is about adjusting. Sometimes we don't adjust. We want to find solutions really quickly. Over time it's possible to see that it's not just solution that's important, it's resolution. A solution is like, "This is the only way to do it." Sometimes following that thinking can cause more problems. A resolution comes from looking again. In the case of two people disagreeing, that means taking into account both sides–

both views–and coming to some consensus based on peace, reason and logic.

It has a lot to do with perspectives. Our perspectives change. How we see things, how we hear things change. Life repeats itself. We all wake up and have a day. How we choose to spend our time creates the uniqueness of each individual. It's unlimited, really. That's choice and that's change.

OK. Now for change culturally–oh, man–that's a big one. I'm Iranian. I have two Iranian parents, but I was born in America. Changes have taken place in Iran that I have not seen. Neither have my parents. The values and things they remember from their childhoods, they brought here. Like any organism, they use those to survive. They adapted, developed traits and passed those traits down to me and to my brother and sister.

However, the generation I'm in, we have American life and Iranian life. The children in the middle who aren't totally Iranian may have learned how to read and write or speak the language, but we don't understand the meaning like someone raised in Iran. We've had to adapt to survive in the environment of our country, America, while still feeling alright with being Iranian. One foot is in American life–we're American–and one foot is in our Iranian heritage. We're straddling this line, you know, these two sides. In the middle things like communication can get lost. The meanings of words change, especially in circumstances of immigration. Everything in that change falls into this bottomless abyss between the generations. Even the impossibility of being 100% American. I'm not–we're not. And we're not 100% Iranian, so seriously, what are we?

We're something that's changing to adapt. We're just an organism like everything else. We're all tied together. We're changing. There isn't any solution. We have to somehow find a resolution–resolving these two cultures and changing. Seems funny to say that–changing to survive.

The best way to survive is with serenity or peace. Being at peace with whatever happens. As long as you're in your right mind, you can know what's right for you as life keeps coming at you. Having that calming factor helps for knowing that no matter what happens I'm alright; as long as I'm breathing and I'm alive and I have my mind.

We each have a mind that changes to help us get through things. And we have a heart. There's always a chance to adapt. And the ground of it all is peace.

090 Dr. Dapo Sobomehin
Starbucks, S.E. Hawthorne Street/Portland, OR

Dr. Dapo (*as he asks to be called*) is Nigerian-American. He immigrated after coming to the United States when he was 19 years old as an exchange student from a small Yoruba village. That was in 1961. Across his career Dr. Dapo has served variously as a law enforcement officer, a religious leader, and an educational tutor. He is recognized throughout the city of Portland and the state of Oregon as an activist for African American children in schools. We sat together at a Starbucks on Hawthorne Street.

Dr. Dapo: I'm a Yoruba from Nigeria, West Africa. My name is Dr. Dapo.

Word, w-o-r-d, means a lot to the Yoruba. We live by the word. The Yoruba proverbs

Dr. Dapo Sobomehin *Portland, Oregon*

are important. They stay with me, because words are very important. We live the word. Americans keep away from that importance. Words don't stick. Americans don't live their word.

This change we talk about–Obama knew what he was talking about. I don't see anybody at present time who would disagree that something has to change. Change is a word. What is it in living? A word that has come to me is k-n-o-w, know. Know what that word, change, means. Know what this time means. Our getting together this morning to talk together, what does it mean? What is in the journey? Where are we going?

I have been in this country for a long time. I came here in 1961 as an exchange. I've been thinking about the people I met at that time. I collected from them wisdom. It was during the Cold War. There wasn't much physical war until we got into Viet Nam. I was at Georgetown University in D.C. Americans brought us to their homes. We were guests of the Soviet Embassy. We didn't know that Americans were watching other countries then. We were foreign students from all over the world. There was no separation. We didn't look at skin color. Nothing. We were just having the best time of our lives.

Look at what is happening to this wonderful country. Do American's really know what this country is about? Where we find ourselves? Do we know this place? What does it mean that Europeans came here and then brought people in shackles. What does it mean that when the Europeans got here, there were Native Americans–people they should have been very curious to get to know–to connect with and say, "OK. This is your land. Let's do it together." Instead it became disconnected.

You Europeans are here. You don't have to kill them. You're here. The whole place was the land of the Native Americans. Unfamiliar with European ways, but full of wisdom. Full of nature. Beautiful people. That is intelligence. That is holiness. To say, "We don't have to cure it. We don't have to mess it up. We just exchange. We have the technology, you understand the natural world." Yes. We change and exchange.

What change means to me is in the key point I am talking and writing on–together. We belong to each other in change. We work together. In community we are related to each other. When I talk about multiculturalism, that's what I'm looking for–that we do it together. With dignity, with respect, with knowledge of nature, together.

So the change we are talking about in America is a change of heart. To get to know my neighbor. To get to know that I belong to all folks. We are the same people. Yes, culture is a beautiful part of our lives. But it doesn't have to separate us. My mind still goes back to the village. Then from village to here. The biggest change of my life. Through it, I as an individual, as Dapo, am connected with all of you. I'm talking about that. The way Dapo has shifted through contact with Americans.

How in the world did my people come to Legos where there was Nigeria's only airport? The whole village moved to Legos to say goodbye to me. I was a little boy all alone. For the first time in my life I was going to the country of the King. I don't know where the Yoruba people got it, but they looked at Europe as the country of the King. My people, especially my grandfather, respected white folks so much. I began saying, "From what I see happening to Nigerians, what did my grandfather see in these folks?" Especially when Kennedy was killed. How can you possibly kill a wonderful man like that?

Then I arrived and I began to experience the loneliness of Americans. Americans are very lonely. There's too much separation. But I have been connected with Americans.

The connection is the constant. And I have been deeply troubled by the exclusion of the African Americans. That's what makes Americans lonely. Too many black people who are American do not see themselves as citizens of this place. They've been here for 400 years. Even the little kids feel like they don't fit. It's so deep, the separation and exclusion of the American people from themselves. That's what is holding us down.

Things will be changing when American people can talk about race. The president is talking about it. But he knows the power of words. It is up to individual consciousness to recognize, "That's my brother. He or she belongs here." It has to be done. We've been so blessed. I would like the African American kids to know that–to feel and trust it.

Of course, all of us take a lot of stuff for granted. But we can't take this country for granted. What we need to do then is to build a community. It is never too late. We're changing for our children's children so we can't know exactly how it will look then.

It is so simple, but it can't be found outside of us. It's here. There's nothing you can apply from the outside. You possess it. The infrastructure is already there. The foundation is there in every person. My optimism and belief in change is based on the Owner. We don't own this stuff. He gives everything. You and I didn't have any input on the creation. I don't knock it anymore. It's not an abstract. It's not an accident. We must move together. It doesn't mean that we are not going to upset each other, but we must get much better at living together. It's natural.

Road Note

"We must talk with each other about race," Dr Dapo had declared, echoing the sentiments of Kelvin Anderson (058) and TC Corbett (059) the young businessmen in Decatur, Emily Lopez (074) the professor on Long Island and Susan Stout (075) the forester in Warren, Pennsylvania. I now found myself in the parking lot of the small Oregon Counseling Center in Beaverton, about to interview another American who has been profoundly affected by immigration and the realities of race relations in our country.

Outside the constraints of geography, I honestly did not plan a particular order for the *EX:Change* interviews. I hadn't selected people so that particular themes would be conveniently harmonized, but by following the interviews as they came, themes like immigration reappeared and fit themselves into place with a natural flow.

091 Marjan Baradar
Beaverton, OR

Marjan Baradar is Avishan's (089) mom. She is Iranian-American, a psychotherapist in her late 40's. The Oregon Counseling Center is her business. Marjan immigrated with her family as a young woman in the late 1970's. Her parents responded to dire political circumstances threatening the family's safety by leaving their homeland. At 17, Marjan did not know the family was doing anything other than taking a trip to the U.S. She would spend years walking through the haze of unrecognizable language and lifeways. She would ache for her friends and the countryside, but she would never know Iran as home again.

Marjan: Something that is certain in this world for all of us is change. It never goes away. If you look at our own bodies, our development; from a little infant we become these adult human beings–that's a big change. And the weather, it's always changing. So change is one thing that is going to be constant whether we like it or not. Whether we are aware of it or not.

Some changes are, of course, better than others. And it is not necessarily that people are going to have an easy time with changes. I know people that, when the weather is rainy, they don't like it. But, you know what? They have no choice. (*laughs*) They have to get used to it until there are sunny days.

A great change is the presidential situation with Obama being there. We all are happy. We were celebrating, screaming with joy because that's change we wanted for a long, long time. We were waiting for this voice, for this face, for these differences to come forward. We were waiting to know that we are all ok. And yes it can happen. Oh, I like that sentence, "Yes, I can. Yes, we can!" It's through not giving up, through perseverance. And here we are. Here we have it.

Some people are not ok with this presidential change. We know that, but we're growing as a nation. The only constant I look for is our health as a country to get stronger. We have problems with the word different in our country. (*laughs*) Allowing others to be different and to be one of us is huge. It may be a time for us to look at difference and finally be ok with it. We don't have to be familiar with everything.

Sometimes change intimidates people. We know that. You've got to be careful about those who are not comfortable with change. They want to stop it, to hurt or get back at you. For a while I was very worried about Obama. I had restless nights. Seriously. I was constantly thinking, "What if something horrible happened? What if?" It has happened before. It concerned me until I said, "I have to allow this to go as it does and experience that, too. This is another new experience for all of us."

It took me a while to let it go of my constant concern. I care so much for the change he represents that I want to protect him in my helpless ways. It took a while for me and to trust that he would be safe. He has body guards. He is more careful about his life than I need to be about mine. It is important to be careful in the change, wary of those others who can't take care of their own responses–who get intimidated and can cause problems and pain.

People have expectations. If some of their expectations are being met–not all of them, because that's impossible–but if they see some expectations fulfilled, that's a good sign. It is necessary be clear on what we want. People often complain, but they don't know what they want. They don't know what and who they are. That's empty. It doesn't go too far. You've got to know your path. For example, a lot of people want to have voices, but is having voices all we need? What are the meanings behind these voices? It's very important to have meanings. How far am I willing to contribute to all this?

For me, I have a responsibility to this world. I truly believe that. I need to be an example for others. My responsibilities are important. It doesn't matter what they are. If it is to clean the house, if it is to take care of my children, if it is to be a counselor or a leader, I have to be a responsible person in this society, in this life that I'm living. That's what has made change always possible for me. Being responsible.

092 Lauren Kraakevik
S.E. Clinton Avenue/Portland, OR

A few mornings later I sat having coffee with Lauren Kraakevik in a living room on Clinton Street in Portland, OR. At 23, Lauren had just gone through another bout of graduate school applications. Her aspiration is to become a nurse midwife. One of Lauren's jobs in the meantime is helping people die – working with very old people tending physical needs and being a companion. Lauren works. She applies to graduate school. She also likes to party, loves blue grass, and regularly stays up late being loud and silly. I watch and listen to Lauren and I think this: Angels often look like regular folk, but they're still angels.

Lauren: I've always liked change. I don't know if that makes me unusual. It's opportunity, it's new, different. We change. We grow as individuals, as a culture and as the world. Still, there's that essential core of being that remains constant. I guess that can mean different things to different people. Call it the value of life or call it God or call it–I don't know. I guess I would call it God or Faith–that core, that soul that stays the same.

It's something I don't really have the words for. The only concrete thing I have, which isn't concrete at all, is a deep soul feeling–the fact that right now as I speak of this constant, I can feel it. I feel it tugging.

I was thinking about this last night. I was driving up Highway 43. It's a beautiful road. Yesterday was the first time I've ever driven this road. I was just driving and looking, and I was awed. I get the same feeling looking out the window now; really acknowledging the beauty of nature, of life, of being here. It's important to me that I can feel that connection. And so quickly.

As I was driving, I realized how privileged I am to be able to feel that. I've always felt it. There are plenty of times I take the world for granted. But I can be in a horrible mood and all of a sudden look around me to see what is here. I see other people walking down the street or I see the trees or the mountains or something. And its, "Oh yeah. That's right. This is beautiful." I feel it. My soul just singing–just praising whatever made all this–whatever brought this about which I believe is a Creator God. It's nothing more than a feeling, but it's there and I can't ignore it.

One of the things I'm learning the last few years is how to be persistent. I enjoy skipping around, seeing a bunch of different things and meeting a bunch of different people. But, for the last 4 years, I've had a constant goal as well–getting into grad school. It sucks, but it's teaching me a lot. It's taught me how to pursue something seriously and to believe I can do it even if I don't see immediate results.

When I was 20, I decided I want to be a nurse midwife, which is weird because up until last September I'd never even been to a birth. So far, I have had amazing teachers. It's easier to see the change in birth than in death because there's so much potential in it. Not only do you have this new creature, this new life, but you have a completely transformed family.

I'm interested in women's overall health–emotionally, spiritually and physically. To see the transformation and know I could help make it positive for women and families gets me excited. I want to help women hold on to the power they have when they are giving birth. I want them to see how that power can remain and work in the rest of their lives. I'm excited about the baby. I'm excited about new life. But the really cool part is that this woman gets to see how awesome her body is, how strong she is. Hopefully I can help her translate so she gets to be this new mama who knows how strong she is as a person, too–as a woman. Maybe it's idealistic of me, but I want to be a part of it.

Pursuing this dream puts me right next to that constant again, the understanding that it's not up to me. It doesn't matter what I think I'm capable of or not capable of. I just have to try. I put myself out there and let my constant, let God take care of it–This being that is more powerful than I am or could ever be. If it's not meant to happen, it won't. Even if I'm brilliantly wonderful at what I do, I will fall flat on my face. Even if I'm struggling to meet the minimal requirements for applying to grad school, if it's the will, then it will happen. I think that's what gets me through. I've been trying for this for 3 years. Nothing's come of it yet. That's ok. It's weird. I can't think of anything else that I want to do. Part of me wonders if I'm just caught in selfish or crazy personal ambitions. But I'm going to keep trying. Until I get there I'm ok with doing these random crappy jobs.

To be who you are to your greatest extent requires change. We have to change how we're doing things or what we're doing or who we're with. Some changes have to occur for us to be our truest selves. A lot of people put themselves in these boxes to say, "Well this is what my life is supposed to look like." Really we all do it. A lot of it is about trying to stay out of conflict. You know, "If I'm contained in this little spot, I'm not going to bump into anybody." But I bump into you anyway because we can't keep ourselves in the little spot all of the time.

It's like in global conflicts where I see America as a little pushy. It's more like we're trying to make our box everybody's box? (*laughs*) There's a difference between power and the abuse of power. If I have power and ability it matters how I use it. It's this idea of looking outward as opposed to looking only inward. For positive change to really happen you have to be more focused on what's outside of you. On an individual level there's this opening up that occurs when you're not just focused on yourself. When you're looking out on the world.

There's this tension a pregnant woman has. She's very concerned about herself because of the new life growing inside her. It's not her, it's something other than her. Maybe I want to make us all into mothers. (*laughs*) Everyone would become someone who's concerned for others–for something outside of themselves. At the same time, everyone would take good care of themselves because you have to take care of yourself to take care of somebody else.

That would work. Think of it. If we were all like mothers. If we had a mother nation, what would she look like?

093 Coleman (Lou) Hall
Portland State University Coffee Shop/Portland, OR

Lou Hall lives change as a man in his 60's who has been a wheel chair user since an accident in his 30's that left him without the use of his legs. Lou and I had become acquainted with one another early in December, 2008 at a post-election community meeting on health care and public policy. We exchanged e-addresses and I had included Lou in the first *EX:Change* e-mail. When he heard of my plans, he offered himself for an interview. Now it was four months later and we had found our time to meet and talk about change.

Coleman: From where I sit, real change would be for our culture to gain genuine understanding of the disability community. There's so much invisibility. That makes me angry.

For example, we're going to have two new bridges. One will connect Portland with Vancouver, WA. A well-circulated schematic depicts the pedestrian part of this bridge, but there are no wheelchair users. Then a foot bridge will go in over here by OMSI (*Oregon Museum of Science and Industry*). Again, plans totally exclude my community. The media tout, "Great new trails for pedestrians and cyclists and moms with strollers," but they don't mention disabled access and use.

Too often I'm the lone voice on these issues. Oddly, I point out narrow doorways or other physical places we can't get into, and they're all over it, "That isn't right!" But there is nary a supporting voice for addressing the attitudinal barriers. Then there's the age old objectifying focus, like with Jerry's Kids. Recently, the disability community in Hollywood catalyzed in a huge rally denouncing that organization and the phone-a-thon. Lewis has been exploiting us for so many years. Finally we got together and said, "Enough is enough." I wish it would go beyond that. I think there should be a disability truth squad with the message, "Don't treat us as if we are pitiful!" We're active. We like, for example, to get out on the public walks and trails.

I'm writing my memoir. I've been working on it for what seems like a century. I think it has a powerful message for a lot of people who struggle with disability conditions. It stresses empowerment and survival. I survived a train accident in Chicago a long, long time ago. I could have died. It was that serious. I was in my late 30's–a loaner drifting around the country. I needed the wake up call. It was horrible, and it was the best thing that ever happened to me.

I ended up in nursing homes where I witnessed huge misuse of power. So many people have been held down and taken advantage of in nursing homes. I survived such a situation. Finally, I couldn't live with myself if I didn't resist. I said, "I've got to get in the game. I can't live with this." Since then I've been a community activist.

Back in the 80's I took on a bus company in Illinois that didn't have lifts. We surrounded a Greyhound in chairs. I loved it. (*laughs*) Then, I went to the governing agency in downtown Chicago–the human rights organization–and said, "Look, you're violating a basic service here." It was long before the Americans with Disabilities Act (ADA), but they used local money to address the problem.

Years later, I single handedly organized the 6th anniversary celebration of ADA in

Coleman Hall *Portland, Oregon*

1996 here in Portland. I drew in people from all kinds of backgrounds. It was probably the most challenging experience I've ever had. When the opportunity arose, I was in a terrible depression. I was living in a place that dishonored me; they had all kinds of barriers. I needed something like a resurrection and knew the anniversary of the ADA had to be my project. In 6 months with hardly any assistance, I organized the whole event. I took the risk to go out there and say, "Alright Universe, here I am. Let's go with it." It went like clock work. I lived through it. I touched a lot of lives. It saved me.

It always reminds me of the Ellen Burnstyn movie called Resurrection. She almost died in a car accident but survived. It's a great movie. Such a beautiful flowering of the soul. She hung in there and so did I. I still go through months of not sleeping well and that sort of thing. Then I reflect back on the experience with the ADA celebration and it's enough to re-energize me.

Right now I'm living alone in my own apartment. I have a morning person and an evening person to help me out. If I have to get up in the middle of the night, I'm on my own. I love the challenge. At times I wish I had a live-in. I've been that route. Most of the time it turns out to be negative–territorial issues, etc. I've tried about every living arrangement you can imagine. Not a pup tent (*laughs*), but I've got all kinds of stories.

Talking of this really turns me on because I have such a wealth of examples in my own lived experience. Including traveling with Servas, an exchange organization that openly welcomes travelers with disabilities. It's a marvelous organization founded on peace and Gandhi. It's been around since 1945. People from different backgrounds come together, share experiences and realize the humanity in all of us.

I want the disability community to be unified that way. The apathy in our community has been so disappointing. It's been surprising to me, the depth of it. My impression is that people are just trying to survive their day-to-day struggles. Still there are issues. Getting to brass tacks, there's been such a watering down of ADA. There have been increases in denying requests for our sisters and brothers who are being marginalized. We need the ADA Restoration Act.

I'll give you an example. There was a guy who needed a breathing tube–a pharmacist at a Wal-Mart. A new supervisor came on board who wouldn't give him lunch hour. He had to stay at his station and try to use this breathing tube there. That's a gross violation of ADA. In the end he got fired. He filed a complaint with a local agency but they didn't support him.

Then there is the fact of people still being warehoused in nursing homes. That's less likely to happen here because Oregon is a model state where we can live in our own apartments and have care givers. But many states still warehouse. That's why we must work toward enhancing public perception, visibility and empowerment of the disability community.

That fires me up. I can't stand to be around misuse of power. Believe you me, I'm a tiger–definitely a warrior. I try to be an example. I just wish there were more people around with that same kind of attitude and determination.

Road Note
Etched by years of experiencing life as a wheelchair user. Lou reflects on change from the perspective of the disability community. Today I sat in a small coffee shop in the Burlingame neighborhood with my friends Jessica and Leah. This mother

and daughter team are connected to my own story. They are the mother and sister of Rose O'Brien (070) from earlier in the *EX:Change*, and Jessica and I have been friends for two decades which means I've known Leah since she was in utero.

There is also a connection here to Lou- the unintended thematic cluster thing happening again. Jessica and Leah both live with disabilities defined by conditions of severe mental illness. The neurochemistry in their bodies lead to their being labeled as "ill" by the medical establishment in our country. That designation can be important when it comes to receiving the care they need, but the disgrace and dishonor associated with mental illness remains powerfully ostracizing. At best, those of us without such conditions feel awkward around them. More often, however, we are just afraid and as a result, tend to ignore both the subject and the people concerned.

While people diagnosed with mental illness are protected by the ADA, it can be as hard for them to access support in cases of discrimination as it is for people with physical disabilities. The stigma of being seen and treated as "crazy" is hard to shake. Listening to these two women speak about change in their lives reveals again how much we miss when our stories of people stop with a label.

094,095 Jessica & Leah O'Brien
SW Terwilliger Parkway/Portland, OR

Jessica is Irish-American and Cherokee. She has professional background in bilingual education, educational administration and is now a family practice MD. Leah is Irish-American, Cherokee and African-American. She is a vastly talented teen, particularly gifted in theater and other performing arts.

Jessica: Well, there's a personal level, a family level and a sort of universe level. My life has been in pretty serious flux lately. Parts of the change in my life complete themselves from moment to moment going from being ok to being way not ok. So at the personal level, that's what change means. There are exceptions, but in general, my life is very difficult with the changes I experience.

At the family level, it's amazing to have Leah home. We sent her to intensive residential treatment. She's home now and I think she's finished being as ill as she was. She has coping skills most adults of 70 years haven't acquired. It killed me to have her gone, but I'll have her longer for having sent her away. The change in her is very good.

Obviously there have been changes in our family around that. My sister wasn't speaking to me and then she put together the money to make Leah's treatment possible. She loaned us the money borrowed against her house. So, there was some positive shifting there. To be reminded of that piece of her has been important to me. Most of us aren't as flat as I was telling myself she was. That's an example of change in family dynamics.

Universally, well I've been hammered for several months at work. Hammered—working like 15 hours, 20 hours at a stretch. So, I don't see changes in the community or country or world. I don't have time. If I have any extra time, I sleep. Family practice doctors are the touchstone of our health care system. Even if people go somewhere else, they come back to us. So our workloads can be enormous.

I only hear what my husband tells me about what is happening in the world. He's my conduit. When Obama was elected, I was blown away. Like a lot of people, I didn't think I'd see this in my lifetime. Now, even without being fully aware and informed, I have great hope. Certainly it's not all Obama. I mean he doesn't get to decide unilaterally on the shape things take. There's administrative, political and social context always.

As all these changes take place, my mainstay is my family. It would be nice to be stable myself. That's not going to happen. I'm in much better shape than I ever have been, though. I finally found a qualified MD who recognized how difficult my life is and set out to change it. He made my improvement a personal goal from the very first visit. That's encouraging even though I know that I will never lose this disability. At this point, I wouldn't even wish for stability in my life that way because it's not possible.

I do recognize when I'm in positive flux. I enjoy those times. I get optimistic and I like what I'm doing. I feel relaxed in my work and at home. Today my level of optimism for me and my world is probably 2 or 3 out of 10. Like I said, it's always changing. But for my daughter I'd go with 150 out of 10. For my husband and my older girl, 100. That's everybody.

Leah: For me, change basically means something different. It doesn't mean something better. It could be worse. I think it was implied in the presidential campaign that it would be something better. I don't know what it's going to be. I didn't get to really follow the election, but I think the hope is always for something better when people say change. I know when I say, "I want this to change," I'm never thinking, "I want things to get worse."

What I rely on is relationships–having people around me and knowing there's going to be something to fall back on. It's funny. Someone once told me that really the only constant is change. So, really the only thing to fall back on is the fact that things are going to be changing. That's not always reassuring. I like to think that I'll always have friends and family to rely on. I'd like to think that through any huge changes people will have other people there to care for them.

I don't know if there's any absolute indicator when it comes to change. There are just little hints or glimpses. You get a different feeling every once and awhile. You feel a little more upbeat, things don't feel as gloomy. I don't think you can ever look at something in life and say, "Oh, this has definitely changed." I don't think it's that simple.

At the same time, there are so many things that could be changed. Something that makes me sad is public school. It's so crowded. I don't go to public school, but I have friends who do. They talk about how they have like 40 kids in each of their classes. That makes me sad, because you don't get any help or individualized attention. Those things are really important when you're trying to learn and to get prepared for the rest of your life. That's something I would like to see changed so people have more of a chance for making it out there. You need to know stuff to make it.

I do volunteer work with kids at Northwest Children's Theater. I feel like that program is a good way for the kids to escape. They are crowded in school all day and the theater is a good place for them to express themselves and have more fun. I know that's the way it is for me with theater. So, being able to support them is really nice. Doing any kind of volunteer work makes me feel better.

096 Sofia Ivlieva
NE Broadway Street/Portland, OR

Leah's motive to provide experiences to youth that are a positive exception are, as she indicated, in keeping with her experience of what has been most helpful, healthful, and empowering for her. Sofia Ivlieva shares Leah's passion. Sophia is another American who lived into her early adulthood in another country -- Russia. She came to the U.S. on her own in her early 20's and speaks of change today with an energetic focus on supporting children and youth to believe in themselves and contribute to their communities.

Sofia: I truly think immigrants appreciate the United States more than people born as Americans because of the things we go through. We see the contrast to experiences in our countries. Freedom is important. Many Americans don't understand that the same way. You fight for your freedom. You really fight to be here where there are so many opportunities–so many things you can do with your life.

I immigrated by myself. I was 22. Everybody else in my family is in Russia. I couldn't visit them for 5 years because of the way it works when you exchange statuses and are between paperwork. It's hard but you get used to it. How it started was in 1997 my English tutor in Russia was invited to teach in Vancouver, Washington. She asked if anybody would like to live for three weeks in an American family. She found me a family and I came. At the time, I was in the third year of university in Russia. I was 19.

I wasn't really impressed at first (*laughs*). In Russia we have a lot of architecture and Portland is very earthy. I was thinking, "Oh my god, this is like a big village. I don't know why people are so excited about it." My town is called Kazail. It's one and a half million people in the Muslim part of Russia. It's really condensed so you can get places by public transportation in pretty much no time. I did love the nature here, though. Here it's got the trees, so beautiful. We don't have that in my town. It's more concrete.

In 1998, my American family visited us in Russia. I graduated in 1999 from the Russian university and decided I would like to study in America. My host family said I could live with them so I left Russia in 2000. I finally finished an American degree just last year in marketing and finance.

I grew up in a Muslim part of Russia that was forced into Russian Orthodoxy under the Soviet Union. So, I had the opportunity to see how religion was going to play out in our republic after the Soviet Union fell apart. There was tension, but our president was so great. His name is Chimere2. He said we all lived here for so many years we could resolve the tension peacefully. He developed policy and programs to make the two religions available in my region. By law it is possible to have mosques and churches equal with no discrimination against either. That was the only way to avoid civil war.

I only speak two languages, although I know a little bit of my regional language, Tatar3. Tatar is part of a Turkish group of languages. From second grade, all the schools teach Tatar. And, of course, Russian. Plus students study a foreign language; usually French, German, or English. By the time all of this was enforced I was already graduated.

America is very rich culturally because you're so many in one big space. It makes me look at things differently and respect all the religions, all the races, all the points of view. That's been the biggest change in the sense that I don't judge anymore by heritage–that's probably the right word. You can be yourself here. There are less hang ups, you know, in clothes, in how you look. It freed me. I don't have complexes I had there. I can see and talk with people in professional lives or corporate America. I can talk with many different people in daily interactions and communications. Just people outside of their work and agendas. That has been liberating. (*laughs*) Very liberating. Change for me has been about open mindedness, understanding we're all the same.

What is constant through all of this is who I am, my values and what I grew up to know. I came here thinking, "I'm Russian, I have an accent and I don't want to stand out of the crowd." But I've learned I don't want to forget my heritage–my Russian roots. It makes me who I am. I don't hide it anymore. It's nice to be able to be who you are.

I think most people don't realize how strong they are. The strength is really deep within. When I went through the change of coming here I didn't have anyone to talk to. It's like ground zero. I knew my American family, but that was different. They didn't know who I was or what I was going to do. When you've got only yourself, you realize you can do it. (*smiles*) You can find the way. There are also people that help when they see the ambition, when they see who you are. It's challenging. But I've done it and I haven't fallen apart; well not yet. (*laughs*) It comes from within.

Sometimes I think love is the best medicine for everything. If you show you're capable of love, people respond. I don't know, though. People often think it's easier to hate than love. I look at it this way. It's hard to change the older generation. They are in concrete because for years they've gotten used to a certain way. I think we should emphasize our children. The new generation is going to bring the change.

We have a lot of kids who are disadvantaged. They didn't choose their family and they see only hate. You start with one child at a time and show them their parents aren't the example of the whole of life. It can be different. Somebody can love you just because you exist. They bore you, yes, but sometimes your parents can be other than biological. With love, kids start changing. They say, "I'm not stealing anymore because I hate my parents. I want to improve."

Most people don't realize what these kids need. In Russia, children in the orphanage become misfits if no one from the outside communicates with them. How can you raise functional individuals in that environment? This is why I came to the United States. In Russia or somewhere else I would like to find a way to work with children who didn't see love and love them for who they are. There is space to improve. They can do it. I did it.

I would involve people who know how to resolve conflicts peacefully. Aggression isn't the problem solver. You should express your anger in a civilized way. That's number one. Number two, I would teach them how to communicate. Education is a big part of it. Education allows you to see outside the box. They need to be shown things to live for and experience. I want to nurture their desire to improve. It's not just holding the hand and saying "I love you." It's showing them what they're capable of. It's like a flower. You water it and it blooms into something beautiful. Everybody is born to be beautiful.

Road Note
When writing fiction, an author has certain tools that can to shape the overall story. Two of these are climax and denouement. The climax is the big moment in the story's arc, while the denouement serves as the resolution that stills the waters

at the end. The resolution generally follows the climax, except in mystery novels where the two may occur at the same time.

If such devices were present here, the *EX:Change* would be more like a mystery. But maybe a symphonic analogy makes more sense; maybe we're we in crescendo. Whatever the metaphor, the voices coming forward to complete the goal of 100 continue both unique and strong. They herald the core values of respect, balance, community, environmental responsibility, peace, kindness, and optimism.

097 Rabbi Ariel Stone
NE Hancock Avenue/Portland, OR

This afternoon, I had coffee with Rabbi Ariel Stone, the 48 year old leader of Congregation Shir Tikvah, a small independent synagogue in Portland. Rabbi Stone is a pioneer, in part because she is one of very few women in her professional and religious position. She is also a pioneer by ancestry. The continuity of her Jewish forebears is due to the remarkable capacity of a people to engage and respond to change after change.

Rabbi Ariel Stone: Today is actually a stunning day to ask about change. Today is Yom HaZikaron which is Israel's Memorial Day. For the 61st year, Israelis and Jews everywhere recognize everyone who has died giving effort toward making change in the Middle East–to bring a Jewish presence back to the Middle East in a sovereign way.

The Jewish people come from this place but they were gone for so long. Bringing them back, even if they have always carried a strong memory of this land as home, has meant a huge change in political power, in social reality and in religious reality. This change has affected everyone around them, and certainly the Jewish people themselves.

On a day like this, when you look at how much change can really be put into effect, it becomes interesting to consider how much change is a lot. In the Middle East 61 years ago, change was revolution. Change was foundational. There was a new state on the map. Change was complete. And it carried the ultimate price for some people.

The next thing I'm going to do this morning is call Israel. I have a 90 year old great aunt there. I'm going to call her and wish her a Happy Independence Day because that's the day that one comes right after this one. They do them back to back so that no one ever forgets what independence costs. Memorial Day comes first.

It's pretty tough on anybody who's actually lost somebody which is most people. You go from mourning the love you lost to celebrating the state. It's rough but the general feeling, even by those in mourning, is that it's not inappropriate. My great aunt was there before the state was founded. She has seen everything. I'm going to call her and ask her what you're asking me. "What have you seen? What change have you seen?"

She left Germany in the 30's. She came to Israel when it was sand. I remember sitting in her son's backyard with her daughter-in-law and the children and the cousins and grandchildren. She casually looked up at the gigantic avocado tree we were all sitting under. It commands the whole backyard. She said, "I remember planting this."

So, I always look at the Israeli pioneers as people who can teach me what change can be. To look at the sand and dream of trees and shade. To look at powerlessness and

Rabbi Ariel Stone *Portland, Oregon*

dream of safety. To look at homelessness and think of home.

With that perspective, I look at the last 100 years in this country. The night Obama was elected I think a lot of people were very excited. I remember bursting into tears when the delegate count went over the top. We opened champagne. It was a big deal. But he is human, too. One of the things he has to be smart about is how much change and how much continuity is good for the country.

There's an interesting kind of wistfulness between what I think he could be and do and what I think he as a pragmatist will try. Given how excitable the American public is by next to nothing, and given the real stresses of the economy, I think people want to be reassured that there won't be anything too revolutionary. Just getting elected was such a change. The four executive orders he signed the first day – that's already huge. And it was quiet. I respect that it's change that is not overtly disruptive. In the long run we'll look back and say, you know, a very great ship can be set on a completely different course with one small change of degree in a rudder.

I would like to see this moment be the beginning of – well, as Obama said, "We can't rebuild capitalism on the same shifting sands." What shifts too damn much is the sense of security people feel in real, meaningful, supportive, responsive connection to other human beings. I would like for us to get to a consistent sense of, "When I do something it really does affect someone."

Speaking as a Jew, I hope human connection continues strong in the values and culture of Jewish community. That nurtures me. As a Rabbi, I'm often in the position of helping other people create connection, but I also need places I can very simply plug into. Each and all of us need the ability to create family where we can't necessarily bring biological family. Family beyond biology is important in terms of who you travel with day to day. I expect there will be people I can identify and spend time with who share the path – who inspire me by the learning we do together.

It can be frightening to teach a deeper sense of connectedness and love. Anybody will tell you, people who try to do that get killed. Martin Luther King. Jesus. People who stand up and say we just need to care for and love each other. It needs to be done. It can be stressful to do it. It is even counter culture in a weird way to talk about all of us being good friends and helping each other. There's something that people don't trust in it. "You'll take advantage of me if I open up and trust you."

Our own natural shyness kicks in and then nobody wants to have anything to do with anybody else. There's little sense that the best way to be a neighbor is to be in touch. We have lost that connection in a tremendously short time, which makes me wonder. Maybe we could recover it in a tremendously short time by appealing to the better angels of our nature or something.

I'm sure it will help to have some overt and very strong message from somebody like the president. If a community organizer can't teach us how to trust each other more and work together, then I don't know who we can turn to. So, one of the things I hope for as change in our society is that the part of President Obama that teaches connection and trust will have a chance to influence us for good.

It's very much like planting and nurturing trees in the sand. The tree in Judaism is the symbol of life for obvious reasons. Surrounded by sand, a tree might bear fruit. That tells you there's water nearby even if you have to dig for it. And then one day you have an avocado tree so tall and so big and it gives everybody shade, you can hang a hammock off it and it can feed you. It takes longer than you thought and it's not easy. A lot of the seedlings die and a lot of the people trying to tend them die. But one day you sit back and look up at this unbelievable tree with all the family underneath.

098 Susan Klapstein
Downtown/Portland, OR

Year in and year out everyday Americans give their lives to the spiritual, social and commercial well being of the nation. They do this often unaware of their contribution. Susan Klapstein epitomizes this way of being. Ms. Klapstein is at the end of her career as an educator. She is in recovery from serious heart disease. In my experience and observation, she is a significant contributor to our shared civic well being and in this she is entirely humble. Sue Klapstine is another American hero.

Susan: If I work next year it will be my 40th. I don't know if I need to work anymore after 40 years. (*laughs*) All those years in human services has taught me an awful lot about people. Then this illness the last 5 years has helped me see how important smart and compassionate human service is. I tell the students I've been a provider and a customer of services for people with disabilities. I know a lot more than I knew 5 years ago.

Part of that came from being in assisted care. Was that a shocker? I remember my insurance made it so I could choose from a couple of places. A friend helped me choose. But I kept thinking, "I want to go home. I don't want to be in here." That really made me think. Those places have people who live there permanently–people who need care. I always figured I'd be getting out, but the thought of living my life there was terrifying.

Fortunately, I'm doing alright. I can still get around. I live on my own, drive, and go to work. That's the way I know change–through my experiences with work and my health and all. I'd like to see change in this nation, too.

I'm thrilled with the current government under President Obama. I think we've been doing awful things in the world. We need great change in what our nation is doing and in our outlook as citizens. We need to be more compassionate. We are so fortunate in this country but we've lost a sense of helping people less fortunate here at home and in the world. Recovering that is change I'd like to see.

Well we elected Barack Obama. I think that's evidence. We're hitting rock bottom in our economy and in our status in the world. People have to think about how we as a nation share responsibility in these bad things. Maybe that can lead us to take a look at our ethics and personal responsibility. I suppose we're going to have to wait a bit longer.

One good sign would be getting out of war. I would like us to stop sending our soldiers to other countries to fight. "Being the world policemen," I guess that's the phrase. With real change we also wouldn't have begging at home. Everyone would have health care resources–a bottom line of health care available to everybody. We'd have places for people with chronic mental illness who aren't receiving any kind of care. There also wouldn't be stigma about having mental illness like we have now. We need a shared sense of looking out for one another, even people we don't know. If somebody falls down, you stop in the street to help them. We don't have that in our culture, now.

There's still a lot of stratification in this country. It would be nice for that to go away–the thinking you're better if you have a lot of wealth. These giant houses really bother me. Change would include people examining the house they built with 50 rooms and asking what they need that for. I think as a culture we still admire acquisition–but boats and houses and fancy cars? The wealthy may think that's wonderful, but I don't think the rest of us have to admire that.

Instead, we could value truly equal educational opportunities. We don't have that. It will be good change when any person in the country has a right and access to good public education and to going as far as they want in advanced education. It sounds hokey, but I do think education is the way for all children to have to better lives. They can get farther with a good educational foundation in knowing how to read, knowing about the world and how to get along with one another. I've always thought that was schools main job: You learn to read and you learn how to get along with other people. That's it.

One place I see potential for local change is with my students. Students in the Graduate School at Lewis & Clark1 tend to be higher in socioeconomic status. When they go in the public schools and see terrible poverty, injustice and the rules we think are going to make everything alright I want them to be outraged. I want them to see how to make it better for those children. They work mostly with kids with disabilities, but I want them also to be thinking and working for all children. Before too many years, I want them to think back on the way it is now as how it used to be. I want them to feel pride and satisfaction in how they've taken part in making things more equitable and fair.

I give them that speech all the time. (*laughs*) I've always worked for schools. I wanted to do that. Maybe that was my generation–late 60s, early 70s. We wanted to do social service work. I don't know whether I see that now in students–wanting to work in tough schools, poor schools, with tough families. But there are some of them who do commit their professional lives to that work. I want them to be honored for that choice. It's easy to go to well-off school systems to work. That's meaningful, but it's better if you're from a privileged background to work to make things better for less fortunate kids and families. So I give them pep talks. I know they go, "Oh no. Another Sue story." But it helps them.

099 Calliope Crane
SE Clinton Street/Portland, OR

A mom, a hippie, a health care provider and a connoisseur of folk and blue grass music, Calliope Crane faces political and personal change as an mother, health care provider, citizen and artist. She wishes to teach this way of being to her young daughter. As a mixed-race woman in a predominantly white community, Calliope finds her stability in community.

Calliope: When I think of change I remember this quote I heard when I was a kid. "If it weren't for change, there wouldn't be butterflies."

I can see how change can be scary, how people can be paralyzed thinking of what might be. At the same time, we can't really know, so why fret? Every second something is different. So why spin out about it? But even with the promise of butterflies, I have to have my feet on the ground. I have to take a deep breath and be right here or I will get lost in the eye (*swirls her hands around*) and won't recognize change to see that everything is as it should be. I have to remember to watch. I go outside. I notice tiny buds. Or I sweat. That helps, too.

These days are a big time of change for my daughter. She's about to start school–to jump into the public school system. I'm hoping the groundwork of her life up to now is solid. Her whole life has been upheaval, but in positive ways like "Surprise, we're going camping! We're going to a festival!" There's so much stimulation. I hope I've instilled adaptability so that when big changes come for her she can handle them. Of course, I can't predict what's about to happen. I don't even know what school she's going to.

Plus she's an alpha female in her current school. I'm hoping there are some big girls at her new school who won't let her be alpha so that she'll have things to work through to get even stronger socially. I can't give her tools for holding things still, but I can remind her that we'll get through it. If we try something and it doesn't work, we'll do something else. Hey, we might move to another neighborhood to get her into a better school. I don't know. As she gets older, I can show her I might not be cool, but I am here for her.

Then there are the changes in the country around her. I don't know if she'll remember, but one of the first laws Obama rescinded made me say, "Wow. This guy means business!" It was the gag law about other countries being prevented from talking to women about choices and women's rights. I can't remember exactly what the law was before, but now these women can be informed of their rights to change their practices around sex for safety and birth control. I told my little miss about it. I didn't talk about sex or anything–but I said, "He's making sure women get information they need to take care of their bodies." I showed her the You Tube clips that come from the White House. How cool for her to remember that fireside chat the way people remember FDR.

Still, as I look out on the world I am definitely feeling the threat of a double edged sword–the fox in Granny's cap kind of thing. I worry that I've let my guard down. In recent years I've had a full fire escape plan. I was on it with emergency safety planning and all those things. On November 4th, I shoved it all into this little pile on my desk saying, "Oh, everything's going to be ok now." Lately, I'm coming back into thinking, "Wait, those were good ideas." Then I say, "Why are you thinking like that? Are you being pessimistic?"

I remember the first time Bush and his crew got elected. I thought, "What can possibly happen in four years?" My girlfriend said, "Calliope! It's four years." I said, "Carrie, he's not going to be elected again." We were in school scurrying through our lives. I said, "Look at us. Look at four years ago for us. Life flew by." Then, when he was elected again, I made the fire escape plan. I remember sitting there with this baby girl who I didn't have in Canada, because I was so sure everything was going to be ok. I came so close to having her there and I didn't do it. I mean, you're growing a baby and everybody's telling you, "Don't have a home birth. Don't have a home birth in Canada. What if you have to go to the ER?" And I was like, "What better country to go to the ER than Canada?" Then her dad said, "We're not taking the risk." And I said "Ok, everything's going to be fine." Then the election happened. I was holding her watching everything go down and

I was like, "Four more years. Oh no."

The whole process leading to this last election has been so much better. The country has already grown and changed so I am better off than I was when Bush first got elected. To be fair, I can ask what Bush did to make my life better. Well, I became very aware of women's lives in the Middle East. Michael Franti went to Palestine, Bagdad and Israel and somewhere else–you know, the four spots–and made a documentary that opened my eyes. I gained huge respect for the people on both sides who still live in occupied territories because of what was done 10 years before Bush. Bush made me an activist.

That led to fire escape planning with the driving force being these big brown eyes. I imagined her saying, "Mama, you knew this was going to happen?" I'm the one, when it comes down to it, who protects and provides for her. She can tie her own shoes and brush her teeth but I'm the one responsible for and to her. She deserves to look into my eyes or the eyes of any adult in her community and to say, "You stopped that from happening? Thanks!" Then as an adult, she'll be able to do that, too.

Here's what it comes down to. I want my daughter and all children to have the option to swim in a river that is crystal clear, to swim with dolphins, to eat nettles that aren't poisonous. To do that, I rely on myself and on the village. I can't grow all of her food right now. I'm living in this tiny apartment with my kid by myself. I have no idea why any of us built four walls to separate ourselves from one another. It's time again for us all to look to the village, to help each other. Part of looking to the village is planning with the village. If we begin to plan together and an emergency comes we will be in it with each other to the end.

100 Kwang Il Kim
Vancouver, WA

My friend Kwang Kim laughingly refers to the two of us as fellow Southerners. Kwang was born in South Korea, spent early childhood years in a refugee camp and immigrated with his family to the Pacific Northwest when he was 8 years old. We are age mates and have been friends for over ten years. Kwang and I enjoy wide ranging conversations over great food (his mother's pickled kale leaves wrapped around steamed rice are my absolute favorite). We speak of politics and philosophy, of economy and art. Without fail we circle out of and into the basis of every one of our conversations – spirit.

Kwang: Change could be about anything. On the one hand there's tremendous hope for significant change. But change requires attention to interdependence.

I wish we would recognize the flawed idea in this country that we can make progress by using up resources. We seem to think that can go on forever, but as somebody said, that's the philosophy of a cancer cell. You eat to grow, but at a certain point you eat yourself out of house and home. Then what? I wish for a change in which we come more into balance with ourselves and with nature.

Following from seeing interdependence with nature is the recognition that workers and CEOs are interdependent. Right now there's an abstracted value system that says CEOs ought to be paid 300 times more than line workers. When you really

Kwang Kim *Vancouver, Washington*

think about who has more value, you can't say. Certainly the CEO gives input and leadership, yet if it weren't for the people putting cars together, you wouldn't have a company at all. So, it's hard to say one is more valuable.

I wonder about how change is actually going to come about. What I know from family work is that change requires focus on the self. All individuals are part of systems. When we change our own attitudes, somehow the family moves along with us. The change is in learning not to have our usual reactions to family members. It requires creativity and a capacity for humor. That then inspires change in the people around us.

Moving into the political arena, those of us interested in change tend to spend over much time thinking about how others should be different. We wait at home being angry at the other side, thinking they'll see the light or somehow be forced to change. But, in the same way change in a family depends on an individual's focus on her or himself, the focus on self is relevant in public change.

You hear this in the polemic discussions on talk radio. There's a violent undertone, an intolerance going back and forth. It's the kind of thing you see in dysfunctional families. Everyone is essentially well-intentioned but invested in the other people making the change. Unfortunately, nothing shifts. In fact, that dynamic only increases enmity, conflict and misunderstanding so people get locked further into their positions. Someone in the system has to say, "I'm going to stop expecting other people to change and focus on changing the knee-jerk reactions that make me say, 'You need to do it.'" When one person finds a new way to respond in a family or political system, movement can happen.

I wonder too if one way to bring about change is to think about our values. Do we actually act in ways that are consistent with our values? Do I really need to use our car today? Why am I forgetting my reusable bags? Is there a way I can carpool? Is there a way to cut down on my use of plastic? There are infinite little things we can do personally to support the change we'd like to bring about. If we just talk about it, if we just wait for someone else to do something about it, of course nothing changes.

This all relates to what R. D. Laing said back in the 60's; that any effort to manipulate people to believe or do as we want them to is violence. I think we all know that violence begets violence. Intolerance begets violence. That's pretty accepted. Still there's all this intolerance between progressives and conservatives. We shouldn't be surprised that rather than contributing to change we're supporting intolerance.

That doesn't mean there aren't public things we can do–protests, being involved in activist organizations, having workplace or neighborhood meetings. Instead of an agenda of making people change to believe as we do, public action can be self expression. Then the attitude is, "Here's what I'm passionate about. How can I share this in a way that is not violent in any way?" Then passion is infectious. Tolerance is infectious.

From R.D. Laing's point of view, each of us grew up in violent circumstances. We learned how to get what we want by manipulating and trying to change others. We actually hunger for passionate tolerance. People are naturally drawn when we express passion for what we believe without needing to change anyone. That can lead to change because people who feel unconditionally connected are freer to consider changing.

Public involvement alongside personal responsibility is important. Let me put it this way. As we feel some kind of emotional connection, we can begin to see the interconnectedness of co-workers and understand the ramifications of our consumption. We go beyond ideas to the actual experience that we're all responsible for each other. We're not out to change people, we're expressing passion for our interdependence.

So, passion and tolerance open up the possibility of connection. In that connection, someone who doesn't have our point of view might feel somewhat safer to consider it. We will feel safer to consider their way of seeing as well. Then we're in conversation instead of conflict. And if you're connected to a few people, pretty soon you might get a sense of being connected to the community. You may start to feel how your health, your neighbor's health and the health of the community are interdependent. What we do either helps the community be healthy or unhealthy whether it's a family, a town, a nation.

So, change for me is thinking about our values in terms of political, economic and environmental well being and considering whether those values are consistent with our behaviors. To the extent they are inconsistent we must make personal changes in the private arena. Finally we take steps to be involved in public activism that is inclusive, passionate and tolerant of other points of view. Rather than protesting to change other people, activism becomes expression, dialogue, and conversation.

Essentially we are all intuitive. We can sense when something done toward us is manipulative or aggressive, even violent. We also intuit when expression is tolerant, welcoming and loving. People are naturally attracted to that. So, change naturally comes back to each of us taking responsibility for our attitudes and behaviors instead of thinking only of ways someone else or the globe ought to change. Big changes follow from the little steps we take individually. Those little steps make ripples, the ripples make waves.

Afterword

Is the cause outside with the effect in here (points to his chest)? Or is it opposite? Could this be the cause (points to his chest) with the effect evident out here? It matters what you put out there.
        ~Russell Hewes (049)

American values and our respect for one another are vital to our success. Sometimes that gets out of whack, but it usually comes back.
        ~Anna (063)

I will likely never be able to describe fully the effect that listening to these people had on me. That description resides in the ineffable constant – the spirit to which so many of them alluded. Certainly each voice resounded individually but the chorus taught me more about human nature and our country that I could ever have imagined. As the collection grew, I realized I was hearing the better angels of our nature – the same ones that President Abraham Lincoln called us to during the American Civil War.

Even among the pointed comments of frustration or disapproval, the bass note across every interview remained the same: Please listen to what I have to say. This is what I feel most passionately about. This is what I want for my family and community because I love and care about them. Of course, the lives behind every voice have elements of struggle and failure, but together they ask us to remember how precious life is and that we are in it together.

From a wide variety of political perspectives, generations, genders and ethnicities, the interviews in the *EX:Change* call on Americans to recognize, emphasize and act from the goodness within ourselves. They tell us that to maintain this goodness, integrity and communication are key. Our corruption, greed and conflict tend to be the elements that attract media attention and this reflects how we can so easily use our energy to complain and criticize. Nonetheless, honor, truth and community are prized values among everyday citizens. They are alive and well, and they residing at the very center of our capacity for survival.

The one hundred Americans of the *EX:Change* offered their thoughts on what change means in their lives as individuals, friends, lovers, community members, and citizens. In the end, I find every interview to be its own meditation on living well, with responsibility, connection and kindness.

One hundred days, one hundred voices. This is what I learned about change in America:

- We are always free to focus on our differences.
- We are free to fear one another.
- We are free to be at war.
- We are free to oppress and to resist oppression.
- We are also free to ground public action in the strength and endurance of our vast similarities.
- We are free to love.
- Being alive demands courage, whatever our choices.
- In life, we may never avoid change and we may never avoid connection. In this we are not free. We are, however, free in our responses given these realities.

Author's Acknowledgements

The *EX:Change* and this book exist because of the countless hands that have touched and thus contributed to them. While I cannot possibly call every name, I am no less grateful. Here, I mention a few people, in particular. First, my eternal thanks to each of the 100 voices, the people of our country who brought their experience and wisdom to talking with me about change. Thanks to the board of the Saraswati Foundation – Marjan Baradar, Melanie Martin, Buz McDonald, and Jennifer McClendon – who approved partial sponsorship of the *EX:Change* trip. Infinite appreciation to the volunteers who have given so generously of their time and intelligence: Kris Alman, Rob Bednark, Hamid Bennett, Allison Brown, Saundra Childs, Ken Farrar, Herman Frankel, Barbara Gutkin, Camille Jarmie, Timothy Kelly, Ken Klees, Tammy Ko, Wendy Lincoln, Damian Miller, Rachel Plett, Roy Sampsel, Bethany Shinkins, Holly Shumway, and Deborah Thomas – and to those who volunteered shelter along the road: Rachel Gaffney, Kathy Goodman, Alicia Henning & Scott Gordon, Bill & Joy Henning, Dot & David Kaylor, Lien Nguyen and her mother, Wendy Parker-Wood & Pat Smith, Dia Paxton, Tim & Judy Schuster, and Mimi Wheatwind. I am especially indebted to long-term volunteers, Dani Hunter, video editor extraordinaire and Rakshith Krishnappa, the galactically skilled web designer. Thanks are also due to the graduate students in my CPSY 550 classes at Lewis & Clark College from the fall term of 2009 through to today. Their brilliance, engagement and courageous inquiry helped to inspire this project and continue to redefine the front edge of thought and action for positive change. I will also be forever grateful to the management and staff of the Sweet Spot Coffee Shoppe in Whitewater, WI where I wrote every day during the winter of 2011. Then there is the immense part played in this project by Loud Mouth Press and, in particular, Gregory Ayres, who has offered tireless creativity, guidance, encouragement and craft to bringing this book to be. Finally, my spirit and my art have been uniquely sustained by my mother, Mary Alice Kemp and my three sisters, Alicia Henning, Nancy Kemp Jones and Rachel Henning; by my sweetheart, Mark McPhail; and at every single step in the process, by the editorial genius and all around stellar human being who has been my inspiration since her birth, my daughter Sara Henning-Stout.